THE POLITICAL ECONOMY OF INNOVATION AND ENTREPRENEURSHIP

T0362148

To my son,

Jón Reginbald Ívarsson

The Political Economy of Innovation and Entrepreneurship
From Theories to Practice

IVAR JONSSON
Østfold University College, Norway

Routledge
Taylor & Francis Group

LONDON AND NEW YORK

First published 2015 by Ashgate Publishing

2 Park Square, Milton Park, Abingdon, Oxfordshire OX14 4RN
52 Vanderbilt Avenue, New York, NY 10017

Routledge is an imprint of the Taylor & Francis Group, an informa business

First issued in paperback 2020

British Library Cataloguing in Publication Data
A catalogue record for this book is available from the British Library

The Library of Congress has cataloged the printed edition as follows:
The Library of Congress Cataloging-in-Publication Data has been applied for.

ISBN 13: 978-1-4724-6682-2 (hbk)
ISBN 13: 978-0-367-59832-7 (pbk)

Contents

List of Figures

List of Tables

Abbreviations

AEF = American Economic Foundation
AEI = American Enterprise Institute for Public Policy Research
ASI = Adam Smith Institute
BBC = British Broadcasting Corporation
CI = Continuous Innovation
CI = Cato Institute
CPRS = Central Policy Review Staff
CPS = Centre for Policy Studies
EC = European Commission
EF = Earhart Foundation
EFTA = European Free Trade Association
ELFS = European Labour Force Survey
EU = European Union
FMS = Flexible manufacturing systems
GATT = General Agreement on Tariffs and Trade
HF = Heritage Foundation
HII = High-involvement innovation
HIS = Institute for Humane Studies
ICT = Information and communications technology
IEA = Institute of Economic Affairs
IMF = International Monetary Fund
IP = Intellectual property
ISI = Intercollegiate Studies Institute, Inc
M&As = Mergers and acquisitions
MI = Manhattan Institute
MPS = Mont Pelerin Society
NC = Numerical control
NIESR = National Institute for Economic and Social Research
PEP = Political and Economic Planning
PS = Philadelphia Society
PSI = Policy Studies Institute
RF = Relm Foundation
R&D = Research and development
TEP = Techno-economic paradigms
TFP= Total factor productivity
USSR = Union of Soviet Socialist Republics
WVF = William Volker Fund

Preface

When I began my studies, in the early 1970s, the situation in academic institutions in Europe was in many ways similar to what it is today. Western societies faced a social and political crisis in the 1960s and 1970s, manifested in the rise of the human rights movement in the USA, the student revolution, the struggle against the Vietnam War, the rise of women's and environmental movements. These movements reflected increasing discontent among the general public, particularly the young generation. The desire for an alternative life style and the request for direct and participatory democracy were pervasive.

In this milieu, students and university teachers became increasingly critical of the role of science and research in society and open to radical analyses and solutions. The request for academic freedom, alternative thinking and the will to improve society was pervasive. The critique of positivism, reification and fragmentation of sciences into more or less isolated disciplines and subcultures was commonly heard. Consequently, there was a widespread demand for interdisciplinary science which would produce more realistic knowledge about society.

Today, the situation is rather similar to that of the 1960s and 1970s. Following the global financial crisis of 2008 and its social and economic consequences, students and academics have again become more critical. Again, they criticise science for being unable to deal with real world problems. This is particularly prominent in economics which is criticised for being reductionist and too limiting in its approaches to mathematical deductions based on the unrealistic world view of utilitarianism and the models of general equilibrium. People realise that orthodox mainstream economics was unable to predict the financial collapse and offers no promising solutions to the current economic, political and social crisis. Recently, students of economics have responded by launching movements which push for a paradigm shift in the economics profession and a heterodox curriculum involving alternative and more realistic economics teaching at universities. Examples of this are the *International Student Initiative for Pluralism in Economics* and the *Kick it Over Manifesto*. The students demand interdisciplinary approaches, teaching of real world debates and pluralism of theories and methods. They claim that theoretical pluralism is missing as neoclassical economics dominates education in economics. The students insist that what is needed is education in classical, post-Keynesian, institutional, ecological, feminist, Marxist and the Austrian tradition among others, besides neoclassical economics. This book responds to this cry for pluralism and interdisciplinarity. Its main aim is to demonstrate why the neoclassical approach is inadequate in studies into innovation and entrepreneurship. The book discusses why it is necessary to approach studies in this field in a pluralist and interdisciplinary way.

I would like to use this opportunity to thank my former supervisors, Michael Dunford and the late Christopher Freeman at the University of Sussex, for inspiring comments while I was working on my doctoral dissertation. Their inspiration sets its mark on the present work. I would also like to thank Ashgate's anonymous reviewers for their helpful comments on my manuscript. Neil Jordan and the staff of Ashgate have been very motivating to collaborate with during the publication process of this book. I am indebted to Rafn Kjartansson for his proofreading and constructive comments on my manuscript. Furthermore, I would like to thank the Østfold University College for supporting the publication of this work and in particular, I am thankful for the good atmosphere and excellent morale among my colleagues at the Faculty of Business, Languages and Social Sciences.

I am especially thankful to my family, Jon Reginbald Ivarsson and Lilja Mosesdottir, for remarkable encouragement to stand my intellectual ground during the past decades and for my wife, Lilja's, constructive comments on my work.

Ivar Jonsson

Chapter 1

Introduction

In recent years, students of social and economic development have often been preoccupied with concepts such as 'the new economy', 'the learning economy', 'knowledge economy' and 'smart economy'. The idea of these various new economies is usually presented as if they were part of an inevitable development. It is presumed that new technology and globalisation unavoidably leads to a transformation of societies and politics, adapting them to the 'new economy'. It is assumed that countries which are not quick enough to adjust to the 'new times' will turn out as losers in the competition to achieve new investments and new enterprises. Hence, they will fail in the race for ever increasing economic welfare.

Similar ideas to those mentioned above have appeared before. Daniel Bell's (1960) theories of the end of ideology are an instance in point. He argued that class struggle was withering away in Western countries because economic welfare was steadfastly increasing together with the growth of the middle classes and the service sector. Thus bitter conflicts between workers and employers had been consigned to the scrap heap of history. Related ideas appeared during the late 1980s in Francis Fukuyama's (1989) theories of the end of history. In his version, human history is reduced to the struggle between advocates of the market economy and Marxists, which culminated in the Cold War and ended in the collapse of the planned economies of Eastern-Europe. The victory of the market economy marked the end of history according to Fukuyama.

The simplified understanding of societal development that we find in the discourse on the new economy and the theory of the end of ideology and history reflects the tendency of Western scholars to view the world in the light of their own dominant ideology, philosophical tradition and history and to postulate that the social 'laws' of their own history are valid for the development of all other societies. This determinism has its roots in the spirit of eighteenth century enlightenment and it has driven them, in a Eurocentric way, to regard the cultures of other areas and countries as obsolete. Typically, they presume that non-Western societies are relegated to some kind of a waiting room of the health centre of human history, where they bide their time until Western scientists and technocrats are ready to give them medical treatment and quicken their maturity so that they can, as soon as possible, become comparable to Western societies. This sort of thinking is to be found in, for example, W.W. Rostow's still appreciated book, *The Stages of Economic Growth: A Non-Communist Manifesto*, from 1960 in which he claims that developing countries must 'modernise' as Western countries have done, if they are to be able to prepare for a 'take-off'.

There are many lapses in the simplified view of society briefly discussed above. *Firstly*, in addition to market forces and opposing class interests, other pressures also shape social development. Gender and ethnic relations are prevailing roots of conflict both in Western societies and other societies. Environmental issues generate political conflict and the foundation of political movements, as well as factions within established political parties.

Secondly, capitalist countries differ significantly. Social and institutional structures are diverse in different countries and affect market forces in various ways. This applies to welfare state institutions, labour market regimes, environmental laws and regulations, etc. Different countries have divergent political systems, culture and history and this affect their economies in different ways. It is more realistic to talk about 'capitalisms' rather than capitalism in the singular (see I. Jonsson, 1989; R.J. Holton, 1992; J. Gray, 1999; P.A. Hall and D.W. Soskice, 2001). Consequently we would claim that it is unrealistic to take economic determinism as a point of departure and adopt a monist view of capitalism.

Thirdly, social scientists are increasingly aware of the varieties of economic systems and have developed models and theories that take into account other factors than those of short term supply, demand and general equilibrium. Business transactions are usually in the form of continuous dealings of inputs and outputs and are based on imperfect information. This makes it difficult to explain economic behaviour in terms of the fundamental idea of economics, namely the idea of the rational '*homo economicus*'. The rational man, it is assumed, always attempts to optimise her/his pleasure or utility and minimise pain or cost and conducts her/his business in an absolutely rational and impersonal way. This simplified picture of the maximising, rational man and of impersonal markets emerged, and was possibly more realistic, in the eighteenth century when markets were predominantly relatively foreseeable small village markets (see R.J. Holton, 1992; J. Gray, 1999). The idea of homo economicus is rather misleading, however, in view of contemporary market transactions in which long term collaboration between buyers and sellers of inputs and outputs in an atmosphere of mutual trust is crucial for business success. There are more points to mention. Collaboration between corporations, various research institutions and universities is of vital importance for high-tech companies. Effective knowledge infrastructures of different economies also play an important role with regard to corporate innovation activities. This does not only refer to communication infrastructures such as the internet and satellite technology, but to various institutionalised forums for formal and informal knowledge exchange.

Finally, ready access by corporations and institutions to a highly educated workforce and accumulated local know-how is important for corporate growth. The same goes for governmental bodies which support business life in contemporary societies.

In short, the view that businesses and markets are the only factors engaged in corporate transactions and corporate competition is obsolete. The same applies to the assumption that social development allows only two alternatives i.e., a choice between private or public enterprises. Real world economics is different; it is characterised by various forms of collaboration between corporations, public institutions and non-profit organisations.

This book concentrates on the driving forces of innovation and entrepreneurship. Research into this field of study is basically twofold. *Firstly*, we come across the '*empiricist*' tradition which builds on research into economic history and actual innovation processes of public and private enterprises. Theories of long waves in economic life, the so called 'Kondratieffs', as well as theories of innovation as learning processes belong to this tradition. *Secondly*, we come across theories based on deductions which generate hypotheses of innovation activity on the basis of *a priori* theoretical assumptions. These theories presume that the driving force of innovation is managers' rational decision-making concerning productivity, as well as marginal use of factors of production or technology and workforce. We may call this tradition '*rationalist*'. That is the ground on which Western orthodox economics is built and the sort of economics that most Western universities teach. However, the orthodox tradition has proved unable to explain the driving forces of innovation activity today. Research shows it is misleading to presume that knowledge necessary for innovation activity can be treated as market goods, bought and sold on impersonal markets. Knowledge is a phenomenon firms and individuals acquire, mediate and actively transform in their interaction with one another. The development and communication of knowledge is based on long term trust between collaborating actors within and outside firms rather than on opportunistic and impersonal short term business transactions.

The preconditions for innovation and entrepreneurship have also changed to some extent in recent decades. International trade has increased, especially within geographically large areas such as Europe, Asia and North and South America. International trade is also largely limited to particular branches of industries such as the financial sector, electronics and automobile industries (L. Weiss, 1998). The role of the nation state in economic and social development has changed as the state has gradually become more active in developing domestic and cross-border infrastructures and laws and regulations which enhance corporate innovation activity and competitiveness. At the same time, 'national' firms participate more than before in research and development activity (R&D) and in the production of transnational corporations, often as subcontractors of such corporations. Internationalisation in this form and a different view on the role of the nation state has generated new conditions for businesses, municipalities and regional governments. These actors increasingly collaborate in order to strengthen the competitiveness of firms, improve their innovation activity and intercorporate cooperation. In many cases, collaboration appears in 'innovation clusters', involving partnerships between competing firms in particular industrial branches. Collaboration can also appear in 'Triple Helix' 'partnerships' of corporations, universities, and governmental bodies. However, we must keep in mind that a discussion on internationalisation and 'globalisation' exaggerates the actual development and one tends to forget that the bulk of world production, or over

85 per cent, is domestic for national use, but not global markets (see N. Fligstein, 2002, pp. 189–90 and 196–98; L. Sklair, 2003; R. Saul, 2005, pp. 18–22).

We claim that research and theories of innovation and entrepreneurship are associated with three levels of innovation activity. *Firstly*, they focus on the *macro-level*; that is the impact of innovation activity on long economic waves, business cycles, economic growth and the development of societies and economies as production systems. *Secondly*, they concentrate on the impact on innovation activity of relationships between firms, research institutes and governmental bodies. Here the focus is on the *meso-level*. *Thirdly*, there is research and theories on the *micro-level* of innovation activity, concerned with the dynamics of innovations within firms and institutions, as well as on personal characteristics of the entrepreneurs themselves. The structure of this book reflects these different levels of innovation and entrepreneurship.

In Chapter 2, we define the main concepts and briefly discuss the principal objects of research into innovation and entrepreneurship in order to clarify the 'territory' or field of study of the political economy of innovation and entrepreneurship. Furthermore, we observe different branches of science which influence research of innovation and technological development, ranging from different disciplines of social sciences to feminist studies. It appears that the basic ideas and methodologies of many of these sciences are diverse and limited to 'intra-disciplinary' approaches rather than 'inter-disciplinary' approaches. We claim that research in the field of innovation and entrepreneurial activity originally developed from classical economics. This adhered to positivism and dealt with the objects from the point of view of macro-economic interests. More recently, different approaches developed that adhered to organisational studies and institutionalist methods which emphasise the interaction between internal, cultural aspects of organisations and external social, political and cultural factors in their environment.

Chapter 3 discusses the main theories of, and research into, the interaction between innovation activity and economic development in order to provide an overview of research engaged with *macro-level* socio-economic impacts of innovation and entrepreneurship. The discussion starts with theories of long waves in economic life i.e., the so-called 'Kondratieff-waves'. This discussion is followed by a presentation of neoclassical theories of innovation which reduces technical change to the idea of production functions. Finally, we present theories of innovation that take theories of learning processes as their point of departure and discuss the contribution of evolutionary theories and neo-Schumpeterianism.

Chapters 4 and 5 yield insights into *meso-level* research and theories of innovation and entrepreneurship. The focus of Chapter 4 is on various forms of corporate collaboration. Companies often engage in various types of cooperation and utilise more than one form. It would appear from the discussion that emphasis has changed in this regard. In recent years, companies have begun to intensify their utilisation of forms such as joint ventures and collaborative networks. Furthermore, corporations have increasingly emphasised external sources of knowledge and implemented new principles in organising their innovation activity. They have become more user oriented and introduced a new model of innovation; that is, the open innovation model which requires new organisational principles concerning innovation activity, particularly in terms of intellectual property rights and reciprocal exchange of internal and external knowledge with a number of innovation collaborators.

In Chapter 5, we focus on the contribution of economic geography to research on innovation and entrepreneurship in order to incorporate the regional dimension into our discussion of studies of innovation and entrepreneurship. The discussion suggests that ideas and theoretical approaches have changed greatly through time. We claim that theories of economic geography have developed from building on the plain ideas of neo-classical economics, concerning minimising production cost in relation to location of production, to institutionalist theories which emphasise the role of collaboration between firms and institutions in advancing competitiveness. Moreover, we highlight the regionally bounded social and cultural conditions of such cooperation. Finally, the discussion turns to the role of social capital, regional innovation clusters and Triple Helix partnerships of corporations, universities, and governmental bodies.

In Chapter 6, we move to the '*micro-level*' of innovation and entrepreneurship and its dynamics within organisations. We observe two approaches to innovation management; that is, one which represents 'top-down' management strategy and another emphasising a 'bottom-up' approach. We highlight the influential theories of P.F. Drucker who approaches innovation from the point of view of top-down management. It appears that Drucker's main object of study is the nature of systematic innovation activity based on well-defined goals. Moreover, it is rooted in seven sources of innovation opportunities which Drucker refers to as *the unexpected; incongruities; process need; industry and market structures; demographics (population changes);changes in perception, mood, and meaning and; new knowledge*. We also discuss a more recent bottom-up approach which emphasises the role of 'active employee participation' in innovation processes. In this context, we present John Bessant's 'high-involvement' approach of active employee participation which is an example of management techniques belonging to the category of 'techniques and methods of innovation'. The main conclusion of the discussion in this chapter is that innovation and entrepreneurship is by a nature group or team activity. Innovation and entrepreneurship is, therefore, a no less 'collective' endeavour on the micro-level than on the meso- and macro-level.

Chapter 7 focuses on social innovations in terms of being processes of defining social problems, as well as representing an active search for solutions and ways of implementing social improvements. We argue that social innovations concern social improvements realised by agents who actively influence the contexts in which social innovation takes place. We highlight common features of processes of social innovation in rather dissimilar contexts and at different levels of social transformation i.e., micro, meso and macro levels. It would appear that processes of social innovation are non-teleological, but at the same time moulded by the particular societal contexts in which social innovators structure and actively transform social relations in a social constructivist way. Finally, we observe the cases of Lord Horatio Nelson, Benjamin Franklin and Margaret Thatcher in order to illustrate processes at these different levels of social innovations.

The final Chapter, 8, gives an account of the various theories and modes of research into innovation and entrepreneurship. A common feature of most of these theories is that they are 'monistic' rather than general and plural i.e., they envisage that one or only a few factors adequately explain the dynamics of innovation and entrepreneurship. They do not emphasise the importance of interaction between diverse explanatory factors. These theories name factors such as inventions in science and technology, market demand, egoism, profit maximisation of firms, etc. We argue in this book that innovation activity is too complicated to be reduced to a single factor or explained within the narrow theoretical framework of a single discipline. A general theory is needed to explain innovation and entrepreneurship; that is, a theory which can illustrate why particular explanatory factors of innovation and entrepreneurship are important during specific historical periods or in particular countries within the different fields of innovation and entrepreneurship. In this concluding chapter, we sketch a framework which includes the main factors such a general theory should incorporate. The main emphasis is on the societal and collective nature of innovation activity. This view proposes that the main precondition for innovation activity is a culture which breeds willingness to collaborate, creativity and tolerance concerning new ways of thinking and generating knowledge. Market mechanisms alone do not create these preconditions and therefore other actors than competing corporations play an important role.

Chapter 2
Innovation and Entrepreneurship as an Interdisciplinary Field of Study

2.1 Introduction

In this chapter, we will observe the field of research into innovation and entrepreneurship in terms of the main sciences that contribute to this field of study. First, we will define its objects of study and subsequently we will discuss the contributions of the various sciences in this field. We will observe contributions from economics, political economy, sociology, psychology, organisation theory and feminism.

2.2 The Main Concepts of Innovation and Entrepreneurship

Research into innovation and entrepreneurship focuses on analysing the impact of technological development on goods and services in terms of design of products, production processes and marketing. Furthermore, the research in this field concentrates on the social and economic conditions as well as consequences of innovation and entrepreneurial activity. This discipline attempts to analyse the dynamics of technological development, a concept referring to machines and tools as well as techniques and organisational forms of work. Consequently technique is to be approached as both a social and engineering phenomenon. The concept of 'technological development' refers to processes that include both inventions and innovations in production and services. Furthermore, the concept of 'innovation' refers to implementation of new technology in corporations, non-profit organisations and public institutions.

'Entrepreneurial activity' comprises realising innovations; that is, implementing a new technology, process of production or service and organisation of work. An 'entrepreneur' is an individual who carries out activities of this kind. Individuals that establish firms are therefore, not to be defined as 'entrepreneurs' unless their work realises innovation. Spin-off companies are cases at hand which illustrate our point. Companies like these are established in order to develop particular goods or services that are new on the market. Such companies are innovative in this sense, although the concept of innovation is wider than this presumes, since innovation refers to the implementation of new technologies and production processes and the organisation of businesses. The concept also covers the improved skills of workers and their work conditions. Thus, concept of innovation and entrepreneurship is not limited to spin-off companies.[1]

Researchers of innovation and entrepreneurship tend to categorise this kind of activity variously. How they categorise it depends on their different theoretical and disciplinary backgrounds as well as different socioeconomic objectives. Moreover, the forms of innovation activity vary in different historical periods of the individual branches of industry and particular countries. They are also diverse, depending on what kind of knowledge they are based. Finally, innovation activities differ depending on the size of the organisations in question.

In general terms one can distinguish between 'process innovation' which relates to the implementation of new technology in the processes of production, and 'product innovation', referring to the implementation of new products or services. Furthermore, innovation activity is categorised with regard to how extensive its impact is on economic systems and societal development. According to this train of thought, innovation may be in the form of small scale improvements of production processes or products that lead to increased productivity of the organisation in question. This kind of innovation is called 'incremental innovation'. However, innovations can also appear in the form of technological revolutions that lead to fundamental change in societal structures. In Chapter 3 (section 3.2) we discuss this matter in more detail.

It appears from our discussion above that innovation activity has various social and economic aspects, but one has to keep in mind that innovation does not take place unless individuals, corporations and institutions work actively on it. It is in this context that innovation teams play their role. Consequently, it is among the main objects of students of innovation to analyse the role of entrepreneurs in the economy. The research that scientists of innovation and entrepreneurship carry out therefore extends into the territory of psychology, particularly social psychology, and management studies. In short, research into innovation and entrepreneurship is highly interdisciplinary as it requires students of innovation and entrepreneurship to make use of approaches and research methods from various disciplines of science. As a consequence, the research is characterised by 'methodological pluralism'. Table 2.1 highlights the main objects of study of innovation and entrepreneurship.

As the table indicates, research into innovation and entrepreneurship is such a wide ranging field of study that interdisciplinary approaches fit it best. However, economics is probably the discipline that has influenced it more than other academic fields. We will start our discussion by scrutinising different approaches within economics, as well as highlighting ways in which economics obstructs research into innovation activity and observing how it enhances innovation research.

---

1   For further discussion see e.g. the definition of entrepreneurship by J.A. Schumpeter (1939, p. 84) and the one provided by the European Commission (1995) in *Green Paper on Innovation* COM 688, p. 1 and by OECD & Eurostat. 3. ed. (2005) *Oslo Manual – Guidelines for Collecting and Interpreting Innovation Data*, p. 46.

Table 2.1   The main objects of study of innovation and entrepreneurship

Actors and factors that influence innovation processes	Disciplines that provide input	Object of study
Individuals	Psychology and history	Personality and history of entrepreneurs
Groups	Social psychology, sociology, organisation theory and management studies	Entrepreneurial teams
Organisations (corporations and institutions)	Organisation and management studies, sociology, industrial economics	Corporate innovation alliances, innovation clusters, globalisation of innovation activity
Governments, public authorities and organised interests	Political science and political sociology, political economy and evolutionary economics	Science and technology policy, national and regional systems of innovation, societal development and techno-economic paradigms
Culture	Anthropology, sociology, organisation studies, institutional economics and history	Corporate culture, social capital, innovation and entrepreneurial activity of different social groups and nations

2.3 Economics and Innovation and Entrepreneurship

2.3.1 Economic Liberalism

Modern economics is rooted in economic liberalism that on the one hand emerged from classical economics of the nineteenth century and neoclassical economics of the twentieth century, on the other (R.J. Holton, 1992). Both classical and the neoclassical economics emerged from the world view of the enlightenment and liberalism of the eighteenth century. The enlightenment opposed the theological worldview of the church. According to the Enlightenment, nature is ruled by its own laws and the same goes for society. The 'Philosophers' as they were called, like Voltaire, Rousseau, Condorcet and Turgot, found the alternative to the worldview of the church in the theories of Isaac Newton who had explained the dynamics of the universe in his book *De Philosophiae Naturalis Principia Mathematica*, published in 1687.[2]

---

2   It is not our aim to write a history of Western ideas in this book. For a short overview see A. Callinincos (1999) *Social Theory: A Historical Introduction*.

The new worldview presumed secularism and the idea of progress. It was built on six main postulates: *Firstly*, human conduct must be based on rational decisions rather than tradition. *Secondly*, explanations of the world must be based on empirical research. *Thirdly*, it was presumed that the methodology of natural sciences must be exploited in all fields of knowledge creation in order to establish scientific laws by which nature and the conduct of humans should be explained. *Fourth*, tolerance should prevail concerning religious and political life. *Fifthly*, economic and social freedom was required for all citizens. *Lastly*, political restructuring was requested and political life was to be built on human rights that were considered to be 'rights of nature'.

The idea of general human rights or 'natural rights' was coined in the French revolution of 1789. A new constitution was implemented and an attempt was made to build a new society based on 'liberty, equality and brotherhood'. With these slogans it was required that the citizens should enjoy freedom of opinion, freedom of speech and all citizens should be treated equally by the courts. Privileges of class and particular religions would be abandoned.

The individualism that appeared in these claims had appeared before in theories on the laws of economic and political life. John Locke (1632–1704) argued for his theory of 'tabula rasa' and declared that the mind and thought of human kind is not prescribed (by god), but is like an unwritten sheet of paper at the birth of the individual. Ideas rise from the experience of the individual according to Locke. Improved environment, increased enlightenment and education will lead to progress. Improvements of the governmental system based on human rights will secure liberty for the citizens, leading to progress. According to Locke, natural rights refer to the right to live, right of free opinion and the right of private ownership. He presumed that the role of the state should be to secure the natural rights or human rights as they are called today (J. Locke, 1690).

The Frenchman C-L. Montesquieu (1689–1755) was preoccupied with comparative studies of the judicial systems and traditions of different societies and cultures. His main contribution to the development of Western ideas of human rights was his idea of the separation of powers; that is judicial power, legislative power and executive power. According to Montesquieu a threefold separation of power would secure the equality of the individuals in society vis-à-vis the government and this would hinder the possibility that particular social groups could abuse the institutions of power to enhance their own interests (C-L. Montesquieu, 1748).

The idea of laissez-faire
The question concerning what kind of organisation of the economy is best suited to its laws was imperative following the rise of the new worldview. The eighteenth century gave birth to the idea of laissez-faire. This is a French concept that means, 'let do'. It is generally believed that the physiocrats (1756–1778) were pioneers of the concept of laissez-faire. They were French economists who believed that the economy was determined by economic laws that were as infallible as the laws of nature. The theories of A.R.J. Turgot (1727–1781) were akin to those of the

physiocrats; he believed that egoism and ambitions of individuals constituted the fundamental source of economic and social progress. The British philosopher David Hume (1711–1776) was also among the pioneers of the idea of laissez-faire. Hume opposed the physiocrats and enlightenment philosophers and criticised Newton's idea of science. He rejected his idea of searching for a few ahistorical and unalterable laws that determine the universe. Hume claimed that it is impossible to prove the infallibility of such laws in the future as the future does not exist as an empirical phenomenon, but is a mere idea. One cannot prove anything that does not yet exist empirically (David Hume, 1739; Book I, Part III, Sect. vi, para. 5–6).

It was Adam Smith (1723–1790) more than anyone who cleared the road for the idea of laissez-faire in economics. He founded 'classical economics', the most important school in economics between 1776–1870. In his book *An Inquiry into the Nature and Causes of the Wealth of Nations* (1776), he argued that individuals, because of their 'self-love', push for the maximisation of their utility in their transactions on a free market and generate a maximum level of production in the economy at large. Smith used the ambiguous metaphor of 'the invisible hand of the market' to illustrate what is at stake. Soon after, and ever since he published his book, social scientists have debated what this invisible hand looks like and how markets work in reality.

If we presume that Adam Smith was the first man to present sound arguments to the effect that egoism and free markets generate maximum economic welfare, then we can assume that John Stuart Mill (1806–1873) was the one who made the idea of laissez-faire popular in the nineteenth century with his book *Principles of Political Economy* (1848), which focuses on the role and extent of the public sector in the economy.

The idea of utilitarian egoism
The idea of laissez-faire became one of the fundamental ideas of classical economics and liberalism in the eighteenth and nineteenth centuries. Another basic element this train of thought was constructed by J. Bentham (1748–1832), i.e. 'utilitarianism'. Utilitarianism presupposed that individuals act rationally and maximise their pleasure, while at the same time minimising the pain caused them by their conduct. It also assumed that individuals are able to calculate the degree of pleasure and pain resulting from every action; thus they use the 'hedonic calculus' when deciding how to act. Every human being is, therefore, by nature '*homo economicus*' who calculates utility and cost resulting from his action and always maximises his utility at minimum cost.

Following the expansion of the market economy in the nineteenth century, poverty became an increasing social problem and the capitalist factories brought greater misery than people had experienced before. Progressive liberalists came forward and began redefining the role of the state in capitalist societies. Mill is the best known liberalist who opposed the view of the older generation which took it for granted that social and economic laws are infallible and ahistorical. He declared that only laws of nature are universal while social laws are 'empirical';

that is, shaped by the particular period of history in question (J.S. Mill, 1843; Chapter 10, Part 3–5). These laws are not imperative; that is, humanity is not doomed to follow them. People can choose between different types of societies in which different kinds of 'empirical laws' prevail. Mill argued that one should not oppose social experiments such as the Saint-Simonian small socialist societies as these are the Saint-Simonians' own choice, but they do not have the right to force other citizens to endure such experiments (J.S. Mill, 1848; Book 2, Chapter 1).

Moreover, Mill not only rejected the determinism of the older generation of classical economists and liberalists (cf. Smith, Bentham and Malthus); he also rejected its naïve progressivism. Their progressivism presumed that history was characterised by a development towards higher stages of improvement. Opposed to this view, Mill felt that progress implied only and simply a change from one social system to the next (J.S. Mill, 1843; Chapter 10, Part 3).

John Stuart Mill criticised the unregulated market system and promoted reformist, social liberalism. As markets are created by human beings, there is no deterministic, natural, scientific or moral necessity for a market system that forces misery and ruthless exploitation upon its citizens. Hence, capitalism can be reformed. Mill cleared the path for new definitions of the role of the state and the development of welfare states. Following this train of thought, he particularly emphasised reforms in the educational system (J.S. Mill, 1845).

Historians (cf. J. Grey, 1999) claim that the period in which an unfettered capitalist market system existed was short, approximately the period 1850–1875, and it was an anomaly in the history of human kind. Liberalists such as John Maynard Keynes developed theories of the scale and scope of state interventions in market economies in the 1930s. Public interventions in the market economy and social reforms do not only have moral value, but are important for economic reasons as public mediation and steering of general demand through welfare expenditure and investments in infrastructure can to large extent even out economic fluctuations and hinder economic depressions (I. Jonsson, 1991a).

The ideas of laissez-faire and utilitarianism are the core concepts of classical and latter time economics. We will now observe these two fundamental notions on which 'economic liberalism' is based. Economic liberalism is one of three main traditions of research into economic life alongside 'social economics' or economic sociology' and 'political economy' that we will discuss below (R.J. Holton, 1992, pp. 50–51).

Utilitarianism presupposes that individuals are rational and that consequently their decisions are rational. The idea of laissez-faire assumes that without state interventions in the economy and with unhindered competition, the level of production will be maximal and law and order and social harmony will be secured. Let us have a closer look at these assumptions and start with the utilitarian presumption of the rationality of '*homo economicus*'.

According to utilitarianism, the individual always maximises his or her utility. This assumption is based on the belief that the needs and personality of the individual are pre given; that is, they are independent of the individual's interaction with other people and are thus pre-social. In short, individuals are 'sovereign' in their transactions on the market. In the nineteenth century the advocates of classical economics postulated *a priori* that human needs are rooted in the inborn psychological and physical characteristics of humans that appear in hedonism and the human need of maximising pleasure and minimising pain. Hedonism would have it that each and every good in the market has particular utility in relation to the pleasure it can realise. But, despite many attempts, no one has been able to prove the existence of a law or causality that can explain the law of hedonism. Modern economists have, therefore, agreed on a more limited premise; that is, the concept of 'revealed preferences' and they claim that it does not matter where the needs originate as the main thing is that they are actually revealed. On the basis of revealed preferences the economists hypothesise that individuals can 1) list their needs in order of priority and 2) they can rearrange the order of priority of goods if their prices change. Modern economics has consequently given up its attempts to explain where human needs come from, but clings to the idea of homo economicus i.e., the idea that individuals maximise their utility when they buy goods on the market.

For a very long time sociologists have criticised the idea of *homo economicus*. They maintain, as for example Talcott Parsons, that if needs are entirely limited to the individual, they are random which would lead to social chaos and no law and order and social harmony would prevail in society. Other sociologists who adhere to 'social reductionism' claim that needs are determined by the social situation of the individuals, such as class, sex and ethnicity. Still other scientists assert that '*homo economicus*' is but a historical phenomenon limited to a particular society; that is, capitalism. According to this view, personalities characterised by egoism and instrumental rationality are only to be found in a society where the economic sphere is separated from other spheres. Finally, sociologists claim that the conditions for rational decision making are historically determined, namely, what individuals presume to be good, bad, beautiful and ugly is determined by the kind of society they life in; for example which religions and what kinds of morality are predominant in the society in question.

In short, the utilitarianism of economics can be criticised for the following points: *Firstly*, the idea that the actions of individuals are based on hedonism does not have any empirical grounds; *Secondly*, the concept of revealed preferences in no way reflects the conditions upon which rational decisions taken by *homo economicus* are based and therefore does not explain the varying formation of revealed preferences in different social contexts. The same applies to sociologists who adhere to social reductionism. They have not been successful in explaining the development of needs or revealed preferences by means of social reductionism. Social reductionism seems the more fruitless the more fragmented societies are.

Let us turn now to the idea of laissez-faire. It presumes, *firstly*, that egoism determines the actions of individuals on the market and, *secondly*, that they act rationally. *Thirdly*, it surmises that free markets are determined by their own laws which constitute sufficient precondition for securing the maximum level of production of the economy and its sustainability i.e., that there is no need for external actors to keep the economy going by intervention. Let us look closer at this point.

One of the fundamental theoretical assumptions of economics is that human interaction is determined by egoism or 'self-love' as Adam Smith called it. Concerning Man, he claimed:

> In civilised society he stands at all times in need of the cooperation and assistance of great multitudes, while his whole life is scarce sufficient to gain the friendship of a few persons. In almost every other race of animals each individual, when it is grown up to maturity, is entirely independent, and in its natural state has occasion for the assistance of no other living creature. But man has almost constant occasion for the help of his brethren, and it is in vain for him to expect it from their benevolence only. He will be more likely to prevail if he can interest their self-love in his favour, and show them that it is for their own advantage to do for him what he requires of them. Whoever offers to another a bargain of any kind, proposes to do this. Give me that which I want, and you shall have this which you want, is the meaning of every such offer; and it is in this manner that we obtain from one another the far greater part of those good offices which we stand in need of. (A. Smith, 1796/1904; Book I, Chapter 2, I.2.2)

This assumption has in recent times been doubted both within and outside economic circles. The claim that egoism controls human conduct is an assumption that does not survive the test of reality. It is so general that it can explain any decisions and hence has very scant explanatory power in terms of different decisions that are based on divergent preferences. In brief, the critique of the assumption that egoism controls human conduct concerns three main subjects:

a. the role of meta-preferences in decisions;
b. the role of morals and feelings in decisions
c. the preconditions of maximisation in decisions

Let us have a closer look at this matter.

Concerning the role of meta-preferences in decisions, we would claim that the needs of people are not all of the same nature and therefore they are not equally easy to evaluate in terms of utility-cost calculation. Some of our preferences are fundamental to other preferences (A. Hirschman, 1984). Such fundamental preferences are not only basic to other preferences, but also influence how our tastes and preferences in different spheres develop over a long period. Hirschman calls these fundamental preferences 'meta-preferences'. Our taste for chocolates or sausages is of different kind than our taste for peace or preservation of the environment. Because of our views of war and the environment we do, as an example, not give our kids toys such as guns or battery driven playthings, or we do not buy shares in polluting corporations. In short, some of our preferences are more important than others.

Concerning the role of morals and feelings in decisions, Nobel-prize winner Amartya Kumar Sen's critique is valuable. His point of departure is decisions of individuals in relation to the welfare of their fellow individuals. Sen claims that decisions of this sort are of two kinds; that is sympathy and commitment. As Sen puts it:

> ... we must distinguish between two separate concepts: (i) sympathy and (ii) commitment.

> The former corresponds to the case in which the concern for others directly affects one's own welfare. If the knowledge of torture of others makes you sick, it is a case of sympathy; if it does not make you feel personally worse off, but you think it is wrong and you are ready to do something to stop it, it is a case of commitment. (A.K. Sen, 1977, p. 326)

Social security systems are examples of decisions based on sympathy while voluntary activity is an example of commitment.[3] Commitments are altruistic decisions which presume that individuals pay costs without gaining pleasure or utility in return.

Economic decisions of individuals are influenced by feelings as well as meta-preferences and moral considerations. Consumers do more than simply calculate cost and utility of goods. Their decisions are influenced by feelings such as pride, joy, guilt and shame. Moreover, economic decisions are affected by prejudices such as sexism and racism, and such cases lead to 'irrational' decisions concerning employing staff, investment and consumption. An example would be a case where a lower skilled white person is hired for a job instead of a higher skilled black person. Moreover, some people avoid doing business with individuals of a particular ethnic background or the corporations they own.

Although some economists agree with this critique of the assumption of egoism the response of most contemporary economists has been to adhere to a contemporary version of utilitarianism. We are here referring to theories of 'rational choice' (cf. G. Becker and J. Elster). The concept of 'free rider' is particularly important in this context. It is deduced from the assumption of egoism or self-love. According to the idea of the free rider, individuals always attempt to gain the advantage of consuming goods or services that other individuals have paid for without paying anything themselves (cf. consuming public services and cheating the tax system). Consequently, it is presumed that individuals always try to cheat each other. Rational choice analyses are based on 'game theory' and the theoretical case of the 'prisoner's dilemma'. The case of the prisoner's dilemma is described thus: Two prisoners are suspected of having committed a crime together.

---

3   This distinction by Sen is similar to Aristotle's analysis of friendship or 'Philia'.

They put into separate cells in a prison. The police tell both of them: If you witness against your comrade and he does not witness against you, he will be released (box 3 in Table 2.2); If they witness against each other, they will both get three years in prison (box 1); If he does not witness against his comrade, but his comrade witnesses against him, he will get five years in prison (box 2); If they do not witness against each other, the police say there is enough evidence for both of them to get one year in prison (box 4). In situations like that of the prisoner's dilemma, fundamental characteristics of human interaction emerge according to advocates of ´rational choice'; that is, the prisoners do not trust each other and believe their comrade will cheat and witness against them. Thus result will be the one in box (1) i.e., they both get three years in prison, but not what is best for them, namely box (4).

The conclusion that advocates of rational choice draw from the table and previous arguments, can be criticised by bringing time and social context into the argument. If the prisoners believe they will work together in the future or can be a threat to each other, they will not witness against each other. Moreover, the conclusion of rational choice scholars can also be criticised like Granovetter (1985) does on the grounds of lack of realism. The prisoner's dilemma describes a very unusual situation that cannot be taken as a general rule. One can point at similar but contrasting cases such as when a family escapes a burning house and the family members tend to trust each other and help each other rather than trampling each other down. The conclusion of the critique of rational choice train of thought is, therefore, that lack of trust is the base for some decisions while trust determines other decisions depending on time and social context.[4]

Table 2.2   Prisoner's dilemma

		Prisoner A	
		Witnesses against B	Does not witness against B
Prisoner B	Witnesses against A	(1) Both get three years in prison	(2) A gets five years in prison (B is released)
	Does not witness against A	(3) B gets five years in prison (A is released)	(4) Both get one year in prison as police have enough evidence

---

4   As we discuss in Chapter 5, trust is an important condition for innovation activity. Consequently we emphasise the critique of egoism discussed here, as egoism is a theoretical assumption that most schools of economics maintain.

C. Perrow (1986) has argued that the egoism or self-interest of individuals is influenced by the context in which individuals find themselves; some contexts reduce egoism while other contexts increase it. R.J. Holton (1992, p. 86) has summed up six types of the contexts at issue. According to Holton, in contexts or workplaces where *interaction between individuals* is minimal, the context encourages self-interest. An example of this is fluid labour markets based on single migrant workers, high turnover of labour and occupations with a heavy emphasis on individual promotion. Opposed to this, in contexts where interaction between individuals is close, self-interest is discouraged. An example would be occupations with group job rotation and occupational communities where workplace and residence are stable and common for most of the workforce.

The *nature of rewards* encourages or discourages self-interest. When work rewards are accrued to individuals rather than teams or groups, self-interest is encouraged. The opposite are contexts in which group based rewards prevail.

Self-interest is encouraged in contexts where the *work effort* of individuals can be measured. This goes for e.g., piece rates, and personal evaluations. In large indivisible projects based on teamwork and job transferability, individually based rewards are rarely possible.

Work design affects as well the degree of self-interest in organisations. When workers interdependence is minimised, e.g., in the case of Taylorist breakdown of work-tasks, self-interest increases. The more work organisation is based on interdependence, the more self-interest is discouraged. Examples of this are cooperative effort and activity which is not based on precise contractual specification.

In organisations where stable and continuous *leadership and authority* is emphasised and individual leaders are presumed to be omnicompetent, self-interest is encouraged. An example is a company established by an entrepreneur, owned and led by her. Contrasting this are organisations in which leadership rotates and all employees are regarded as potential leaders and hence skills develop in group context.

Finally, Holton refers to the role of *hierarchy* in organisations. In cases where rewards are unequally distributed, better rewards require pursuit of self-interest. In cases in which flat hierarchy prevails self-interest is discouraged as greater participation and less inequality is the condition for advance.

It would appear from the discussion above and Perrow's contribution that the concept of self-love or egoism is flawed in many ways when analysed in terms of social contexts, and the assumption of economics of maximising decisions also appears to be faulty. Let us discuss this concept.

Concerning the preconditions of maximisation in decisions, the utilitarian assumption of economics that individuals always maximise their utility has been criticised in many ways. The critique expressed by Herbert Simon (1982) is well known. He has shown that many factors in the organisation of work and motivation undermine the relationship between egoism and maximising behaviour. According to Simon, the information upon which decisions are made is always imperfect and bounded in the particular context in which the decisions take place. He uses the concept 'bounded rationality' to reflect this situation and claims that because decisions are determined by bounded rationality they can never be maximising as they are only 'satisficing' depending on the information at hand.

It seems reasonable to conclude from the discussion above that the *a priori* assumption of economics that individuals make rational decisions is flawed. In terms of summary: *Firstly*, it is unlikely that individuals can measure their preferences or utility as accurately as economics presupposes. As a consequence, we must reject naïve utilitarianism. *Secondly*, pure egoism seems to characterise relatively few situations and consequently we would doubt its explanatory power. *Thirdly*, information is imperfect and therefore decisions cannot be maximising.

The idea of general equilibrium
Beside the idea of the rational *homo economicus*, the notion of self-regulating markets that always tend to be in a state of equilibrium is among the fundamental theoretical assumptions of economics ever since Adam Smith. The main postulate is that markets work in such a way that prices of goods and services are determined by supply and demand and individuals and corporations on the markets always buy goods and services that maximise their utility at minimal cost. As all actors maximise their utility, the production of the economy is at optimum level given the factors of production that exist at that particular point in time and current preferences. Now, if this idea is to work, many preconditions must be met: Information has to be perfect concerning prices of goods and services on the market and the same applies to supply and demand with regard to all factors of production in the economy. Moreover, all factors of production must move freely in the markets without hindrances. In reality these preconditions never exist. No one has perfect information concerning all current market choices. Furthermore, there are many social and cultural reasons that generate 'market imperfections'. For various moral reasons investment is hindered in fields such as organised crime, projects that threaten nature, etc. There are many social hindrances in the labour market as people are for example reluctant to move between regions for family reasons.

Let us put aside the arguments above against the realism of the notion of how markets work. We may still accept that the market system has the advantage of securing 'allocative efficiency' and surmise that markets, by means of price signals, steer resources to uses that maximise outputs relative to inputs. Moreover, the price system responds to consumer choices, takes advantage of specialisation and hence optimises performance for a given level of resources (R. Kuttner, 1999, pp. 23–24). Allocative efficiency refers to a situation according to which investments in terms of their scale and scope lead to optimum level of production of the economy. The problem with this formulation is that this is limited to only one kind of efficiency and has scant explanatory power concerning the economy as a whole and its long term development. The main shortcoming is that it draws a static state picture of the economy and economic growth is analysed in terms of 'static growth'. This view is based on the assumption that the economy tends to stay in a state of equilibrium, since all factors of the economy, such as preferences or tastes of consumers, technology and labour, remain unchanged. Thus, information regarding their prices is a sufficient base for the market laws (of demand and supply) to secure optimum uses of those factors. If the price of one factor increases; the price of labour, for example, this will lead to decreasing demand for that particular factor as production costs have increased. Demand for labour will not rise again until its price has decreased so much that it is profitable to produce. According to this view, the same process of adjustment takes place in all markets and therefore the result will be a state of equilibrium in the economy.

As Joseph A. Schumpeter (1911/1934) has highlighted, there are three main reasons why a static condition like this is disturbed. *Firstly*, because of external disturbances in nature; *secondly*, because of noneconomic occurrences in society (war, changed economic or social policy) and; *thirdly*, because consumers' tastes change. Economics cannot explain why this happens, but can only *post festum* describe how adjustment to a new equilibrium took place. (J.A. Schumpeter, 1911/1934, p. 62). Economic theories cannot explain economic evolution as such; that is, the development of the factors of the economy themselves. Schumpeter claimed that: ' ... "static" analysis is not only unable to predict the consequences of discontinuous changes in the traditional way of doing things; it can neither explain the occurrence of such productive revolutions nor the phenomena which accompany them. It can only investigate the new equilibrium position after the changes have occurred'. (ibid., pp. 62–3)

Following Schumpeter's critique, it is clear that the emphasis in economics on analysis of equilibrium substantially limits the scope of economic research. An important part of economic life falls outside the research, namely the factors and dynamics of economic development.

We will now set aside Schumpeter's critique and focus on the postulation of economics that the free market system, or laissez-faire, secures optimum level of production of the economy and at the same time optimum efficiency in the use of factors of production. In this context it is worthwhile discussing the concept of efficiency itself. This concept is not as unambiguous as it seems at first sight. R. Kuttner (1999, pp. 23–4) has criticised this concept and recommends a distinction between three kinds of efficiencies; *firstly*, 'allocative efficiency' that we mentioned above; *secondly*, he mentions 'Schumpeterian efficiency' that we could call 'innovation efficiency' and; *thirdly*, 'Keynesian efficiency' that we could call 'employment efficiency'. Economics can only explain the first mentioned type of efficiency, but not the other two types.

'Innovation efficiency' refers to how efficient actors and economies at large are in stimulating and realising social and industrial innovations. Innovations refer to the implementation of technological changes that lead to increased productivity lasting for long periods (as we will discuss in more detail in chapter 3 below). Schumpeter analysed the role that oligopoly and imperfect competition plays in technological development and came to a very different conclusion than classical and neoclassical economics. Large oligopoly corporations frequently have the financial resources to reproduce and develop new technology so as to secure their privileged market position and to defend themselves against potential competitors that would enter the market in question. The innovation activity of oligopoly corporations is often more viable than the innovation activity of companies situated in markets characterised by fierce competition. Collaboration between oligopoly corporations in countries like Japan, Germany and South-Korea are examples of innovation activities that models of economics cannot explain with their concept of allocative efficiency (R. Kuttner, 1999, p. 26). Later in this book we will discuss in more detail various forms of innovation collaboration between corporations, but the public sector also plays an important role in maximising innovation efficiency.

The third type of efficiency, employment innovation, refers to the question of how well the economy uses its factors of production. Employment efficiency is at its peak when unemployment is at its lowest point. The economy can be in a state of equilibrium which is characterised by inadequate uses of the factors of production of the economy. The high level of unemployment in Western countries in the 1930s is a clear example of such a situation which remained unchanged for many years until military production was amplified and the Second World War started. J.M. Keynes (1983, p. 293) stated in his groundbreaking book, *The General Theory of Employment, Interest and Money*, that one has to make a distinction between 'stationary equilibrium' and 'shifting equilibrium'. He claimed that expectations concerning the future development of the economy affect its current state. Keynes argued that by controlling interest levels and the supply of money governments can influence the expectations of capitalists concerning the profitability of their investments. Low interest rates and positive expectations motivate capitalists to invest. The same goes for the supply of money realised in the economy by means of public expenditure. An increased money supply leads to inflation that decreases real wages and cost of production in the short run and hence stimulates investment in production. Increased public expenditure leads to rising general demand in the economy which generates the positive expectations of producers as this means that they will be able to sell their goods. With these measures the equilibrium of a crisis with its high level of unemployment can be transformed into another state of equilibrium characterised by a maximum level of employment (I. Jonsson, 1991a).

Keynes presented his theories in 1936 in *The General Theory of Employment, Interest and Money* but J.A. Schumpeter (1936, p. 793) immediately criticised them. He claimed that expectations conceal problems rather than solving them. The most important of Keynes's ideas is that his economic policy only works if current general preconditions for innovation and technological change generate a long-term increase in productivity combined with reduced cost of production in the economy. Keynes accepts the fundamental assumption of classical and neoclassical economics that capitalist economies are characterised by an underlying tendency towards equilibrium. Schumpeter and his followers claim the opposite, namely that innovation and entrepreneurship constantly creates new goods and ways of producing goods. With innovation, corporations increase their profits and consequently the capitalist economies are characterised by fundamental tendency of undermining rather than creating equilibrium (I. Jonsson, 1991a).

In brief, we would claim that the tradition within economics we have discussed above and has been called economic liberalism (i.e., classical and neoclassical economics) (R.J. Holton, 1992) is, on the one hand, based on the utilitarianism of classical economics, the concept of the sovereign rational individual and the view that laissez-faire will autonomously generate a state of equilibrium. On the other hand, economic liberalism rests on the idea of neoclassical economics of 'general equilibrium' and 'marginalism'. We focused on classical economics above. Now we will discuss the main concepts of neoclassical economics.

The founding fathers of marginalism and what came to be called 'the marginalist revolution' were W.S. Jevons, C. Menger and L. Walras who all wrote their most important works in the 1870s. According to marginalism, individuals are determined in their conduct by the law of diminishing marginal utility. This law presumes that the greater the quantity an individual buys of a particular good, the lower becomes the utility of each unit he or she adds to the quantity he or she already has of the good. The utility (or pleasure) of the first unit bought is much higher than the utility of unit number 1000 and therefore he or she will pay a lower price for unit number 1000 than the first unit bought. Marginalists generalise this law, deduce that it is valid for all goods in the economy and claim that prices are determined by how individuals, corporations other actors on the market evaluate their marginal utility of the goods in question. Prices are, therefore, determined by subjective factors rather than objective factors such as the amount of work that is put into the production of the goods as D. Ricardo and other classical economists concluded.

According to the theories of 'general equilibrium' proposed by the neoclassical economists, equilibrium exists in the economy when no economic actor (individual or company) can increase her or his utility with further transactions or by buying more units of goods; that is, supply is equal to demand in all markets in the economy (R.J. Holton, 1992, p. 83). Moreover, the marginalists presume that market imperfections obstruct the realisation of general equilibrium and reduce the allocative efficiency of markets. Economists have pointed out an infinite number of market imperfections, the most important of which are: *Sticky prices* as for example when wages and interest rates do not change according to fluctuations in supply and demand; *Institutional barriers* as for example when price is determined by an actor's monopoly position such as in the case of a monopoly corporation or trade unions; *Wrong responses to price signals* e.g., when actors believe that price signals are wrong because of uncertainty concerning current or future market developments or because of wrong expectations or an unsupported hypothesis concerning a market situation. Economists of this persuasion are called 'imperfectionists' because they believe that a general equilibrium is an inevitable result in circumstances where all market imperfections have been abolished (J. Eatwell and M. Milgate, 1982, p. 3). These assumptions are highly unrealistic as are the presumptions of economic liberalism that we discussed above. Later in this book we argue that such unrealistic speculations render economics of little use for research into innovation and entrepreneurship. The main reason is that utilitarianism, the idea of the egoistic actor and the marginalist concept of 'production function' reflect only very limited aspects of the process of innovation and technical change.

The main theoretical assumptions of economic liberalism appear in their purest form in neoclassical economics that emerged and developed during the last three decades of the eighteenth century. The assumptions of this school of economics are seen as the preconditions that have to be realised if a market economy is to be able to deliver maximum level of production and economic welfare. These preconditions therefore serve as a legitimation for policies of laissez-faire and minimum state interventionism. Despite the fact that neoclassical economics is almost one and a half century old, it remains the foundation of contemporary mainstream economics and the textbooks in practically all introductory courses in economics in Western societies are neoclassical. However, the theoretical assumptions of neoclassical economics are strangely unrealistic. As P.A. Wickham (2006, pp. 124–5) highlights, all the main neoclassical assumptions can be reduced to four a priori postulates, that is ideas concerning how transactions work, human nature, the nature of industries and the nature of the firm.

As for how *transactions* are presumed to work, on the one hand, neoclassical economics supposes that sell-buy transactions are simply determined by and reducible to the prices of goods that determine supply and demand of goods. On the other hand, neoclassical economics assumes that markets are costless to set up and run. Hence transactions are 'free' and 'frictionless'.

In terms of the neoclassical ideas of *the nature of human beings*, it is claimed that all individuals in an economy are rational and aim to maximise their personal pleasure (utility) from the goods they may acquire. Humans are also assumed to be perfectly efficient processors of information. In addition, they know all there is to know, know what others know and know that others know what they know … ad infinitum (referred to as *common knowledge*). Furthermore, all economic decisions made by humans are based on evaluation of marginal utility. This assumption takes it that an individual's demand for a particular good and the price he/she is willing to pay to gain an extra unit of that good, will diminish as the number of the units of her or his good increases.

As for neoclassical ideas of *the nature of industries*, it is assumed that, all goods are *homogeneous* within an industry. Hence, on the one hand, the goods have exactly the same utility and, on the other hand, the goods from one firm within an industry can be exchanged for those of another firm within the same industry without the buyer noticing a difference. Furthermore, it is assumed that there is an infinite number of firms within an industry and it is indeed presumed to be costless for the buyer to switch from one supplier to another supplier within the same industry. Finally, between industries all goods are *heterogeneous*. Hence, no two goods from different industries can be switched in any way because all goods have entirely different utility as far as the buyer is concerned

Concerning assumptions related to *the nature of the firm*, neoclassical economics presumes that each and every firm is totally independent of other firms in its decision making and that each firms makes one and only one product. Furthermore, each firm is 'atomic' and has no internal structure of interests, that is, all inputs and resources of the firm are delivered through market exchanges, including labour. Moreover, it is presumed that it does not require any extra costs for firms to enter markets compared to the firms that already operate on the market. Finally, neoclassical economics presume that firms can sell their assets without loss when they leave an industry.

As we will discuss below, these apparently unrealistic theoretical assumptions of neoclassical economics have been criticised by various heterodox schools in economics. Political economy is the heterodox tradition that has the longest history of such a critique. We will now discuss its contribution and highlight its relevance for studies of innovation and entrepreneurship.

2.3.2 Political Economy

Political economy in the modern sense has its roots in the economics of the eighteenth century. This train of thought differs from economic liberalism, classical and neoclassical economics, as it postulates that the spheres of the economy and politics cannot be separated. Accordingly, the market system cannot autonomously generate economic equilibrium, social harmony or law and order in society. Markets need constant public interventions in order to secure that 'market laws' work as they are supposed to do in reality. This modern understanding of what political economy stands for thus opposes the understanding that, for example, Adam Smith, who called himself a political economist, had of this discipline, but he (J.R. Holton, 1992, pp. 104–5).

Contemporary political economists argue that the market system is characterised by inequality and a struggle between ruling classes and exploited classes; socioeconomic inequality is maintained by means of power resources and structures of power. Political economy constitutes an independent scientific tradition whose founding fathers were scholars of the nineteenth century such as D. Ricardo, Karl Marx and their followers. As an example of contemporary political economists one should mention I. Wallerstein and his 'World System Theory'.

In brief, we would claim that the critique of the market system which finds expression in political economy is twofold. On the one hand, the critique is often called romantic and, on the other, scientific. The romantic critique focuses on the narrow picture of humanity that economic liberalism draws. The idea of homo economicus that reduces human relations to egoism excludes close emotional relations between individuals as in the family and small communities. Without emotional relations societies cannot exist, they would break apart. Romantic critique appears in different forms such as nostalgic notions of turning back to the forms of societies that existed in the past, or it is manifested in nationalism and patriotism. The romantic tradition also appears in ideas of social revolutions in the spirit of Robert Owen who advocated that societies should be based on cooperatives. The other type of critique of political economists of the market system has its point of departure in science and rationalism and the world view of the enlightenment. Here, the main emphasis is to analyse how forms of ownership of wealth and the market systems limit the potential of individuals for realising their physical and spiritual welfare. This approach is different from the point of departure of economic liberalism which emphasises that market systems and capitalist society tend to be in autonomous or spontaneous state of harmony if, and only if, the state does not intervene. Political economy, on the other hand, emphasises that market systems and capitalist society are anything but harmonious but characterised by conflicts between social groups, particularly classes and contradictory class interests. It also underlines that without intervention the market systems suffer from regular economic crises.

The analysis by political economy of power structures and economic interests in society is probably the clearest difference between political economy and economic liberalism. The latter maintains that markets are primarily characterised by decentralised power relations and independent individuals, corporations and institutions. Unlike this, political economists claim that the power system is fundamental to the economic system and determines the objectives of economic activity and how wealth and resources are distributed in society. While economic liberalism presumes that concentration of power is an exception in the market system, political economists claim that this is the main principle of the market system and a precondition for its reproduction through force and, indeed without it privileged groups in society could not secure their position (J.R. Holton, 1992, pp. 106 and 108).

This train of thought, i.e. the view that the power position of different social groups or classes determines how large a portion of the surplus of production and wealth they gain, can be traced back to D. Ricardo and Marx. Ricardo distinguished between three main classes in capitalist society; landowners, capitalists and labourers. He came to the conclusion that, following the growth of the population, more and more unproductive land would be exploited and therefore income from land would gradually diminish and thus the income of landowners, the land rent, would dwindle. At the same time, the profit of capitalists would decrease, according to Ricardo, due to increasing labour costs leading to rising prices of agricultural products. Declining profits would render capitalists unwilling to invest in increased production and consequently the development would slow down. Ricardo's conclusion was, therefore, pessimistic compared to economic liberalism. Contemporary neo-Ricardians emphasise that the development of wages and profits is determined by the negotiating power of labourers and capitalists and the strength of their associations (ibid., pp. 115–116; A. Glyn and B. Sutcliffe, 1972). The development of wages and profits constitutes the frame within which investment opportunities, capital accumulation and innovation activity can be realised.

Many other political economists take the qualitative changes in Western market systems over the long run as their point of departure. Eighteenth and nineteenth century economists like Adam Smith, D. Ricardo, Karl Marx and neoclassical economists built their theories on their contemporary economic systems. The capitalism of the nineteenth century was characterised by competition between small family companies. In the twentieth century oligopoly and monopoly became the ruling principles of economic life in Western societies and the power of large corporations steadily increased. As a result, a new breed of economists appeared, such as J. Robinson and the post Keynesians, who rejected neoclassical theories of perfect markets. They base their theories on the works of M. Kalecki and claim that large corporations, imperfect markets, oligopoly and monopoly are the main characteristics of contemporary capitalism and that economic life is *a fortiori* determined by the interests of oligo- and monopolies.

Theories of 'monopoly capitalism' by 'neo-Marxists' follow a similar train of thought as that of the post Keynesians. The Marxist prediction that capitalism would crumble in a general economic crisis failed to materialise and after the Second World War a boom era set in, lasting until the 1970s. It was about time, many Marxists thought, for something to be done about Marxist crisis theory. The theories of P.A. Baran and P.M. Sweezy are probably the best known theories in this field of economics. Their views were presented in *Monopoly Capitalism: An Essay on the American Economic and Social Order*. Baran and Sweezy claimed that:

> Today, the typical economic unit in the capitalist world is not the small firm producing a negligible fraction of a homogeneous output for an anonymous market but a large-scale enterprise producing a significant share of the output of an industry, or even several industries, and able to control its prices, the volume of its production, and the types and amounts of its investments. The typical economic unit, in other words, has the attributes which were once thought to be possessed only by monopolies. (P.A. Baran and P.M. Sweezy, 1973, p. 19)

According to Baran and Sweezy, among the main characteristics of contemporary capitalism is a persistent crisis tendency generated by overproduction and insufficient demand for goods. The capitalist system is, therefore, doomed to generate ever new ways of keeping up demand. The solution is large scale 'waste production'. Among the important conditions for waste production is innovation activity that focuses on developing goods for the military sector, product differentiation and design of goods that will not last long and finally the opening of markets in the Third World; a process which often requires military intervention and imperialist measures. Military measures incur a waste of military technology and public military expenditure.

Research into innovation and entrepreneurship influenced by the theories of Baran and Sweezy concentrates on the role and dynamics of innovation activity in developing waste production.

Another tradition in political economy that, similar to the theories of Baran and Sweezy, has been called neo-Marxism is the work of J. Habermas (1971 and 1978) and the Frankfurt school. This tradition has generated a wide field of studies; however, the critique of the ideological essence of technology and technological development in capitalism is a subfield within the studies of the Frankfurt school most directly related to the examination of innovation and entrepreneurship. In line with the Frankfurt school, J. Habermas emphasises the phenomenon 'alienation' in capitalist societies; that is, a trend in which individuals become increasingly powerless in their private lives, work and society. The laws of the market and the capitalists gain increasing power over individuals, determining what is produced and with what technology. Technological development is charged with conflicts due to contradictory interests of workers and corporations, but experts and engineers have the ideological role of preventing real confrontation concerning for whom and in what form technology is developed. On the surface it appears that the experts are ideologically neutral in their work and technological development seems inevitable. However, the experts do not play a neutral role according to the Frankfurt school as they satisfy the interests of corporations and the ruling class in the wider social context. This clearly appears in conflicts concerning work organisation, environmental issues and the role of military production.

By way of summary, we would claim that in relation to innovation and entrepreneurship, political economy emphasises analysing how the interests of corporations and military authorities mould the objectives and forms of technological development and innovation activity. It also highlights the alienating effects of technological development in the private and social life of individuals.

2.3.3 The Austrian School

Around 1900 some Austrian economists criticised neoclassical economics for its idea of homo economicus and the conditions for general equilibrium. The best known members of the Austrian school are C. Menger, F. von Wieser and E. Bohm-Bawerk. Furthermore L. von Mises, Friedrich von Hayek and I.M. Kirzner.

The Austrian school rejected the neoclassical school emphasis on showing that pure market laws generate equilibrium and harmony in society. They claimed that according this view the economy appears to be frozen and timeless. The state of equilibrium appears to be an end state that cannot develop further. In reality, the economy is very different from this picture and is constantly developing. Competition is a process, according to the Austrian school, which leads to continuous changes in the economy, but not a force that engenders a state of equilibrium. Although competition forces the economy in the direction of equilibrium it never reaches that stage, as the individuals are not the perfect beings as neoclassical economics appears to assume. The Austrian school claims that the needs of the human being are never satisfied and therefore he or she is never content, constantly imagines that the world can be improved and consequently attempts to change it. Hence, communication and transactions between people are constantly determined by uncertainty. 'Man' is therefore not as rational as the notion of homo economicus would have us believe and is not capable of creating economic equilibrium with impersonal business transactions in the market.

With this view of human beings, the Austrian school reintroduced individuals and their views to economics after neoclassical economics and homo economicus had swept them out to sea. Individuals who imagine that there are unsatisfied needs and try to satisfy them are the driving force of market competition. This is precisely the role played by the entrepreneur; that is, a person who sees business opportunities and offers new goods or services to satisfy needs that hitherto had not been met. However, the ideas of the entrepreneur are always imperfect because there is always uncertainty as to what and how to produce, as well as knowing when the time is ripe to supply the new goods or services. Entrepreneurs are at all times bound by the context in which they find themselves concerning the business opportunities at hand. No one can have full knowledge or all information about all available business opportunities in the economy at all times. Thus the economy is subject to constant uncertainty and general equilibrium is unattainable (F. von Hayek, 1937; L. von Mises, 1949, pp. 706–707 and 871; J.A. Schumpeter, 1942, p. 77).

Joseph A. Schumpeter, who was a disciple of Egen Bohm-Bawerk and Ludwig von Mises, built on these grounds of the Austrian school concerning the individual, the entrepreneur and the idea that general equilibrium will never be realised in the economy. General equilibrium is at best an 'imaginary construction' in the minds of mathematical economists (L. von Mises, 1949, pp. 697–8). J.A. Schumpeter (1942, p. 77) claimed that theories of equilibrium hardly ever yield a true picture of economic reality because they fail to describe the processes that are fundamental to capitalist economies; that is, human efforts and innovation activity that lead to continuous evolution. He further developed his ideas in his theories of the relationship between innovation and long waves in the history of capitalism. We will discuss Schumpeter's theories in the following chapter.

2.3.4 Heterogeneous Demand Theory

Among the many assumptions of neoclassical economics is the notion that goods produced in a particular branch of industry are homogeneous; this being a precondition for consumers to be able to decide rationally which goods to buy. According to this premise, the goods of a particular branch of industry are perfectly comparable and interchangeable. These conjectures are highly unrealistic. Consumers are often in the situation of choosing between buying meat, fish or vegetables when they buy groceries; all these goods being products of different branches of industry. According to the theory, however, they are all comparable and interchangeable and are therefore identical 'substitutes'. This view does not hold water according to the 'heterogeneous demand theory'. Joan Robinson (1933) and Edward H. Chamberlin (1933) presented theories in the 1930s on monopoly and imperfect competition and laid the grounds for heterogeneous demand theory. The main idea of these theories is that companies do not sell homogeneous goods or services on the market of the branch of industry in question and their supply is, therefore, not determined by the prices set by the market. Corporations *marketise* their goods in a way that suits particular groups of consumer or market niches that are willing to pay higher prices for the goods than the average price on the market. The goods and services offered for sale by the branch of industry in question are thus heterogeneous and not homogeneous. One can point out examples of cars, restaurants and tourist agencies. From the consumer's point of view, there is a large difference between car trademarks, or the cooks in restaurants. Similarly, different holiday beaches generate different experiences. For the consumer, goods and services like these are not perfectly comparable substitutes. The profitability of production depends on the ability of producers to establish the specificity of their products and introduce valuable trademarks to the market.

Hetereogeneous demand theory and related research is useful for the science of research into innovation and entrepreneurship. A large proportion of innovation activity is in the form of 'incremental innovation' which focuses on small scale improvements of products and production processes in order to increase the level of added value, as well as productivity. Achieving differentiation by means of consistent design work, the market specificity of goods and services is created and companies can sell their products at higher prices. The interaction of innovation and design is, therefore, an important aspect of the competitiveness of corporations (K. Halldórsdóttir, 2005).

2.3.5 Differential Advantage Theory

Heterogeneous demand theory is an alternative to the naïve view of neoclassical economics concerning the nature of goods. The problem with the latter is that it has little to contribute to an analysis of competition and the processes by which it is determined. Differential advantage theory focuses on the strategies of competition and its conclusion contradicts neoclassical economics. J.M. Clarke (1940) is among the founding fathers of this new approach to competition. He maintains that the relationship between sellers and consumers is dynamic and different from the mechanical decisions involved in the concept of *homo economicus*. He claims that the relationship is not random and impersonal, but most often a long-term arrangement where the companies in question satisfy the needs of particular groups of consumers. He also argued that companies cannot increase the price of their products at will because, in the last instance, the consumers can go elsewhere if they like. The most important of Clarke's arguments is his claim that companies compete for the demand and attention of consumers and hence they are obliged to improve the goods in order to better satisfy the needs of consumers.

In addition, Clarke claimed that corporations do not maximise their profits in the way neoclassical economics suggests. Although companies attempt to maximise their profits in the long run, they temporarily accept low level of profits for various reasons, for example in order to minimise uncertainty; to be able to invest in capital resources and skills that will increase profitability in the future or; to invest in social responsibility in order to sustain the communities of their customers and ensure lasting demand for their products. The directors of corporations aim at realising the long term interests of the corporations, rather than maximising profits in the short run.

Moreover, many students of innovation activities have emphasised the importance of collaboration between those who develop and produce goods and those who buy the goods. The concept 'user-producer relations' reflects such relationships and highlights the importance of collaboration between users and producers concerning innovation activity (B.Å. Lundvall et al, 1983 and B.Å. Lundvall, 1988).

2.3.6 Industrial Organisation Economics

Industrial organisation economics deals with a problem that neoclassical economics cannot explain; namely, why profitability varies in different branches of industry. Industrial organisation economics attempts to explain this difference with reference to 'imperfect competition'. An example of this is seen in markets where few producers prevail which leads to oligopoly or monopoly. Another example is a market situation where entry or exit costs are high. Production of scale or differentiation of goods (cf. the discussion above) also leads to imperfect competition.

Industrial organisation economics has developed in three stages. In the first stage, in the 1960s, industrial organisation economists believed that each company builds on a particular mixture of imperfect competition and thus has a specific competitive advantage over other companies. Accordingly, managers exploit the specificity of the company in relation to imperfect competition and are successful if they use the right methods or resources that fit the company in question.

In the second stage of Industrial organisation economics, in the 1980s, theories of scholars like M. Porter (1980 and 1985) appeared which emphasised that the success of companies is not merely rooted in implementing the right management strategies that adjust management to the specific advantages of the firm. The main idea in this stage was that the environment of the corporations can be changed with the right kind of strategies. Porter consequently presented a model of five forces that summarised the new way of thinking. According to the model, five forces determine the development of the branch of industry in question: a) the nature of the relation between the firms and their customers (how many and important the firms' customers are); b) the mode of competition in the branch of industry; c) obstacles to entry (i.e., the costs incurred by new competitors entering the market); d) the firms' power position in relation to suppliers of inputs and; e) consumers' opportunities to buy substitutes produced in other branches of industry.

Porter's model is based on very general conditions that emphasise structural characteristics of the environment in which the corporations or institutions find themselves at a particular time. The concept the model is based on, and indeed the same mode of thinking that predominated the first stage, is characterised by a static view; that is, one postulates that imperfect competition is pre-given rather than being the result of actions or decisions made by conscious actors. In the third stage of industrial organisation economics a new approach emerges which emphasises a dynamic view of markets; here it is assumed that markets develop as a result of conscious action of the actors on markets.[5] The methodology that follows as a consequence of this new approach is a game theoretical analysis of limited number of branches of industry rather than large number of industries as was the trend before. Consequently, the concept of 'the new industrial organisation economics' is used in order to distinguish it from the former stages in the development of this discipline (P. Wickham, 2006, p. 130).

In relation to research of innovation and entrepreneurship, the role of the entrepreneur is different in the 'new' and 'old' industrial organisation economics. In the first two stages the entrepreneur has the role of adjusting the firm's resources, namely raw materials, equipment, knowledge and labour, to the conditions of imperfect market competition. In the new version, entrepreneurs still have this same role, but fulfil it in an active strategic way. The entrepreneurs do not simply make decisions on the basis of the given conditions on the markets, but predict what the responses of other competitors on the market will be to their actions and come up with new strategies on the basis of anticipated reactions from the competitors (ibid., p. 130).

2.3.7 Transaction Cost Economics

In the 1970s some economists tried to answer the question why there are two ways of coordinating economic activity in the market system. On the one hand, large corporations exploit hierarchy to coordinate diverse activities within their administrative structures. On the other, the market coordinates economic activity by means of competition between independent firms. This situation i.e., that there are organisations in economic life which are not ruled by market laws, contradicts the assumptions of neoclassical economics concerning how markets work. If the world were organised according to neoclassical economics, firms would dissolve into aggregates of independent individuals whose transactions are short term and impersonal and who maximise their utilities. The reason why this is not the case is that individuals do not possess the information they need to take perfectly rational decisions that maximise their utilities.

Oliver Williamson (1975), who is one of the founding fathers of 'new institutionalism' in economics, is the best known scholar who has attempted to answer the question mentioned above. His answer is the theory of 'transaction costs' that he developed on the grounds of the work of R. Coase (1937). Williamson's explanation is that it would be too expensive for firms to make

---

5   An approach of this kind is similar to the approaches of the economic sociology or socioeconomics of Max Weber, i.e., a tradition in social sciences that rejects the separation of economics and sociology.

daily contracts with other firms or individuals concerning the execution of every task the firm needs to have done. What each task constitutes and how it must be executed is impossible to define in detail. Moreover, there are unforeseen changes in the environment and conditions of production one would need to respond to with new unforeseen measures. In short, one cannot extinguish uncertainties in business. It is, therefore, cheaper in many instances to hire staff for considerable time to execute the work needed.

Williamson's solution has its shortcomings. The main problem is that his analysis presupposes only two kinds of organisational forms; that is, market and bureaucratic hierarchy. In reality there are various organisational forms and various forms of collaboration between corporations as we will discuss in Chapter 4 in this book regarding alliances and networks.

In relation to studies of innovation and entrepreneurship, the theory of transaction costs is important as it highlights the problem of uncertainty in running corporations. It is the role of entrepreneurs to organise firms in a way that generates increasing added value. They realise this function by determining what to produce and execute indoors and which parts of the production to buy from external suppliers and by deciding what to sell here and now rather than developing the products further in the hope of getting higher levels of added value in the future. One may presume that the theory of transaction costs would predict that firms would prefer intramural R&D rather than buying from external suppliers when uncertainty is high in supplier markets concerning prices and standards. The theory would also predict that entrepreneurs prefer to sell products rather than develop them further when uncertainty is high concerning demand and this would be costly to estimate.

2.3.8 Evolutionary Economics and Neo-Schumpeterianism

Evolutionary economics is a school in economics that has gained an increasing number of followers in the past two decades, both in economics and in other social sciences. Those who advocate this train of thought emphasise historical and social contexts as important factors in explaining economic development. Moreover, they stress that economic systems and their organisation changes over time. Apart from these general assumptions, evolutionary economists are rather diverse and they define the concept of 'evolution' in various ways. The basic ideas that most of them accept are, on the one hand, Darwin's idea of the 'survival of the fittest' i.e., that species which best fit the environment they live in survive while others die. On the other hand, there are ideas which postulate that mutation of genes creates new species (J. Foster, 1991, pp. 221–2). Evolutionary economists also agree that the concept of evolution presumes irreversible changes. However, within this school economists disagree whether evolution is gradual or whether it is a large scale structural change in economic systems. They also disagree on the role of social institutions in economic development and how important the interaction between actors and the environment is in economic development. Finally, they have different views concerning the speed of development; that is, some of them consider development to be gradual while others assume that it is fundamental and revolutionary, taking place over a relatively short period and causing structural changes that last for long time.

The concept of evolution in relation to heterogeneous goods and consumers has a similar meaning in economics as it has in biology. The process of adjusting appears in the development of new goods and changes in consumers' tastes. The economy itself is the environment that consists of individuals, social groups and corporations (S. Keen, 2001, p. 310). Many evolutionary economists follow K.E. Boulding (1981) who, as Kropotkin (1904) did in his book *Mutual Aid: a Factor in Evolution*, emphasises that cooperation creates new conditions for evolution and, as a consequence, evolution is not a simple mechanical adjustment to the environment. Cooperation creates new opportunities (J. Foster, 1991, p. 222). Kropotkin criticised nineteenth century Darwinism and argued that it is true both for humans and for animals that cooperation is a more important force in the development of the species than competition (P. Kropotkin, 1904, pp. xiv–xv). Hence, Kropotkin rejected the social-Darwinism of H. Spencer, Huxley and others.

Theories and studies on alliances and networks of corporations, innovation clusters and the hypotheses of R. Nelson and S. Winter of routines in firms that affect their innovation activity are examples of research that would be categorised as evolutionary economics. These theories will be discussed in more detail in the following chapter; in short, however, we would claim that research into innovation clusters became an established field of research in management studies following M.J. Piore and C. Sabel's book *The Second Industrial Divide* that observes forms of collaboration of small firms in France and North-Italy. With their collaboration these small firms have been able to improve their competitiveness and have managed to compete successfully with large firms that exploit economies of scale and mass production. Small firms are able to adjust their production to demand in market niches and to changing tastes of consumers faster than large corporations focused on mass production. A similar train of thought can be found in works like C. Freeman's (1987), *Technology Policy and Economic Performance: Lessons from Japan*, that observe the macro economic importance of collaboration between corporations and public institutions in 'national systems of innovation' that affect the competitiveness of corporations and economies.

The theories of R. Nelson and S. Winter on routines in firms and how they affect their innovation activity are based on a Lamarckian concept of evolution. Lamarck claimed that the traits of animal species are acquired rather than pre-given. Nelson and Winter compare routines in firms to genes that contain acquired traits and are essential for corporate survival in market competition. They focus on the innovation activity of firms and label their research 'neo-Schumpeterian'. However, as G.M. Hodgson (1993, pp. 149–50) claims, the theories of Nelson and Winter have very little in common with Schumpeter's concept of evolution. Schumpeter assumed that evolution in an economic sense consists of changes in the inner conditions of the economy that lead to fundamental shifts in its traditions and institutional conditions. Economic evolution in the sense of Schumpeter does not comprise adjustment to changing external conditions such as changing tastes of consumers, but is restricted to innovations that change consumer taste. Adjusting to the environment, independent of whether it is in a Lamarckian or Darwinian sense, is therefore not in accordance with Schumpeter's concept of evolution (ibid., p. 145).

Population ecology theory

Population ecology theory is based on Darwin's theory of natural selection; instead of focusing on firms, however, the emphasis is on species of firms similar to species of animals.

According to this theory, the structure of firms and organisations is determined by inertia that prevents them – and at the same time the species of organisations they belong to – from adjusting to fundamental changes that take place in their environment. The firms die in groups rather than individually because the species cannot adjust (G. Morgan, 1996; Chapter 3).

Population ecology theory assumes that corporations and organisations can neither change themselves nor their environment. It is anticipated that corporations in different branches of industry are homogeneous and can at best decide into which markets they move and which corporations they collaborate with. But basically it is envisaged that corporations, their management styles and strategies, cannot be changed and that they are entirely dominated by their original characteristics. The number of corporations in the different branches of industry is determined by the carrying power of the industry in question, the resources it has access to and especially the buying power of its customers (P.A. Wickham, 2006, p. 136).

Theories like these downplay the role of the entrepreneur in economic development. The role of the entrepreneur is limited to creating the original characteristics of the firm and defining its objectives.

Theories like these are unrealistic as can be seen from the fact that firms are often capable of implementing new management strategies and they often collaborate in networks with other firms that make it easier from them to adjust to market developments and empower them in their efforts to influence the markets. Moreover they can also move from one market niche to another.

Institutionalist economics

Institutionalist economics is rooted in the type of economics that dominated this discipline in USA from around 1900 to the 1950s. Torsten Bunde Veblen was its founding father, but it is in many ways similar to the German school of historical economics that developed in the same period. Gustav von Schmoller was the best known of the Germans historical economists. This type of economics highlights the role of culture, morals and traditions in economic life and development. The theoretical and methodological approach of institutionalist economics tends to adhere to anthropologist approaches.

Contemporary institutionalist economics usually presumes that corporations are influenced by their culture and their culture is difficult to change. Corporations do not have a tendency to change and develop according to this train of thought. However, this view differs from the perspective of population ecology theory which assumes that corporations cannot influence and change their environment. Institutionalists see corporate culture as a crucial factor that determines corporate and organisational ability to influence and change their environment. However, the precondition for this ability is that the corporations create a positive reputation and earn trust from the actors in the environment. According to this point of view, it is the cultural rather than financial resources of the firms which are important concerning their ability to influence their environment. Entrepreneurs who launch their activity in a new branch of industry or found a new branch have to be able to establish an image of trustworthiness of themselves among investors, customers, employees, suppliers and even actors in the public sector. Otherwise the project will *not* be realised. Entrepreneurs legitimate their projects in many ways. They may create an image according to which they have become representatives of new times while the competitors are presented as old timers in business or advocates of privileges that obstruct the welfare of the general public. Entrepreneurs have the role of legitimating the new values they promote (P.A. Wickham, 2006, p. 136).

Evolutionary theory of organisations
The theories of R.R. Nelson and S.G. Winter (1982) of how routines in firms influence their innovation activity are important in the field of evolutionary theories of organisations. According to these theories, it is firms and not branches of industry that are defined and determined by laws of evolution as population ecology theory assumes. Evolutionary theories of organisations assume that directors of firms cannot change their environment, but the firms themselves can be changed. This view is in accordance with heterogeneous demand theory that we discussed above. The difference between these theories is substantial, however, in relation to how they analyse the processes by which firms change themselves. Heterogeneous demand theory takes the view that firms adjust to market developments with general change strategies which cover all their corporate aspects. Changes in the environment are analysed and the management and operations of the firm adjusted according to predetermined plans. Evolutionary theories of organisations reject this view and claim it is impossible to realise changes on the basis of totalising plans. Firms adjust to changes in the environment by gradually shifting their operations. They constantly search for the right ways to adjust since there is no perfect information and consequently no plans one knows in advance to be right.

According to this view, entrepreneurs are not the actors who execute predetermined plans of change; they rather take on the role of moulding the firm in question so that it has the capacity to adjust to its environment and ever changing information in this context as well as responding to and defining new opportunities.

Industrial community theory

This theory goes further than the evolutionary theories of organisations in the sense that it assumes that firms and organisations can change both themselves and the environment. The external environment is, therefore, not a pre-given unchangeable factor that the firm has simply to adjust to. Industrial community theory is straightforward and its followers concentrate on detailed empirical descriptions of entrepreneurial activity rather than theoretical excellence. They presume that each firm is unique and different from other firms in terms of its position in the branch of industry in question and in terms of the capacity of its employees. Corporations differ in their ability to actively adjust to their environment and change it. Corporate capacity to create and reproduce networks in the business community is a crucial factor in this respect. By creating networks and mutual support of corporations, firms are able to generate communities that are important for their survival and support their adjustment to requirements of the environment as well as changing it. The role of the entrepreneur is important in this context; that is in creating and reproducing corporate networks. The approach of industrial community theory is to a large extent sociological (A.H. Van de Ven and R. Garud, 1989; R. Garud and A.H. Van de Ven, 1992). We will now discuss the relationship between sociology and research into innovation and entrepreneurial activity.

2.4 Sociology

In the 1980s, when it had become clear to many politicians and social scientists that the competitiveness of US and European industries was declining compared to Japanese industries (P. Armstrong, A. Glyn and J. Harrison 1984, pp. 218–24), various scientists looked for explanations of these developments in the culture specific to the countries concerned, including social factors like class structure, history and differences in the role of the state. In sociology there is a tradition which is valuable in this context; that is, the economic sociology of Max Weber. He is particularly well known for introducing German historicism in social sciences and for being a pioneer in research that focuses on '*verstehen*' or understanding the meaning of individuals' actions. '*Verstehen*' refers to a research approach in which the researcher analyses the ideas and modes of thinking that lie behind the actions of individuals. As an example, Weber explained the development of capitalism by analysing the spread of the 'spirit of capitalism' and its roots in the ethics of Protestants and their fear of belonging to those who are not 'chosen' (M. Weber, 1958). Weber assumed that economic activities of individuals did not simply reflect the need to maximise utility. Economic actions are influenced by culture and traditions (R. Swedberg, 2000, p. 163).

In recent years, research related to M. Weber's approach has flourished in studies of 'social capital' and economic phenomena such as innovation activity and competitiveness of economies and regions. Culture and traditions are important for regional and national competitiveness according to theories of social capital. Research into social capital is, however, in its infant stages and the concept is defined in various ways; measures of social capital are unclear and empirical research is scant concerning how social capital affects productivity and competitiveness (B. Fine, 1999; G. Torsvik, 2000). This is no surprise as we are referring to a relatively new field of study. In short, the main idea is that social capital affects trust between corporations, between managers and other employees and between corporations, governments and public institutions. When trust is high, information flows easily between different actors and transaction cost is low. This situation leads to enhanced innovation activity and economic productivity. Consequently we would claim that social capital plays a crucial role in the economic development of regions and countries. We will discuss the concept and research of social capital in more detail in Chapter 5 of this book.

Another field in research on innovation and entrepreneurship which is influenced by sociology is research into the social background and context of scientists and entrepreneurs. Sociology of knowledge and sociology of sciences are disciplines that can be traced back to the first decades of the twentieth century and the works of Karl Mannheim, for example. At that time sociologists analysed the relationship between class position of individuals and their world view and how this influences theories and scientific research. In the latter half of the twentieth century the focus was on scientific communities; processes of socialisation in such communities were observed that led to stagnation in sciences thus undermining technological development. The historian of science, T.S. Kuhn (1970), was highly influential in this field and also the American ethno-methodological sociologist, H. Garfinkel. Kuhn described long periods in sciences in which stagnation prevails and scientists approve fundamental concepts and theories in the sciences in question. This is the period of 'normal science' according to Kuhn. The reason for normal science is that the scientists are (mass)socialised in the same way. They read very similar textbooks, attend uniform courses in universities and do standardised experiments in the labs. Sciences face a crisis when ruling theories cannot explain a growing number of 'anomalies' and finally a revolution takes place when the elite of scientists of the discipline in question agree to start anew with new theoretical foundations which can explain the anomalies. Those who adhere to Garfinkel, as for example the 'strong program in science' emphasise analysing how world views are reproduced in everyday situations (J. Barnes, D. Bloor and J. Henry, 1996). They have observed conduct and communication in research labs, scientific conferences etc. and analysed how ruling ideas can act as 'blinkers' and delay scientific progress. Research of this kind observes how orthodoxy is reproduced in science. The method of Garfinkel and 'ethno-methodologists' has also been used in relation to research into communication in workplaces. These studies uncover obstacles to creativity and innovation activity in workplaces.

Finally we should discuss the contribution of the sociologist Gabriel Tarde who defined some concepts that later became fundamental to research into innovation and entrepreneurship (G. Tarde, 1890, 1894 and 1897). He made a distinction between 'innovation' and 'invention'. He presumed that innovations develop in waves; that is to say, innovations are relatively more frequent in particular periods than other periods. J.A. Schumpeter later developed a consistent theory on the basis of similar ideas as we will discuss in the following chapter. Tarde contributed important concepts but he never developed a consistent theory of innovation activity as his object of study was to explain societal change (J. Sundbo, 1998, pp. 49–51).

2.5 Organisation Theory and Management

Management and organisation studies are a branch of science that concentrates on organisations, especially workplaces. The discipline exploits both theories and research of sociology and psychology. James March and Herbert Simon (1958) prepared the grounds for a 'decision making approach'. They conclude that organisations are aggregates of units which make decisions on the grounds of imperfect information. Simon (1959) contributed with the concept of 'bounded rationality'. According to this view, the structure of work roles and departments in organisations cannot be reduced to definitions of occupations and work, since organisational patterns guide and control how and what kind of information is collected and how it is interpreted. The way this information is processed has fundamental effects on how organisations operate, according to Simon.

Besides being moulded by the organisational patterns, the information basic to decision making is imperfect in three respects: *firstly*, concerning work processes and related detailed operations; *secondly*, information is limited in scope but it determines what decision making alternatives are at hand and; *thirdly*, the limited information defines how management plans and predicts the output of operations although it is impossible to define operations in detail. Consequently, Simon turned against homo economicus and utilitarianism in economics and claimed that decisions can never be perfect and thus maximise output as they can only be 'satisficing'.

The approach outlined by Simon and his followers has led to voluminous research of organisations in recent decades. This research has emphasised 'learning processes' and 'trial and error' procedures employed in organisations. This kind of research has generated new theories and research i.e., theories of 'learning organisations'. The relation of these theories to innovation and entrepreneurship is evident. Organisations are observed as experiments and processes in which new organisational structures, as well as knowledge and skills of employees, are constantly developed in order to adjust to an ever-shifting environment of organisations, involving changing markets, technological development and institutional development. Research in the spirit of 'learning organisations' yields a fuller picture of organisational processes which are basic to innovation activity in organisations; that is, processes like 'learning by doing', 'learning by using' and 'learning by interaction'. In addition, research of this kind provides insight into 'incremental innovation' which refers to small scale improvements of products and production processes. Incremental innovations improve productivity but do not result in fundamental transformation of products or production processes. We will discuss innovation of this kind in detail in Chapter 3 and 6 of this book.

2.6 Psychology

Numerous psychological research projects with regard to entrepreneurs were undertaken some years ago. The focus was on the personality of the entrepreneur and the aim was to explain why some individuals become entrepreneurs and others do not, and why some entrepreneurs are successful and others are not. Most contemporary scholars of innovation and entrepreneurship agree that this research has not been fruitful and that no strong links exist between personality traits and success in entrepreneurship. In other words, research has not shown a strong relationship between personality traits such as the need to show efficiency, independence, persistence, authority and the urge to organise, and the likelihood of becoming entrepreneurs. Moreover, personality traits are no better explanatory variables than social background (Mescon, T.S., Montanari, J.R., and T., Tinker, 1981). The factors of uncertainty in the work of entrepreneurs are so numerous that one cannot identify one class of factors that explains success. Research indicates that experience from entrepreneurial activity and strategic management better explains the success of entrepreneurs than factors such as age, how long they have managed a firm, how long they have been managers or their technological know-how (Stuart, R.W. and Abetti, P.A., 1990). Personality is only one among a great many factors that explain entrepreneurial success.

Psychology is a wide ranging discipline and there are various types of research in psychology which are not quantitative or statistical. The research of many psychologists involving studies of innovation and entrepreneurship is qualitative. As an example of such research are Freudian studies of anxiety, but such studies highlight forces that hinder innovation activity in organisations (G. Morgan, 1996, pp. 230–239).

Melanie Klein (1981) is a Freudian psychologist who has developed theories of the effects of anxiety in childhood on the personalities of adults. She traced childhood anxiety to the fear of the child in relation to 'bad breast' in breast feeding; that is, the child experiences constant fear because sometimes there is enough milk while sometimes there is too little. Consequently, the child develops a love-and-hate relationship with one object i.e., the mother's breast. Love-and-hate feeling leads to guilt complex and sorrow. If the child is not able to control these feelings, it will suffer from personality disorders later in its life and behaviour that the individual does not fully control. Feelings like fear, hate, greed, anger, envy, sadism, guilt, paranoia, obsession or depression control the individual. This love-and-hate relationship and anxiety is transformed into different objects which control the subconscious behaviour of the individual in adulthood.

W. Bion (1959) builds his theories of group behaviour in organisations on Klein's theories and thus explains their reactions to changes inside organisations and in their environment. Group responses to changes can be an obstacle to innovation activities in organisations. Bion claims that when groups face new circumstances and traditional work procedures do not succeed, they may react in three ways: *firstly*, 'dependency mode': the group believes it needs guidance, a kind of parent, to lead them out of the situation. The leader is cheered and the group feels he or she will solve the problem like no one else can do; *secondly*, the messianic 'pairing': the group believes that a messianic person will appear and solve the problems; *thirdly*, 'fight-flight: the group transforms its incapability and fear into an enemy. All of the three forms of reactions indicate that the group is incapable of solving the problems on its own and seeks refuge in fantasy and myths. Frequently the group looks for a scapegoat inside the group or in the organisation; that is, individuals who think differently compared to most members of the group, who are 'trouble makers' or 'always in the way', difficult to work with etc. The result of these psychological responses of the employees frequently leads to restructuring of the organisation. Thus the final outcome is more a product of the psychological state of the employees than rational measures that increase productivity.

D.W. Winnicott (1958) is another psychologist who also builds on Klein's theories, but who takes the point of departure in 'transitional objects'. Winnicott claims that children's toys have the function of bridging the internal and external reality of the child. They seek consolation in teddy bears and dolls, for example, and establish with them their own dream-world and illusion. The relations between the toys and the individuals hold for life, but as the individual grows older, new toys enter the scene. The toys become more complicated and function as transitional objects. People identify with these objects and protect them as part of their self-image. When their job or workplace becomes a transitional object of this kind they fight against changes as if they were an assault against themselves. This happens subconsciously and works against innovation activity in the organisation if the theory is right.

2.7 History

Historical studies create important material for research into innovation and entrepreneurship. This is particularly true in terms of history of technology and science and entrepreneurs' biographies. In the period of classical economics in the eighteenth and nineteenth centuries scholars like Adam Smith (1776) and Karl Marx (1976; Chapter 15) spent much time on analysing how technological development contributed to the growth of modern production systems, especially Marx (P.F. Drucker 2004, p. 24). Around the middle of the twentieth century important improvements took place in the history of technology as scholars started to analyse the history of inventions and innovation of new technology and categorise them according to their significance for the history of technology and economic history of Western economies. The knowledge base that emerged became an important base for those who build on Schumpeter's theories of innovation and long waves in the history of capitalism. Neo-Schumpeterians like G. Mensch (1979) and C. Freeman, made use of the improvements in historical research of technological development in their analysis of long waves and the role of innovation in economic history (C. Freeman, J. Clark and L. Soete, 1982) as we will discuss in detail in the following Chapter 3.

2.8 Feminist Approaches

Finally it is important to discuss briefly the increasing influence feminist approaches have in social sciences and their impact on innovation and entrepreneurship studies (R. Collins and M. Makowsky, 1998, p. 294). The views of feminists will doubtless influence future research on innovation activity as they will concerning other sciences. Feminists have already made important contributions to innovation research. In this respect, one should highlight their influence in philosophy of science, sociology of science as well as critique of the gendered content of scientific research and technological development. Feminists have been notable among those who advocate relativism and criticise all views which presume that science produces objective and ahistorical knowledge of universal natural and social laws (A. Sayer, 2000, pp. 74–5 and 77–9; L. Nicholson, 1989). Among leading feminists in the field of philosophy of science and epistemology is Sandra Harding (1991) who is one of those feminists who have prepared the grounds for 'standpoint epistemology'. The main concept of this epistemology is that the ideas of individuals of phenomena are in reality moulded by their social background, environment and practice. The background and experience world of men and women differs and therefore their ideas, knowledge and research concerning phenomena in the real world are different. Men have for centuries ruled most spheres of society. Science is an example of this. Sciences, their methodologies and fundamental ideas are male dominated. Since the standpoint of women has not moulded science, the result is that scientific knowledge is biased, fragmented and insufficient.

Following standpoint epistemology, feminists have criticised science and technological development in different ways. As an example, the tradition of comparing women with nature is criticised and the idea that nature can be exploited and abused without limits. The experiential world of women is dominated by care and interactive, emotional communication; as a consequence, women in feminist science emphasise the protection of nature and strengthening the competence of individuals to take part in emotional and interactive communication. Emphasis of this kind is important for innovation studies as this can improve our understanding of the conditions for better communication of individuals and teams that take part in innovation activity in organisations and how to enhance their learning capacity. Feminist views have also directed attention towards new fields of research into the history of science and technology. As an example, feminists in medical research have criticised the fact that diseases from which women in particular suffer from have been researched to a very limited extent. Moreover, feminists have criticised and analysed power relations which ensure that technological development serves male interests rather than those of women. In relation to this, one should highlight C. Cockburn's research which has analysed how males used trade unions in the printing industry, in the period when information technology was implemented in this industry, as a means to define women out of jobs that would secure higher wages for women than male dominated jobs in printing. At that time women's jobs in offices were better suited

Chapter 3
The Dynamics of Innovation and Entrepreneurship

3.1 Introduction

Briefly, we would claim that theories in the field of innovation studies have developed from emphasising macroeconomic concerns to taking an interest in institutional, regional and country specific conditions of innovation activity. In this chapter we will observe the main theories and research approaches to the interrelation between innovation activity and economic development. Theories of long waves in economic life will be discussed i.e., the so called Kondratieffs. Furthermore, we will discuss the ideas of neoclassical economics which reduce the dynamics of technical change to the concept of 'production function'. Moreover, theories that approach innovation activity in terms of learning processes will be noted and, finally, evolutionary economic theories and neo-Schumpeterian theories will be highlighted.

3.2 Innovation and Long Waves in Economic Life

The concept of innovation has been defined in different ways, but most contemporary interpretations are based on Joseph Alois Schumpeter's definition. According to him, innovation presumes any kind of improvement of production processes, products or marketing that makes business more profitable. He claims that the concept comprises:

> ... introduction of new commodities which may even serve as the standard case. Technical change in the production of commodities already in use, the opening up of new markets or of new sources of supply, Taylorisation of work, improved handling of material, the setting up of new business organisations such as department stores – in short, any 'doing things differently' in the realm of economic life – all these are instances of what we shall refer to by the term Innovation. It should be noticed at once that that concept is not synonymous with 'invention'. Whatever the latter term may mean, it has but a distant relation to ours. (J.A. Schumpeter, 1939, p. 84)

Schumpeter made a clear distinction between innovations and inventions. Inventions involve the discovery of new knowledge, equipment or objects, but innovations comprise the application of inventions. The relationship between inventions and innovations is not linear in the sense that when inventions appear, they would be applied in innovation activity: It is also the other way around as innovation activity leads to new inventions that lead to new innovations that lead to new inventions etc. However, not all inventions are caused by new ideas resulting from the implementation of new technology because scientific inventions emerge which are independent of economic life in the narrow sense and some of them become sources of innovation (J.A. Schumpeter, 1911/1934, pp. 88–9).

The main aim of Schumpeter's analysis of inventions and innovations was to explain economic development. He focused on the economic history of capitalism and paid particular attention to the question why there appears to be regularity in shifting periods of slumps and booms i.e., business cycles. At first he concentrated on cycles that last 7–11 years (J.A. Schumpeter, 1911/1934), but later he focused on explaining long term cycles that go on for 45–60 years (J.A. Schumpeter, 1939). Schumpeter argued that this regularity was due to innovation activity; that is, the introduction of new technology, new production processes, raw materials and new markets. However, innovations are not isolated events and are not evenly distributed in time. They tend to cluster and occur in bunches (J.A. Schumpeter, 1964 [1939], p. 98). When innovation activity is weak, crisis sets in, while in periods when innovation activity is extensive, economic expansion prevails.

But, what is the reason for the shifts in innovation activity? Why do innovations appear in clusters? This part of Schumpeter's theory has been considered inadequate from early on by his critics. Nevertheless, this assumption is fundamental to his explanation and theory of economic development. As J.J. van Duijn highlights (1985), Schumpeter (1911/1934, pp. 228–30) explains this phenomenon as follows:

1. The carrying out of new combinations is a difficult task, only accessible to people with certain qualities. During periods of stagnation only a few people can succeed in this direction. However, if one or a few have advanced with success, many of the difficulties disappear. Success makes it easier for more people to follow suit, until finally the innovation becomes familiar and its acceptance a matter of free choice.

2. As entrepreneurial qualifications will be distributed according to the 'law of error', the number of individuals who satisfy progressively diminishing standards in this respect continually increases. Hence, the successful appearance of an entrepreneur is followed by the appearance not simply of some others, but of ever greater numbers, though they may be progressively less qualified.

3. Reality shows that every boom starts in one or a few branches of industry (railway building, electrical and chemical industries, and so forth), and that it derives its character from innovations in the industry where it begins. *But* pioneers remove the obstacles for others, not only in the branch of production in which they first appear but, owing to the nature of these obstacles, *ipso facto* also in other branches.

4. The more familiar the process of development becomes and a mere matter of calculation to all concerned, and the weaker the obstacles grow in the course of time, the less the 'leadership' needed to call forth innovations. Hence, the less pronounced will become the swarm-like appearance of entrepreneurs and the milder the cyclical movement.
5. The swarm-like appearance of new combinations easily and necessarily explains the fundamental features of periods of boom. It explains why increasing capital investment is the very first symptom of the approaching boom and why industries manufacturing means of production are the first to show supernormal stimulation. (Duijn, 1985, pp. 99–100).

All booms caused by the bunching of innovations sooner or later come to an end. Depressions are the outcome of disturbances that follow prosperity. The essence of disturbance generated by the boom lies in the following three circumstances, according to Schumpeter:

a. New entrepreneurs' demand for means of production drives up their prices.
b. New products (innovations) come on the market after a few years and compete with the old. At the beginning of the boom costs, therefore, rise in the old businesses (argument a); later their receipts are reduced, first in those companies with which the innovation competes, but then in all old businesses, insofar as consumer demand changes in favour of the innovation. The average time which elapses before the new products appear fundamentally explains the length of the boom. This appearance of new products causes the fall in prices, which on its part terminates the boom, *may* lead to a crisis, *must* lead to a depression, and starts all the rest.
c. The appearance of the results of the new enterprises leads to a credit deflation, because entrepreneurs are now in a position to pay off their debts; since no other borrowers step into their place, this leads to the disappearance of the recently created purchasing power just when its complement in goods emerges (ibid., p. 100).

Schumpeter generalised this hypothesis and envisaged that it explained all kinds of business cycles; that is, both short term and long term cycles, as outlined in his book, *Business Cycles,* from 1939. His hypothesis was also supposed to explain Kondratieff cycles which are characterised by economic downturns that take place every 45–60 years in the history of capitalism. Instead of analysing only two stages in each cycle i.e., prosperity and recession, Schumpeter added two other stages, namely depression and recovery. The period of recovery drives the economy towards equilibrium.

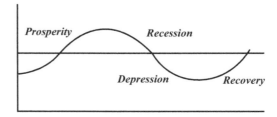

Figure 3.1   Four stages of business cycles

In his analysis of long term cycles, or Kondratieff cycles, Schumpeter distinguished major or basic innovations from other types of innovations and claimed that they cause Kondratieffs. Innovation activity constantly takes place, but it is only basic innovations that have the capability of causing reduction in cost of production in a large enough number of industries to lead to long term cycles. According to Schumpeter, Kondratieffs emerge due to introduction of basic innovations and they develop through the four phases of recovery, repression, depression and prosperity. Schumpeter presumed that steam power was the basic innovation that generated the first Kondratieff was and spurred growth in cotton and steel production. The first Kondratieff was characterised by a period of recovery in 1787–1800 that developed into recession in 1801–13. The period of recession was followed by depression during 1814–27 and prosperity in 1828–42. The second Kondratieff was due railroadisation according to Schumpeter and had a period of recovery in 1843–57 that was followed by recession in 1858–69. Depression set in during 1870–84/5 and prosperity in 1886–97. Electricity and motors were the basic innovations that generated the third Kondratieff which was characterised by recovery in 1898–1911 that developed into recession in 1912–24/5. The period of recession was followed by depression during 1925/6–39 (Schumpeter, 1939).

Schumpeter explained the relationship between innovations and business cycles, but he did not explain the nature of innovation activity as such. His analysis is to be criticised for its lack of scrutiny of the social innovations necessary for new technology, new organisational forms and patterns of consumption to be implemented in society. Neither does he note the dynamics of social innovations in the development of institutions in the corporate environment, nor social innovations concerning interaction of employees inside firms, constituting the internal conditions of innovation activity.

In his early works, Schumpeter was satisfied with explaining innovation activity by referring to personality characteristics of entrepreneur(s), but in his work *Business Cycles* (1939) he further advanced his theory and highlighted the role of research and development departments in large corporations. At that time, it was apparent that large, departmental corporations played a leading part in the economic development of Western countries and had captured the role of firms based on individual entrepreneurs. Following increased interest in research into innovation activity in the 1980s and 1990s, scholars began to analyse the complicated processes of social innovation and internal as well as external conditions for the innovation activity of corporations. We will take note of this research and related theories in the following discussion.

Among important research products in recent decades is a more sophisticated taxonomy of innovations than was available before. Much research is based on the categorisation of innovation Christopher Freeman (1987) developed in the 1980s. His definition of different kinds of innovation reflects the need to widen the concept of innovations so that it covers both social and technological innovation in the strict sense. In addition to distinguishing between 'process innovation' and 'product innovation', he makes a distinction between four kinds of innovation:

1. *Incremental innovation* refers to constant improvement to processes of production and products in manufacturing or service corporations although this does not imply fundamental changes. Such improvements are introduced by engineers, foremen or other employees that work directly 'on the floor' in manufacturing or service industries.[1]

2. *Radical innovation* appears as a result of determined research and development work. Innovations of this kind fundamentally change the conditions of production in particular branches of industry, but do not significantly affect other branches of industry or the economy as a whole. Nylon and the P-pill are examples of radical innovations. In terms of their aggregate economic impact they are relatively small and localised, unless clusters of radical innovations are linked together in the creation of new industries and services, such as the synthetic materials industry or semiconductor industry.

3. *Changes of technology systems* lead to fundamental alterations in technology which affect many branches of industry in the economy and lead to entirely new industrial concerns. The changes are based on incremental and radical innovations, as well as organisational and administrative improvements affecting a large number of corporations. Changes of this kind comprise 'constellations' of innovations that are technically and economically interrelated; for example the clusters of synthetic materials, petro-chemical and machinery injection innovations introduced in the 1920s, 1930s, 1940s and 1950s.

4. *Changes in techno-economic paradigms ('technological revolutions')* involve far reaching changes in technology systems which exert a major influence on the behaviour of the entire economy. Such changes are accompanied by many clusters of radical and incremental innovations, and may eventually embody a number of new technology systems. However, a fundamental characteristic of this fourth type of innovations is that they have *pervasive* effects throughout the economy; that is, they lead both to the

---

1   We will discuss incremental innovation in detail in Chapter 5 of this book.

emergence of a new range of products, services, systems and industries in their own right and they also directly or indirectly affect almost every other branch of the economy, Furthermore, techno-economic paradigms involve changes which transcend engineering trajectories for specific product or process technologies and affect input cost structure and conditions of production and distribution throughout the system. Moreover, once established as the dominant influence on engineers, designers and managers, they become 'technological regimes' for several decades, implemented and reproduced on societal scale by accompanying institutional frameworks, which, however, only emerge after a painful process of societal structural change. (C. Freeman and C. Perez, 1988, pp. 45–7)

Research based on the categorisation of innovation we have highlighted above emphasises 'externalities' in the socioeconomic context of firms. The focus is on the institutional milieu of firms, such as the role of public research institutions, and their relations. However, the interaction and collaboration of these bodies varies in different countries. This difference has led scholars of innovation activity to observe divergences in 'national systems of innovation' that appear to influence how effective this kind of activity is. Students of innovation claim that national systems of innovation; that is, the scale, scope and organisation of research and development (R&D) in different economies, influence competitiveness of firms and are an important determining factor of economic growth in the long run (C. Freeman, 1987; J. Fagerberg, 1988).

In recent years, students of innovation have also focused on differences in corporate innovation capacity from a perspective other than that discussed above. The research interest has been in the learning capacity of firms; namely, in terms of analysing which factors affect their ability to internalise and exploit new knowledge and technology and, consequently, strengthen their competitiveness. We will discuss research and theories of this kind i.e., 'evolutionary' theories, below in sub-section 3.3.2. However, before turning our attention to these concepts we should briefly discuss theories of long waves.

In short, we would claim that the history of theories of long waves or 'Kondratieff waves' can be divided into three main periods. In the first period, 1847–1928, long waves were discovered for the first time, but theories of these waves were primitive. In the second period, 1939–76, theories developed based on Schumpeter's hypothesis of the relationship between innovation activity and long waves. In the third period, since 1982, the role of 'institutionalist' factors has been increasingly emphasised, such as public institutions, organised interests, corporate cultures and corporate networks of collaboration.

Hyde Clark, the English engineer and editor of the *Railway Register* was probably the first person to present a hypothesis of long waves. He wrote an article in his journal in 1847 entitled 'Physical economy a preliminary inquiry into the physical laws governing the periods of famines and panics' in which he argued for long waves of 54 years' duration. His meteorological explanation of long waves was, however, poorly founded (J.A. Schumpeter, 1954, p. 743). The Russian Marxist, Parvus, or Alexander Israel Helpland, as was his real name, developed a hypothesis of long waves in the 1890s. Parvus (1901) assumed that the long wave which began in 1896 was caused by the opening of new markets, increased gold production, electrical power and electronic technology. He did not, however, explain why depressions change into recovery (the lower turning point of a wave) and prosperity changes into recession (upper turning point). Thus he did not have a useful theory of long waves (Duijn, 1985, pp. 60–61).

The hypothesis by Parvus were taken over and developed further by the Dutch economists and Marxists, Van Gelderen and De Wolff. Van Gelderen (1913) was the first scholar to verify the statistical relation between long waves and the development of prices in Western economies. He analysed, among other things, the long term development of the volume of production of manufacturing goods, international trade and transportation of goods. Van Gelderen concluded that an upswing is generated by: 1) discovery or exploitation of new countries or regions, and 2) production of new goods that satisfy hitherto unsatisfied needs (e.g., cars and electricity). Increased demand leads, in the beginning, to consumption driven multiplier effects in the economy, but it is followed by recession. The reason is that: Firstly, increased production leads to overproduction and, secondly, lack of raw materials leads to higher price levels and increased production costs. Hence, demand decreases, profits shrink and recession is inevitable ((Duijn, 1985, p. 62). Unfortunately, Van Gelderen could not explain what happens at the lower turning point of a long wave. He was, however, able to indicate which factors need to be present when recovery starts, but was at a loss to explain how and when these factors emerge.

De Wolff (1924 and 1929) followed Van Gelderen's train of thought, but claimed that long waves are due to the depreciation of fixed capital that loses value over a long period of time, such as factories, bridges, harbours, railways etc. Depreciation of fixed capital of this kind is 2.615 per cent per year according to his calculations, and a long wave spans 38 years. He considered the upper turning point of the long waves that he observed to be 1873 and 1913, while the lower turning points took place in 1894 and 1930. Each recovery and recession period of a long wave includes two and a half shorter cycles, according to De Wolff, and the duration of these cycles is becoming ever shorter and, consequently, crises in capitalist economies are becoming ever more frequent. De Wolff's long waves are determined by their own laws of motion, although external factors bring them about, such as innovation activity and technical changes that took place in the industrial revolution (Duijn, 1985, pp. 62–3).

Nikolai Dimitriyevich Kondratyev, or Kondratieff as he is usually referred to in economic texts, is the best known student of long waves from the first decades of the twentieth century. Long waves bear his name and called 'Kondratieff cycles'. He established the Institute of Conjuncture in Moscow in 1920 and was its director until 1928 when Stalin arranged his removal from the directorship. He was arrested in 1930 and sent to Siberia where he 'disappeared'. In the Soviet

Russian Encyclopedia from 1929 his theories were deemed 'wrong and counter-revolutionary' (M. Marshall, 1987, p. 24).

Kondratieff (1926) developed similar theories as De Wolff and assumed that the main reason for long waves is the depreciation of 'basic capital goods' like factories, railway systems, canals, major land improvement projects etc. (Duijn, 1985, pp. 66–7). But, why do basic capital goods present themselves in clusters; that is, why is investment in them concentrated in particular periods but does not emerge evenly over time? Or, put differently, how does Kondratieff explain the turning points of long waves? To answer this question, Kondratieff borrowed a theory from his former economics tutor, Mikhayl Ivanovich Tugan-Baranovsky, that of free capital funds. At the start of recovery periods, there exists a large amount of capital that can be borrowed at low interest rates. Propensity to save is also great at this point in time and prices of goods are low. Following increased investment in basic capital goods, funds of investment capital decrease and interest rates rise. Consequently, investment decreases and recession follows with falling prices and dwindling activity in the economy as a whole. During recession, propensity to save increases again, especially among those who enjoy increased purchasing power due to lower prices. Increased savings, lower interest rates and decreasing prices generate the conditions for a new recovery.

Kondratieff was not fully convinced that his theory was adequate and agreed that a new upswing did not necessarily follow a downswing. He accepted that he was unable to explain the lower turning point of long waves. Kondratieff built his theory on the presumed influence of overinvestments, but he also emphasised the role of innovation and technical change in the development of long waves. In addition, he analysed in which periods major innovations emerge in relation to periods of upswings and downswings. He also realised that upswings within long waves are related to increased production of basic capital goods. However, he did not manage to connect these phenomena and develop a theory of the endogenous development of long waves; that is, a theory which presumes that innovation and technical change create the conditions for new branches of industry requiring investment in new infrastructures and, consequently, generate the conditions for a new long wave (ibid., p. 67). As we discussed above, it was Schumpeter, the first student of long waves, who provided that kind of theory.

In recent years, various theories of long waves have emerged. In brief, they fall into four categories: 1) price cycle theories; 2) theories of innovation and the development of industries; 3) theories of disproportionate investment in capital and; 4) Marxist theories.

3.2.1 Price Cycle Theories

W.W. Rostow (1960), like Kondratieff, developed a theory of long waves which is based on price cycles. In his book, *The Stages of Growth: A Non-Communist Manifesto*, he claimed that all societies develop through particular developmental stages. The first stage is the stage of 'traditional society'. The second stage he refers to as 'preconditions for take-off'. The third stage is the 'industrial take-off' when economic growth becomes the natural state of the economy. The fourth stage, the 'drive to maturity', implies that manufacturing becomes the basic source of national income. Finally, the fifth stage emerges as the stage of 'high mass consumption'. The precondition for the development of societies through these stages is that surplus production in traditional industries such as agriculture accumulates in the hands of a new class i.e., the 'entrepreneurial class', which is farsighted enough to invest in new technology and new industries and, as a result, increase the national income. Democratic development and the introduction of human rights is also a precondition for the full maturity of societies according to Rostow. In short, all societies need to develop similar social structures as those that characterise the Western world.

Rostow analysed the evolution of societies from one stage to the next in his book *The World Economy* (1978) by observing the development of different branches of industries in Western economies and some Third World Countries. Kondratieff waves are the main explanatory factor in his explanation of the development of societies through his developmental stages. Britain, as an example, had its 'industrial take-off' based on cotton production in the period 1783–1830. Britain's 'drive to maturity' was between 1870 and 1913 when the railway system became the precondition for growth, followed by steel, electricity, automobile and chemical industry. After 1920, Britain finally entered the stage of 'high mass consumption'.

Rostow explains this development with his theory of Kondratieff waves. Periods of upswings and downswings are caused by a mismatch between prices of, on the one hand, agricultural products and raw materials, and, on the other, manufacturing goods. This mismatch leads to altered income distribution, channelled investment into different industries and regions, simultaneously changing lending interest rates and prices in the economy. But, why were the long waves so long compared to, as an example, 10 year cycles? Rostow argues that it takes a long time before the conditions are ripe for new kinds of food and raw materials. Increasing prices of food and raw materials in upswings lead to overproduction. The following oversupply of these goods leads to a gradual fall in prices until demand rises again in the upswing of the next Kondratieff wave (M. Marshall, 1987, p. 27). Rostow claims that high prices of food and raw materials lead to labour demands for higher wages and increasing production costs in industrial manufacture. The rising production costs push for the development of new technology. Technical change leads to decreasing prices of capital goods in the long run and creates the preconditions for a long wave. Rostow has, however, failed to link these two dimensions of long waves; that is, price cycles and technological development and, furthermore, he has not explained the dynamics of technological development which therefore remains an unexplained external factor in his theory (ibid., p. 28).

3.2.2 Theories of Innovation and the Development of Industries

The 1970s were stricken by recessions and it appeared that they were part of a long wave. Keynesian economic policies were largely useless in a situation where increased public expenditure did not reduce unemployment as easily as it had in the post war boom era. Indeed, increasing unemployment developed alongside rising inflation and the result was 'stagflation'. Economists reacted in two ways. On the one hand, the monetarists under Milton Friedman's leadership, claimed that an explicit monetary policy of cuts in public expenditure and wages was necessary to reduce high levels of inflation in Western economies. On the other hand, there were those who considered the problems to be more fundamental and pointed out the fact that investment in technological innovation and technical change was increasingly ineffective in terms of improving productivity. Consequently, they claimed, profits had decreased in the long run. Following this train of thought, interest in Schumpeter's theory of long waves reawakened. Among the first economists to make his mark on the development of 'neo-Schumpeterian' theories was Gerhard Mensch.

In his book, *Stalemate in Technology: Innovations Overcome the Depression* (1979), Mensch discussed the lower turning point of Kondratieff waves. Basic innovations emerge in clusters according to his research that are unevenly distributed through time. It is these clusters of basic innovations that lead to long waves. Such clusters appeared in 1770, 1825, 1885 and 1935. Kuznets (1940) had criticised Schumpeter's theories maintaining that their empirical testimony was not sufficient. Mensch presented a new empirical study into the history of technology that substantiated Schumpeter's theory of clusters of basic innovations. His studies confirmed that innovation activity and implementation of new technology is bolstered in depressions; that is to say, basic innovations are most frequent in depressions and ignite upswings. He explained this phenomenon with his concept of 'technological stalemate' which always precedes an upswing. Downswings of Kondratieffs are characterised by increasing improvements of existing technology and 'pseudo innovations' that lead to decreasing productivity. As the crisis deepens, capitalists become more desperate and more willing to invest in new technology. In the end a new basic technology is introduced and clusters of new technology emerge which substantially increase productivity. Mensch claims, furthermore, that it is in depressions that basic inventions emerge, but when they are actually implemented in production depends on how desperate capitalists are and how willing they are to take risks in investments. According to Mensch, basic technological innovations have a lifespan which appears in a pattern; in early stages they lead to large increases in productivity, but gradually pseudo innovations appear which do not raise productivity. At this point, the upper turning point of the long wave creeps in and the downswing takes over (Mensch, 1975, p. 180).

Mensch's theory has been criticised by many students of long waves. G.F. Ray (1980) claims that it is not the main issue whether innovations are 'basic' or 'improvements' in terms of explaining long waves. What is most important in this context is how new technology is *diffused* in the economy and how *fast* it spreads.

A different critique emanated from a research group at the Science Policy Research Unit at the University of Sussex i.e., from C. Freeman, J. Clark and L. Soete (1982). They conducted research in the history of technology along the same lines as Mensch. They came to the conclusion that basic technological inventions come about in clusters, but their emergence is not limited to depressions alone. They appear, as an example, in the recession period before the following long wave takes off. Freeman, Clark and Soete used statistics on patents in USA and Britain from the eighteenth century to 1971 in their research. They were able to show that the frequency of technological inventions and their implementation, measured in terms of number of patents, is not linear, but appear in clusters. They also showed that these clusters are not limited to depressions, like Mensch presumed, because besides appearing in depression periods (1874–89 and 1928–36) they emerge in upswings (1897–1903 and 1956–61) and in wars (1806–15) (C. Freeman, J. Clark and L. Soete, 1982, pp. 59–63). Their conclusion was that the reason for innovation clusters is much more complicated than simple desperation among capitalists. Freeman claimed that the explanation for the phenomena of innovation clusters is to be found in the interplay between technological and social innovations that together constitute 'techno-economic paradigms'. We will discuss techno-economic paradigms and their relation to long waves in section 3.3.3.

3.2.3 Marxist Theories

Ernest Mandel published his book, *Der Spätkapitalismus* (1972), in English translation in 1976 as *Late Capitalism* (Mandel, 1976). In his book, Mandel attempted to join together Schumpeter's theories of Kondratieff waves and the Marxist theory of surplus-value. He based his approach to long waves on the idea of clusters of basic innovations and maintained that they caused long waves, claiming, however, that the privileged competitiveness corporations achieve by exploiting technological rents disappears in the long run (ibid., pp. 137–45 and 257–8).

In his theories, Mandel follows Trotsky, the Russian revolutionary and Marxist. Trotsky, or Leo Bronstein as his real name was, accepted Kondratieff's analysis of short term cycles, but claimed that his theories of the dynamics of short term cycles could be generalised and used to explain long waves. Trotsky presumed that long waves are not determined by internal economic laws in the same way as short term cycles, but determined by external social and political forces (M. Marshall, 1987, p. 39).

In this respect, Mandel follows Trotsky concerning Kondratieff waves. He observes external forces and claims that they reduce the general crisis tendency of capitalist economies. Capitalist market economies are characterised by 'the tendency of the rate of profit to fall'.[2] This propensity is the basis of the internal crisis tendency of capitalist economies. The tendency of the rate of profits of firms to fall is due to the need of corporations, in their competition with other firms, to constantly improve their productivity by implementing new technology. The cost of equipment and machines rises faster than that of wages and profits in the long run as the corporations must necessarily invest in ever more expensive technology. In Mandel's and Marxist terminology this means that 'the organic composition of capital' increases. With increased organic composition of capital, the rate of profit falls as the general production cost of the branch of industry in question has increased. As an example, Mandel claims that over a period of one decade the structure of the production cost of manufacture changes as follows:

Equation 1:
300 million c + 100 million v + 100 million s = £500

changes to:

Equation 2:
400 million c + 100 million v + 100 million s = £600
c = buildings, machines, raw material and energy; v = wages; s = profit[3]

The rate of profit is defined as the ratio of s to the sum of c and v or s/(c+v). According to this formula the rate of profit has decreased from 25 per cent to 20 per cent over the decade (i.e., 100*100/400 =25% to 100*100/500 =20%). As there is competition on the market and the good in the example is sold for £500, but not £600, the firms must cut the cost of wages (v) in order to receive profit from the production. In order to hinder the falling rate of profit the corporation must make workers redundant and save labour costs. However, if the rate of unemployment is high in the economy, the demand for goods decreases and crisis creeps in. This process appears in technological development which is characterised by the changing value constitution of capital as c has become relatively higher than v compared to previous period. In Marxist terms, the organic composition of capital has increased. To illustrate his point, Mandel observes the development of US manufacture in the eighteenth and nineteenth century (E. Mandel, 1962/1974, p. 166 and 1976, p. 41).

If this was really the case, capitalism and its economy would have crashed a long time ago. This has not happened, according to Mandel, due to counteracting forces that are able to reduce the crisis tendency and the likelihood of the rate

---

2   Trotsky got the theory of the tendency of profits to fall from Karl Marx who analysed it in Chapters 13–15 in the third volume of *Capital* (K. Marx, 1981). Marx had received this theory from John Stuart Mill (1848) who analysed it in his book *The Principles of Political Economy*, cf. Volume 4, Chapter 4.

3   In order to simplify, s is here called profit instead of surplus-value.

of profit to fall:[4] *Firstly*, the higher organic composition of capital can lead to increased productivity and hence increase the rate of profit. A counter-effect of this kind, however, has its limits in the long run as increased productivity may lead to boosting needs and consumption of workers, leading to an intensification of trade union struggles for higher wages. Furthermore, there is an 'absolute' limit to reducing the number of workers in the production processes (ibid., pp. 166–7). *Secondly*, increased organic composition of capital leads to heightened productivity in the capital goods sector. This leads to lower prices and consequently cost of production falls as prices of equipment and machines decrease (cf. cost of c in Mandel's equations above). However, the effect of a higher organic composition of capital gradually diminishes as the more equipment and machines are installed and overproduction capacity builds up. *Thirdly*, the expansion of capitalist production counteracts the tendency of profits to fall. International trade secures a supply of cheap raw materials and labour. However, as production is moved abroad to countries with cheap labour and raw materials, the competitiveness of domestic corporations diminishes and, sooner or later, firms will have to increase their organic composition of capital, which will generate a crisis tendency in the long run. *Fourthly*, the sum of profits increases with increased production, but while the rate of profit falls only minimally the capitalist is satisfied that the sum of profits has increased following increased investment. Similarly, higher velocity of turnover can counteract diminishing rates of profit (ibid., pp. 167–9).

In *Late Capitalism* (1976), Mandel mentions three factors that explain the first half of the long wave that lasted from 1940(45) to 1966. *Firstly*, he points out the historical defeat of the working classes that made it possible for the countries of fascism and the allied countries to increase rates of profit. Secondly, he mentions technological development and increased velocity of production technology that created conditions for increased production on a world scale. The explanation, therefore, relates to both technological and historical external factors that led to increased profits (E. Mandel, 1976, p. 442).

Mandel agrees with Mensch that basic innovations typically emerge in depressions, but he also criticises Mensch for emphasising technical change as the main reason for upswings. According to Mandel, wide ranging technological innovations do not create long waves unless, at the same time, markets expand and demand for labour rises (E. Mandel, 1984, p. 197). Mandel claims that the lower and upper turning points of long waves are characterised by different laws. Lower turning points; that is, the transformation from depression to recovery, were generated by the bourgeois revolutions of 1848 as well as the gold rush in California in 1848 and Transvaal in 1893 that led to an expansion of the world

---

4 In his analysis of counter effects to the tendency of the rate of profit, Mandel follows John Stuart Mill's (1848) train of thought in the fourth chapter of the fourth volume of his *The Principles of Political Economy* and Karl Marx (1981) in Chapters 13–15 of the third volume of his *Capital*.

market. The defeat of the working classes in the Second World War and the Cold War era were later turning points which led to a sudden rise in the rate of profits and this impact lasted for decades. As Mandel puts it: ' ... the turn from the long depression into the long boom is essentially *not predetermined*, i.e. it depends on the outcome of momentous political and social struggles – class struggles, inter-imperialist struggles, wars, revolutions, counter – revolutions – ... '. (E. Mandel, 1984, p. 201). The upper turning point does not result from such external factors, but from the internal laws of capital accumulation i.e., falling rates of profits in most branches of industry, developments which are to be explained by increasing organic composition of capital (ibid., pp. 200–201).

Mandel's theories have been criticised, among other things, for not taking into consideration the conditions which influence the power position of the working classes, despite the fact that class struggle plays a central role in his theory. In addition, his theory is criticised for presuming that the boom era after the Second World War is due to the defeat of the working classes in the war economies of the allied countries and the countries of fascism. Quite the contrary is claimed; namely, the strong power position of the working classes after the war was the precondition for a strong general demand for goods on a world scale and consequently for a long new term boom era (I. Wallerstein, 1997).

In terms of research into innovation activity, the most important critique of Mandel's theory is that it uncritically accepts Mensch's argument that basic innovations emerge in periods of depression when capitalists are presumed to be especially desperate and more willing to take risks in investment. Mandel does not develop any theory of the internal dynamics of innovation activity within corporations and he only presents a general hypothesis concerning the role of the class struggle as well as conflict among imperialist countries as they create the necessary 'institutional' conditions; that is, social and political, for the implementation of new production technology.

The so called 'evolutionary theories' in economics take these considerations into account concerning internal corporate dynamics of innovation activity, as well as the role of the social institutional context of business environments. We will discuss this approach below, but first we will observe how the main contemporary orthodox economics i.e., neoclassical economics, approaches innovation activity.

3.3 From Neoclassical Theories to Evolutionary Theories

3.3.1 Neoclassical Theories of Innovation and Technical Change

Neoclassical economics has very little to contribute to research into innovation activity as we highlighted above in chapter 2. Technical change is observed by neoclassical economics as a choice between two 'factors of production' i.e., labour and capital (J. Elster, 1985, p. 96). It is presumed that the capitalists are in a position in which they have to choose between these factors of production in the so called 'production function'. In theory this choice is simplified so that the capitalists only have to choose between capital and labour. This function is formulated as:

$q = f(K,L)$

where K = aggregate capital and L is aggregate labour and q is quantity of output.

It is presumed that the variables K and L are interchangeable so that they can be substituted for each other in indefinitely small numbers and that labour can be substituted for capital and vice versa. Furthermore, it is anticipated that diminishing returns prevail so that if one of the variables is kept constant, let us say K, then an increase in the quantity of L will lead to a diminishing return of L. In other words, if for example labour is increased at the same time as capital is kept constant, then the increase in output will be less than the increase in labour. Finally, a static relationship is presumed to exist in the relations between the variables so that constant returns to scale prevail. If 10 K and 20 L are needed to produce 60 items of a particular model of cars, then 20 K and 40 L will be needed to produce 120 items of the cars. This assumption leads to the equation:

$f(aK,aL) = a \cdot f(K,L)$

If we accept all these assumptions, the resulting equation prevails:

$f(K,L) = f_K (K,L) \cdot K + f_L (K,L) \cdot L$

The production function is usually explained by means of a figure of 'isoquants', which shows different combinations of capital and labour in relation to output. An isoquant is the locus of factor combinations which give the same output, so that $f(K_1, L_1) = f(K_2, L_2)$. With constant returns to scale all the information in the production function can be conveyed by the isoquant corresponding to one unit of output, since all other processes are simple multiplies of this. The straight lines, PP' and QQ' are called 'iso-cost curves' i.e., the locus of input combinations with the same total cost, given the factor prices. The figure below is an example of a production function that has particular iso-cost curves or possible combinations of capital and labour at a particular level of output.

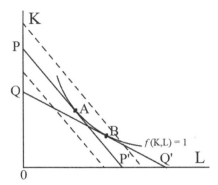

Figure 3.2   Production function

The vertical axis measures costs due to capital while the horizontal axis measures labour costs. The line PP' shows possible combinations of costs of K and L presuming a particular relative difference in costs of K and L. The line QQ' shows combination possibilities of K and L after changes in cost differences of K and L i.e., following a decrease in the cost of labour (L) which has come considerably cheaper than capital (K). Facing this change, the capitalist chooses the combination shown in point B instead of A that he/she choose before. At point B the capitalist uses more L and less K. The curve $f(K,L) = 1$ is the isoquant of the production function and is characterised by the fact that all combinations of K and L result in the same quantity of output.

The discussion above sums up neoclassical theory of production and technical change. They presume that the actor's decisions are rational (i.e., optimising in utilitarian sense) and based on prices of factors of production. The model above is based on three main assumptions which have all been criticised. *Firstly*, the presumptions of the model are behavioural i.e., it is presumed that the actor; that is, the capitalist, always attempts to optimise her/his profits. This assumption of neoclassical economics has been criticised by many scholars, among them John Kenneth Galbraith who criticised it in his book, *The New Industrial State*. According to Galbraith, modern corporations are managed by managers who do not own the companies' shares. They manage the corporations on behalf of others; that is, the shareholders, and their purpose is to maximise their dividends. However, profits and corporate performance are not reflected in managers' remuneration; only a minority of managers receive astronomical compensation. However, managers have their interests. As their income is not according to corporate performance, they tend to seek compensation in a different way (J.K. Galbraith, 1974, p. 127). Their interests are transformed into boosting their power by maximising the growth of their corporations and the number of employees, as well as by participating in various decision making processes in the social and political environment of the corporations.[5] These interests often conflict with profit maximisation (ibid., pp. 132 and 137. See also P. Baran and P. Sweezy, 1973, p. 34). If this is correct, one should not expect managers to consistently attempt to maximise profits when they consider combinations of capital and labour with regard to production functions, since deciding to save labour costs might undermine the power position of the managers within the corporation and/or the power position of the corporation in society.

Secondly, the model of production function assumes that perfect information is available concerning technological potential or its limits at any given time. Furthermore, the model presumes that all isoquants i.e., all points on the 'iso cost curve', are equally accessible to the manager who can, without hindrance, move on the curve and the isoquant remains static. Let us put it differently; it is presumed to be unproblematic to implement a new technology in the production processes vis-à-vis the employees. Training of employees, their present skills and their acquisition of new necessary skills that the new technology requires is neither problematic nor a hindrance. Labour is simply exchanged for capital in the production function. These assumptions have been criticised for being unrealistic by scholars who adhere to evolutionary theories of innovation and technical change. Their point of departure is the special characteristics of knowledge and learning processes that do not fit into the neoclassical theoretical framework of the production function. We will discuss evolutionary approaches below in the following section (3.3.2).

Thirdly, the neoclassical economic concept of production function is rooted in the orthodox postulate of perfect competition, or the idea that capital and other production factors flow freely between markets (J. Elster, 1983, p. 99). This theoretical postulate is empirically dreadfully unrealistic as various hindrances prevail on markets, both in terms of wage formation and labour conditions and concerning social and legal obstacles, such as for example laws on patents. Furthermore, lack of information and knowledge hinders the smooth flow of equipment, machines and knowledge on and between markets.[6]

Jon Elster, (1983, pp. 101–111) has observed the explanatory power of neoclassical, orthodox theories of production functions with reference to technical

---

5   Galbraith (1974, p. 137) quotes Frank Abrams, former board chairman of the mega sized Standard Oil Company of New Jersey, who claimed that the primary goal is a just distribution of income i.e., 'to maintain an equitable and working balance among the claims of various directly interested groups – stockholders, employees, customers, and the public at large – to pronouncements of a primary concern for improving higher education, increasing economic literacy, resisting Communist subversion, supporting American foreign policy, building the community, strengthening the two-party system, upholding the Constitution, amending the Constitution to preserve its original intent, defending freedom and free enterprise and rehabilitating the environment'.

6   Neoclassical economists have answered this critique by claiming that if these hindrances did not exist, markets would work according to theory. This assumption is both unrealistic and illogical according to John Eatwell and Murray Milgate (1983, p. 261).

change. He looks, on the one hand, at their explanatory power in relation to the *choice between capital and labour* as the history of Western industries shows that the general developmental trend is in the direction of labour saving. On the other hand, he considers the explanatory power of the orthodox theories in relation to the *speed of technical change*; that is, with reference to explaining why technical change varies in space and time, as it is faster in particular periods and countries.

Neoclassical economists traditionally presumed that a high price of labour leads to labour saving technology and vice versa; furthermore that a high price of capital leads to capital saving innovations. If we accept that the orthodox postulate of perfect competition is right, we face the problem of explaining why the prevailing tendency is to choose capital rather than labour: If wages are generally increasing on the market in question, all capitalists on the market will respond by investing in capital rather than labour. Demand for labour diminishes, its price decreases, equilibrium returns to the market and the ratio between capital and labour becomes the same as before. If capital increases in price, a similar process will emerge leading to the same result. The theoretical assumptions of neoclassical economics are, consequently, unable to explain why the development of technical change has in fact been in the direction of capital intensive and labour saving technologies.

In addition to the above-mentioned critique of the explanatory power inherent in the idea of production function, it can be criticised from the point of view of 'rational choice'. If we assume that each and every capitalist attempts to maximise his utility, then our conclusion will be that the combination of factors will be unchanged and contrary to what actually has happened in the history of Western economies. Let us conjecture that the capitalist needs to pay the cost for developing new technology. She finds herself in a situation called 'prisoner's dilemma' which we discussed in Chapter 2 of this book: It is better for all capitalists that they all invest in new technology than that no one does it. However, it is tempting for them individually not to invest and gain from labour saving innovation activity that others finance, rather than investing themselves in the necessary R&D. If no individual capitalist invests in developing the new technology, then no one is willing to do it as this would only lead to increased costs which would not be matched by increased profits to cover the extra cost of the endeavour. This is, as we discussed above, because the new technology would save labour which consequently would become cheaper and this would strengthen the competitiveness of other capitalists on the market in question. We may put the case differently. Let us presume that the cost is equal, regardless of whether technical change is in the form of capital saving or labour saving, respectively. This context leads to conditions for a specific game. It is the collective interest of all capitalists to implement labour saving technology, as this will lead to decreasing wages, but for each and every one of them it does not matter whether they choose capital saving or labour saving technology. Why is it then that the labour saving option has prevailed? The reason is apparently that capitalists choose the alternative that is in their collective interests as long as it does not harm them or lead to expenses (Jon Elster, 1983, p. 103). Other reasons may be that, on the one hand, the capitalists presume that in general it is less problematic in the long run to choose capital due to possible labour unrest and, on the other hand, it might be because they want to secure their power in the firms.

William Fellner (1961) has argued why it is rational for firms to choose labour saving technology even though this incurs extra costs. If we reject the idea of perfect competition and envisage that companies have a monopoly position, then it would be rational to choose labour saving technology and control labour costs or wages because no one else will be competing for the labour. Companies also learn from experience. They learn that wages have tended to increase in the past and on the grounds of this experience they presume that wages will increase in the future. Consequently, the company will choose labour saving technology in order to respond to anticipated wage increases. This option may be irrational, however, in a game in which there are many competing companies on the market. If the managers of the company expect other firms to implement labour saving technology in order to protect themselves against future wage increases, it is best for the company to wait. The reason is that demand for labour will diminish, as well as wages, if the other companies implement labour saving technology. However, after some further contemplation the managers will come to the conclusion that other companies will think in the same way as they do, so they presume that the other companies are likely to wait as well. If they all wait, wages will increase in the future which forces them to the conclusion that it is wise to invest in labour saving technology. Thus, the conclusion drawn from these observations is the following: Each company has reason to implement labour saving technology if no other firms do so, but they have no reason to, if all other companies act along the same lines. It is, therefore, difficult to explain why companies choose labour saving technology by surmising that their decisions are rational in the utilitarian sense. The reason for this is that companies' expectations are not based on rational assumptions as they do not have access to perfect information (Jon Elster, 1983, p. 104).

Let us continue our discussion of the critique of the neoclassical idea of production function and now focus on the question of *speed of technical change*; that is, the question why technical change is faster in different periods and countries. Technical change has been slow in less industrialised countries and among most nations not belonging to the Western world. The model of production functions is unable to explain this phenomenon as technical change falls outside the scope of the model which is limited to choices between pre-given factors of production i.e., capital and labour. The model is unable to explain why it is rational for companies to take risks and invest in innovation in particular periods rather than other periods. Neoclassical economists have, therefore, moved to other grounds and tried to build different models to explain the difference in speed of technical change. If it is assumed that technical change is caused by external forces – such as for example that sciences produce new technology that corporations evaluate in terms of the model of production function – then the firm is unable to make rational decisions, unless it is known in advance what the demand for the products will be. As long as the demand is unknown, it will be rational for the company to wait and let other companies bear the cost and risk of investing in development of new technology or products. The neoclassical economist J. Schmookler (1966) rejected the hypothesis that technical change is a direct product of science; that is, according to the theory of 'technology push'. Instead he presented a theory of 'technology pull'. He analysed in detail the development of patents in USA and came to the conclusion that growth and reduction of inventions follows growth and reduction of investment in the economy. His conclusion was, therefore, that the development of demand is the fundamental factor that explains technical change, but not external independent scientific inventions. Schmookler was criticised in the 1970s both for his incorrect analysis of his own research material and with reference to new empirical material. Mowery and Rosenberg (1979) claimed that the demand pull theory confuses the concepts of 'need' and 'demand' and the same goes for the concepts of 'potential demand' and 'effective demand'. 'Needs' are quite various and are often not satisfied over long periods of time; therefore they cannot explain why a particular innovation takes place at a particular point in time. It is neither possible to view innovations as a linear process in terms of independent scientific inventions ('technology push') nor with reference to demand on markets. Innovation is, according to them, a complicated interactive process that knits together potential users and inventions in science and technology (C. Freeman, 1994, pp. 479–80). Innovation activity is, therefore, more similar to learning processes than linear processes of production.

A comparable critique has been aimed at Schumpeterian theories of diffusion of new technology. In the 1950s and 1960s it was presumed that new technology spreads more or less unchanged in the economy and the economies themselves change slowly. Research in the 1970s and 1980s showed the opposite, namely that the process of diffusion of technology and innovation in economies is a learning process according to which new technology undergoes modifications while diffusing in the economy. Furthermore, increased productivity can partly be traced to these changes and adjustments (ibid., p. 479). However, it has appeared that it depends on the branches of industry in question how much the new technology alters during the process of diffusion. As an example, new technology changes substantially in the automobile industry and computer industry while adaptations are small in the pharmaceutical and food industries (ibid., p. 480).

In recent years theories have been developed that focus on corporate alliances and networks of collaboration concerning innovation and the diffusion of new technology. These theories emphasise both the supply side (science and technology push) and the demand side (D.F. Midgley et al., 1992). Research and theories of this kind, which emphasise innovation activity as an interactive learning process and highlight corporate alliances, as well as institutional conditions for innovation activity, are termed institutionalist theories of innovation. In recent years evolutionary theories have been important in the field of institutionalist theories and research. We will now look closer at such theories.

3.3.2 Evolutionary Theories of Innovation and Technical Change

It is above all scholars who adhere to evolutionary theories of innovation and technical change that have criticised the oversimplified view of technical change endorsed by neoclassical orthodox theories. In this group we find a wide range of students of management and organisation, economists, business majors, sociologists and psychologists who approach this object of study in terms of the specific nature of knowledge as a factor of production and the learning processes that are necessary for innovation activity.

Evolutionary theories are a reaction against neoclassical orthodox theories; that is, theories resting on weak empirical foundations, but particularly characterised by deductions based on raw utilitarian postulates and the ideas of general equilibrium of neoclassical economics. Evolutionary research into innovation activity grew fast in the 1980s, especially following R.R. Nelson and S.G. Winter's book, *An Evolutionary Theory of Economic Change*, in 1982. However, the concept of 'evolution' has not been rigorously defined in most of these studies, although Nelson and Winter clearly illustrated the concept in their book (G.M. Hodgson, 1993, p. 37). A common feature of evolutionary theories is that they reject neoclassical theories of equilibrium and radical approaches that emphasise the role of social revolutions in the development of economies. Neoclassical orthodox economics is unable to explain processes of economic development because it oversimplifies the conditions and contexts which economic actors, such as individuals and firms, take into consideration in their decisions. Ideas of perfect information, maximisation (usually maximisation of profits) and general equilibrium are nothing more than thought constructions that inadequately describe what really takes place in firms and the economy as a whole. In reality information is imperfect and managers can never optimise profits. They can only realise 'satisficing' performance according to minimum standards of achievement that they hope will ensure the firm's viability over a long period. According to Nelson and Winter, managers' decisions are, on the one hand, based on 'routines' and on the other, on 'search'. 'Routines' refer to habitual ways of doing things in the firm that are known to work well, while 'search' refers to hunting for new knowledge on which new routines will be based. The new 'routines' take over the old 'routines' and become habitual ways of doing things. 'Routines' are, therefore, similar to genes in organisms; that is, their growth and development is grounded in the control mechanisms that are part of their internal being. 'Search' is constantly going on, but it is based on knowledge and ideas that already exist in the firm in question. However, as the environment of firms, markets and technology, is continuously changing, the existing knowledge and 'routines' in the firm are constantly revised and developed further at the same time as new knowledge accumulates. The 'search' in firms is determined by rules distinctive to the firm in question. These rules and the resources of firms, such as their R&D activities, condition their potential for survival and capacity to achieve satisficing performance.

The concept of 'routines' is similar to that of 'genes' in biological theories in the sense that 'routines' by which the development of firms is determined, dictate how easily firms can be transformed so as to adjust to new contexts and/or environments. If the routines cannot be adjusted, then the firms will not survive. Firms that successfully transform and adjust their 'routines' will increase their profits and survive (R.R. Nelson and S.G. Winter, 1982, pp. 14–19). As Nelson and Winter presume that firms learn from accumulating experience, their approach is not to be taken as a simple Darwinian theory as it also reflects the ideas of Jean Baptiste de Lamarck concerning the evolution of organisms.

Schumpeter's theories have traditionally been criticised for being too general to be useful for analysis of what characterises innovation activity in companies in the short run. Nelson and Winter responded to this problem by developing their theory of 'routines' and 'search' which we outlined above. With their contribution, we would claim that they knitted together Herbert Simon's theory of 'satisficing' performance and Schumpeter's theories that reject the idea of maximisation and general equilibrium. Nelson and Winter distinguish between two approaches in business studies; on the one hand, managerial approaches and, on the other, behavioural approaches. The former share the view that managers maximise whatever they are working on and that they have perfect information on all possible alternatives and consequences of choosing between them. Among 'managerialists' in this sense are scholars such as W.J. Baumol (1959) and E.O. Williamson (1964). The latter mentioned, or behavioural, approaches to business studies emphasise some or all of the following issues:

> Man's rationality is 'bounded': real life decision problems are too complex to comprehend and therefore firms cannot maximise over the set of all conceivable alternatives. Relatively simple decision rules and procedures are used to guide action; because of the bounded rationality problem these rules and procedures cannot be too complicated and cannot be characterised as 'optimal' in the sense that they reflect the results of global calculation taking into account information and decision costs; however, they may be quite satisfactory for the purposes of the firm given the problems the firm faces. Firms satisfice; a firm is unlikely to possess a well-articulated global objective function in part because individuals have not thought through all of their utility trade-offs and in part because firms are coalitions of decision makers with different interests that are unlikely to be fully accommodated in an intrafirm social welfare function. (R.R. Nelson and S.G. Winter 1982, p. 35)

Nelson and Winter emphasise that behavioural theories first and foremost focus on short term decisions in firms, but they are also interested in analysing the relationship between the development of rules of decisions within firms and trends in their environment (ibid., p. 36). The critique that behaviouralists and Nelson and Winter express against the maximisation premises of neoclassical economics is very important in terms of innovation studies, as we will discuss in Chapter 5.

The roots of the theories of Nelson and Winter can also be traced back to other theoreticians than Schumpeter and Simon. The theories of the social philosopher, M. Polanyi, constitute an important part of their approaches, especially the concept of 'tacit knowledge' (M. Polanyi, 1967). Polanyi built a whole philosophical school on the basis of the proposition 'we know more than we can tell' (ibid., p. 4). By this phrase, he meant that much of our knowledge is rooted in experience that we have not formalised in written texts, but is hidden in our emotions and practical experience that we can repeat without substantial thought or even unconsciously. Much of practical knowledge is based on 'tacit knowledge' of this kind that is transferred between individuals by way of imitation rather than in textual form.[7] Despite these similarities, there is a difference between Nelson and Winter's theory of tacit knowledge and Polanyi's work as he limits his observations to individuals, while they presume that organisations possess such knowledge as well, due to the collaboration of their employees or members. As Winter claims:

> The coordination displayed in the performance of organisational routines is, like that displayed in the exercise of individual skills, the fruit of practice. What requires emphasis is that ... the learning experience is a shared experience of organisation members ... Thus, even if the contents of the organisational memory are stored only in the form of memory traces in the memories of individual members, it is still an organisational knowledge in the sense that the fragment stored by each individual member is not fully meaningful or effective except in the context provided by the fragments stored by other members. (S.G. Winter, 1982, p. 76)

Knowledge and learning processes in organisations; that is, analysis of how knowledge spreads among employees and how new knowledge comes about, is as important an object of study in Nelson and Winter's research as are their observations of technical change and firms' externalities. Considerable interest developed in the 1980s in research into learning processes in firms following Nelson and Winter's contribution. However, research and theories had been developed earlier in this field that influenced recent studies. Briefly, we would claim that this research focused on three aspects of learning i.e., 'learning by doing', 'learning by using' and 'learning by interacting'.

The concept of 'learning by doing' was first presented by the neoclassical economist K.J. Arrow (1962). With this concept Arrow meant to explain an interesting phenomenon related to production, namely that productivity increases despite the fact that the volume of inputs does not increase at the same time. Arrow's point of departure was the so called 'Horndal effect'. Arrow based his

---

7   See a detailed analysis of Polanyi's work and its importance for innovation studies by Kristin Atladottir (2007).

theory on Erik Lundberg's (1961) analysis of a steel mill in Horndal in Sweden where productivity had increased by 2 per cent over a 15 year period, although production technology had remained more or less unchanged. Arrow came to the conclusion that this example showed that employees learn skills or knowledge while they work and this emerges as a kind of by-product of the production. Problems related to the production processes are solved as soon as they emerge: thus related knowledge accumulates and leads to increased productivity in subsequent production processes.

Arrow postulates that the marginal efficiency of work experience diminishes through time as production technology does not continuously create new problems to be solved. Consequently, Arrow concludes that in order to reproduce productivity increases based on learning processes and the 'Horndal effects' it is necessary to implement new technology. This conclusion of his undermines the neoclassical model of production function as increased productivity is presumed to stem from the development of skills and knowledge of the employees, or labour. This conclusion opposes the main postulate of the production function model which assumes that capital can be exchanged for labour and vice versa without affecting output. This means that capital and labour are not reciprocal substitutes. Furthermore, Arrow's conclusion supports the view that technical change is due to internal factors of production i.e., that employees' learning processes call for innovation, the implementation of new technology and production procedures rooted in the external environment of the firms concerned. Obviously, this view opposes the neoclassical presumption that technical change is solely caused by external forces, particularly from scientific inventions.

Arrow's contribution has been particularly important in terms of influencing the focus of research into innovations in such a way that researchers emphasise endogenous dynamics of innovation activity. However, it is a serious shortcoming of his contribution that it has very little to say about the nature of learning processes. Furthermore, Arrow narrows his analysis to quantitative aspects of 'learning by doing' but fails to observe qualitative aspects of production relationships such as firms' relations to suppliers and or customers. In addition, he does not analyse external institutional conditions for 'learning by doing' within firms, such as R&D in research institutions, the role of the educational system in this respect and the general educational level of society (S. Eliasen, 2001, p. 25).

The contribution of N. Rosenberg to research into innovation activity is probably more important than that of Arrow. Rosenberg (1982) developed the concept of 'learning by using' which he originally used in his study of research and development activity in the aerospace industry. Innovation activity of this kind is built on collaboration between the firm in question and the research institutions and other research actors in its environment. The concept refers to learning processes related both to product development and actual research and experimental work. According to Rosenberg, several forms of learning are relevant to the innovation process. As he puts it:

At the research end of the spectrum, the learning process involves the acquisition of knowledge concerning the laws of nature. Some of this knowledge turns out to have useful applications to productive activity. At the development end of R&D are learning processes that consist of searching out and discovering the optimal design characteristics of a product. At this stage, the learning is oriented toward the commercial dimensions of the innovation process: discovering the nature and combination of product characteristics desired in the market (and in relevant submarkets), and incorporating these in a final product in ways that take into account scientific and engineering knowledge. (N. Rosenberg, 1982, p. 121)

It is the commercial end of the innovation process that Rosenberg is referring to with the concept of 'learning by using'. The concept implies that the experience of those who use the products is transferred to the producers. The user interprets her/his experience of using the product and the producer exploits this knowledge by merging it with existing knowledge in order to improve products and processes of production or to develop new products and processes. In this manner, the producer gains resources that can be used in R&D and experimental activity in relation to products and production processes. Experiments such as these are often risky, but the goal is to improve the knowledge base of the firm, its competitiveness and its customer relations.

Rosenberg's work has had a significant impact on research into technical change and innovation. It has directed the focus of consequent research into studies of forms of collaboration between users and producers of products. Furthermore, his contribution and that of his associate, S.J. Kline (1985), undermined prevailing ideas that there is a linear relationship between scientific inventions and technical change. The linear view of innovation is postulates the process of innovation is characterised by five stages: *Step 1*: Universities and research institutions work on basic research and produce knowledge and inventions that are common goods; *Step 2*: Universities, research institutions and corporations work on applied research and produce patents and scientific reports; *Step 3*: Research departments of corporations work on experiments and development work and produce patents, engineering blue-prints etc.; *Step 4*: Factories introduce new production processes and generate new products and: *Step 5*: Factories, service units, and shops distribute the products on markets.

Kline and Rosenberg opposed the linear innovation model and claimed that the relationship between science, research and technical change is very different from what is envisaged in this model. They emphasise reciprocal influence of all the factors of research, production and markets in innovation activity, arguing that the innovation process comprises five stages which reflect different types of activity. The activity in each stage contributes knowledge to the following stage in the innovation process and market experience and information is processed at each stage. Moreover, the technological and scientific knowledge created in each stage is influenced by the common societal pool of external research which is, at the same time, influenced by the knowledge generated in the innovation process. Figure 3.3 summarises Rosenberg and Kline's model of innovation.

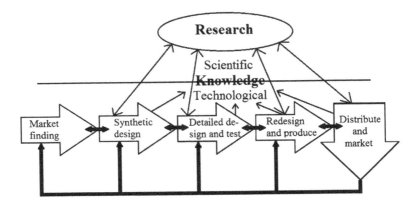

Figure 3.3   Rosenberg and Kline's model of innovation
Source: Based on S.J. Kline and N. Rosenberg, 1986 and S.J. Kline, 1989.

Finally, as an example of theories that emphasise learning processes in innovation activity, we should mention the third theoretical framework; that is, B.Å. Lundvall's (1988) theory of 'learning by interaction'. Lundvall's theory is rooted in economic sociology and institutional economics (J. Foster, 1991).[8] Lundvall, like Kline and Rosenberg, studies what characterises interaction between users and producers, but the difference is that he emphasises the role of 'trust' in their relations. Trust has the fundamental role of minimising risk in investment in innovation and, consequently, it is an important factor in the competitiveness of corporations (B.Å. Lundvall, 1988, pp. 352–3).

Lundvall compares the goals and performance of users and producers of technological equipment. Producers of new technology have an interest in the following: *Firstly*, securing that competitors cannot access information concerning the new technology that the user will apply in her/his production processes. *Secondly*, new products that result from innovation activity, may lead to demand for new technology needed to generate the new products. *Thirdly*, it is only possible to transfer the knowledge that emerges from 'learning by using' into new products if the producer has a direct relationship with the user. *Fourthly*, thresholds and technological problems that the user faces may become sources of new markets for the producer. *Finally*, the producer may be interested in how the knowledge and capacity of the user develops and acquire information on the user's learning capacity as well as her/his ability to use the new products or technology.

---

8   The concept of 'institution' is used here in the wide sense that is common in sociology and comprises ideas, habits, behaviour and values. It is not limited to 'institutions' in the narrow physical sense, such as research institutions, governmental bodies etc.

The objectives and gains that users achieve from the collaboration are as follows: *Firstly*, information on new technology and especially detailed information concerning how it fits the particular needs of the user's production. *Secondly*, it is in the interest of the user to collaborate with the producer at times when thresholds or technological problems appear in the production if the user does not have the technical knowledge. *Thirdly*, when the user needs complicated and specialised technology it is necessary for him/her to collaborate closely with the producer in the innovation activity itself, so that the nature of the problems will be as clear as possible. In this context, it is important for the producer to be able to help the user if needed when production starts and employees need to be trained.

As innovation activity usually takes a long time, even decades, it is necessary, for reasons of competitiveness, that users and producers keep information to themselves, but this is only possible if strong ties of trust exist between them (ibid., pp. 352–3).[9]

In his early studies, Lundvall analysed innovation collaboration of cooperative dairy producers and manufacturers of dairy production technology in Jutland in Denmark. This collaboration had historical roots and was built on strong and reciprocal trust among these actors (B.Å. Lundvall et al., 1983). Lundvall has recently concentrated more on macroeconomic research and observed 'the knowledge economy' and 'the learning economy' (e.g., B.Å. Lundvall and D. Foray, 1996), but he has also studied 'national systems of innovation' (B.Å. Lundvall, 1992) and joined hands with neo-Schumpeterian scholars such as C. Freeman (1987). Let us finish this chapter by discussing C. Freeman's theories of long waves and 'national systems of innovation'.

We highlighted earlier in this chapter that C. Freeman and C. Perez have analysed Kondratieff waves on the grounds of wide ranging changes in the economic, social and political conditions of societies. Their main concept in this respect is 'techno-economic paradigms' (TEP). Changes in TEPs lead to situations in which huge volumes emerge of new products, services, technological systems and branches of industry. These changes also lead to new ways of thinking which gain ground involving ideas of best practice technology, organisation and transport in the economy. These changes also presage alterations in basic economic and technological paradigms concerning the reorganisation of association between firms, the role of the state and relationships between organised interests and industrial relations within firms and other organisations. In brief, these changes refer to what usually is called 'institutional' conditions of economies.

National systems of innovation are part of the institutional conditions of the economies in different countries. This concept refers to the particular relations in the field of innovation activity that we find among firms, on the one hand, and, on the other, firms and public research institutions and government bodies

---

9   Concerning the role of trust in business and economic life see M. Granovetter 1973 and sub-section 5.4 in this book.

such as ministries. Many scholars focused on national systems of innovation in the 1980s as it appeared that the increasing trend of relatively improved competitiveness of Japanese industries seemed to be rooted in the particular characteristics of the Japanese national system of innovation compared to the degenerating competitiveness of European and American industries (C. Freeman, 1987). The superior competitiveness of Japanese corporations was explained by pointing out the Japanese capacity to introduce the techno-economic paradigm characteristic of a new Kondratieff wave i.e., the fifth Kondratieff. Europeans and Americans, however, appeared stuck in the institutional conditions of the fourth Kondratieff wave. C. Freeman and C. Perez (1988, pp. 52–57) have provided valuable comparison of various long waves and their constituent techno-economic paradigms. Their analysis emphasises the role of various institutional factors that shape the socio-technological development of Kondratieffs.

In terms of a comparison of the fourth and fifth Kondratieffs, C. Freeman and C. Perez highlight differences concerning how firms are organised and differences in terms of forms of cooperation and competition. The fourth Kondratieff (1930s and 1940s to 1980s and 1990s) was characterised by oligopolistic competition and the leading role multinational corporations played in global economic growth with their direct foreign investment and multi-plant locations. Competitive subcontracting on 'arm's length' basis or vertical integration spread fast leading to increasing concentration, divisionalisation and hierarchical control. 'Techno-structure' characterised large corporations. In the fifth Kondratieff (1980s and 1990s to ?), networks of large and small firms prevail. They are based on computer networks and close cooperation in technology, quality control, training, investment planning and production planning ('just-in-time') etc. 'Keiretsu' and similar structures became important in terms of providing internal capital markets, according to C. Freeman and C. Perez.

The fourth and fifth Kondratieff differ as well in terms of features of national regimes of regulation. The fourth Kondratieff was characterised by the growth of 'welfare state' and the 'warfare state'. Investment, growth and employment was regulated by means of Keynesian techniques that involved high levels of state expenditure and involvement. Furthermore, following the collapse of fascism, 'social partnership' with unions and new political structures developed. Moreover, during crisis of adjustment, the welfare state was 'rolled-back' and deregulation and privatisation entered the scene. Unlike this, the fifth Kondratieff has seen the growth and regulation of strategic ICT infrastructures. Deregulation and reregulation of national financial institutions and capital markets took place. Furthermore, participatory decentralised welfare state has emerged based on ICT and red-green alliance, according to C. Freeman and C. Perez.

Kondratieffs differ as well in terms of aspects of the subsequent international regulatory regimes. The fourth Kondratieff was characterised by 'Pax Americana', that is US economic and military dominance. Decolonisation took place following the Second World War alongside arms race and the cold war with USSR. Moreover, the international financial and trade regime (GATT, IMF,

World Bank) was dominated by the USA. In the 1970s the Bretton Woods regime destabilised and stagflation crept in. Characteristic for the fifth Kondratieff has been the development of a different international regulatory regime. 'Multi-polarity' rather than cold war 'duo-polarity' has emerged with the rise of China and large economies in the South. Moreover, new regional blocs have developed. Finally, problems have increased concerning developing appropriate international institutions capable of regulating global finance, capital, ICT and transnational companies.

Furthermore, diverse Kondratieffs are characterised by different features of national systems of innovation. During the fourth Kondratieff, specialised R&D departments spread in most industries. Large scale state involvement in military R&D took place through contracts and national laboratories. State involvement in civil science and technology increased as well. Rapid expansion of secondary and higher education and of industrial training took place. Investment by multinational corporations secured transfer of technology through extensive licensing and know-how agreements. Learning by doing, using and interacting was typical. National systems of innovation that have developed in the fifth Kondratieff are characterised by horizontal integration of R&D, design, production and process engineering and marketing. Process design is integrated with multi-skill training. Computer networking makes collaborative research possible. The state initiates support for generic technologies and university-industry collaboration. New types of proprietary regimes have emerged for software and biotechnology and corporations have developed into 'factories as laboratory'.

Behind the development of the different institutional structures discussed above is technological and economic development. C. Freeman and C. Perez highlight in this respect main 'carrier branches' and induced growth sector infrastructure. As for the fourth Kondratieff, the main carrier branches were automobiles providing trucks, tractors and tanks. Armaments for motorised warfare were also important as well as the aircraft industry. Consumer durables production increased fast and so did the spread process plants. Synthetic materials, petro-chemicals production grew fast. Investment in infrastructures like highways and airports grew fast as well. Airlines played a significant role. The main carrier branches of the fifth Kondratieff are those producing computers and electronic capital goods. Also to be mentioned is the software industry and production of telecommunications equipment. Furthermore, optical fibres, robotics, FMS, ceramics, data banks and information services are important carrier branches. Subsequent induced growth sector infrastructures of the fifth Kondratieff are digital telecommunications networks and satellites.

Finally, key factor industries that offer abundant supply at descending prices are among the fundamental factors of Kondratieffs. In the case of the fourth Kondratieff, energy production (especially oil) was a key factor industry, while chips production (microelectronics) is the key industry in the fifth Kondratieff.

It appears from the discussion above that institutional factors play a substantive role in neo-Schumpeterian analysis. The emphasis is on basic ideas or *techno-economic paradigms* that prevail over long periods concerning best practice socioeconomic organisation. The conditions for the realisation of these basic ideas are institutional such as law on property rights; regulation of competition and corporate collaboration; political conditions for collaboration of organised interests; conditions that determine forms of collaboration between firms and public institutions such as in the case of national systems of innovation; educational and training systems. Finally, forms of alliances and collaboration of firms which appear to be of increasing importance in recent decades. Such networks of collaboration are becoming voluminous in scale and scope and play an ever more important role in corporate innovation activity, as we will discuss in the following chapter.

Neo-Schumpeterian theories emphasise that the history of capitalism is characterised by a mismatch between the technological and institutional conditions of societal development. Institutional conditions can hinder technical change so that it is interesting to compare different countries with various institutional setups and look for explanations for disparities in competitiveness and levels of economic growth over long periods. Approaches of this kind have been criticised for technological determinism, but it would take too much space to elaborate on this critique here (see K. Grint, 1998, Chapter 8; C. Cockburn, 1981).[10]

3.4. Summary

In this chapter we have discussed the main theories and research relating to the interaction between innovation activity and economic development. The discussion started by observing theories of long waves in economic life; that is, the so called 'Kondratieff waves'. This discussion was followed by a presentation of neoclassical theories of innovation which reduce technical change to the idea of production functions. Finally, we observed theories of innovation that take theories of learning processes as their point of departure and discussed the contribution of evolutionary theories and neo-Schumpeterianism. Figure 3.4 highlights the main features of our discussion in this chapter.

---

10   In short, we would claim that technological determinism presumes that social and economic development is to be explained by technical change. The best known and possibly the simplest example of this is K. Marx's and F. Engels's thesis in the *Communist Manifesto*. There they explain in a deliberately simplified way the advent of feudal society by reference to the innovation of the plough in agriculture and capitalism with reference to the development and diffusion of steam-power based technology.

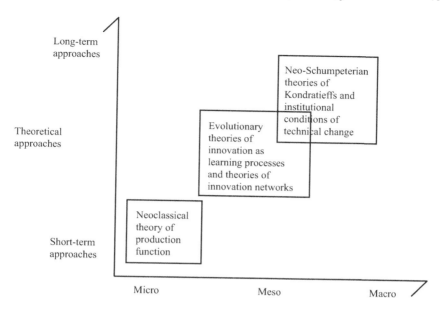

Figure 3.4   Main theoretical approaches to innovation activity

Chapter 4
Corporate Alliances and Open Innovation

4.1 Introduction

Academic interest in intercorporate cooperation has increased dramatically in recent years. At the same time, academic perspectives and general public opinion concerning cooperation between companies have been radically transformed. Previous research, particularly in the field of oligopoly and monopoly, focused on the economic effects of imperfect competition on markets, price trends and growth. Furthermore, many of the studies highlighted the power position of large firms in terms of impact on legislation and the ways in which they gain market privileges (D. Lowery and H. Brasker, 2004). Such privileges appear in the form of protectionist tariffs or monopolies which exclude competitors on certain markets. Such studies have mainly been led by American economists.

Berle and Means published their influential book, *The Modern Corporation and Private Property,* in 1932. In this book they claimed that a revolution had taken place in the US economy as equity and shares ownership had become so widespread that there was no longer a direct relationship between ownership and control of companies. Or, in other words, the owners of capital today are rarely those who manage companies. Berle and Means also argued that corporations are subject to a tendency which causes minority of shareholders to achieve power over them, as ownership of 20 per cent of the shares is enough to dominate a business.

In the sixties and seventies more critical research on control systems appeared, focusing on the power of companies in a broader social context. Gabriel Kolko's (1971) critical analysis of Berle and Means in his book, *Wealth and Power in America*, was published in 1962. According to Kolko, shareholding is far from being as equally distributed as Berle and Means assumed. In addition, the economy is characterised by a high level of concentration of ownership of equity and control in the hands of a power elite which ties corporations together in a network of interlocking directorships. 'Interlocking directorships' refers to the fact that some persons are members of the boards of two are more corporations.

Kolko's analysis focused on the relationship of wealth and power, but political scientist C.W. Mills had, in his book, *The Power Elite* (1956), analysed a corporate elite whose influence reaches into the political life of the United States. This power elite led the economic and military system (economic military complex), which, in his opinion, had made the United States an unstoppable war economy.

Analysis in the spirit Kolkos and Mills is limited to partnerships between large corporations and the societal consequences of their dominance in contemporary societies. Such analysis has little to say about partnerships comprising small businesses and the general motivation underlying them. Studies focusing on small businesses and their collaboration spread in the eighties, following the work of Oliver Williamson (1975), one of the instigators within economics of the so called 'new institutionalism', who sought to answer the question why there exist in the economy two separate ways of coordinating economic activity: *Firstly*, large corporations use bureaucratic hierarchy in order to coordinate manifold and heterogeneous activities within their sphere of activity. *Secondly*, the market coordinates the economic activity of independent companies by way of competition. Williamson's answer was his theory of 'transaction costs', which was rooted in R. Coase's '*The Nature of the Firm*' (1937). Williamson's explanation as to why bureaucratic hierarchies arise is that it would be too expensive for a company to make daily contracts with outside persons or organisations for the implementation of any and all projects that the business requires. It is cheaper in many cases to hire employees for the long term to perform the tasks needed. The prime problem with his analysis is, however, that he envisages only two kinds of organisational forms i.e., market and bureaucratic hierarchy. In reality, organisational forms are more complex.

Williamson's incomplete analysis urged students of organisations to investigate further forms of business structures. Perhaps the most important reason, however, for the following shift in the focus of organisational research was that Japanese companies appeared to have achieved a superior competitive position because their organisational principles differed from those of their American and European counterparts. While the latter were characterised by the fact that their parent companies owned a majority of shares, Japanese corporations formed networks of companies organised by and around large banks and the corporations owned minority shares in each other. This form of organisation is called 'Keiretzu' (M. Gerlach, 1992, pp. 3–6).

G. Richardson (1972) was the first student of organisations to write a milestone work in the field of research of corporate networks. He attacked the view that he had himself held for decades, that companies are a kind of islands in the market which compete with one another totally independent of each other. Consequently, Richardson focused his analysis of corporate alliances as follows:

> I shall have occasion to refer to cooperation and market transactions as distinct and alternative modes of coordinating economic activity, we must not imagine that reality exhibits a sharp line of distinction; what confronts us is a continuum passing from transactions, such as those on organised commodity markets, where the cooperative element is minimal, through intermediate areas in which there are linkages of traditional connection and goodwill, and finally to those complex and interlocking clusters, groups and alliances which represent cooperation fully and formally developed. (G.B. Richardson, 1972, p. 887)

K. Blois (1972) took this view further in his analysis of 'quasi-integration' of companies. W. Ouchi's (1980) analysis of the organisational forms of Japanese companies in which he compared them with tribal organisations, marked a shift in the study of corporate networks. Without a doubt, however, M. Piore and C. Sabel's book (1984), *The Second Industrial Divide*, had the greatest impact on the new focus of research in this area. In this book they analysed the close network collaboration of small businesses in the so called 'industrial districts' of Northern Italy. This book stirred research interest into 'industrial clusters' which has flourished since the 1990s. In Chapter 5 we will discuss those studies with particular emphasis on innovation clusters. Let us now turn our attention to research on collaborative business forms as they have evolved since the 1990s.

4.2 Why do Corporations Collaborate?

In general, the reasons why companies work with other companies are fourfold:

- Reduction in the cost of developing new technology and marketing
- Risk diminishes due to new technology and marketing
- It is easier to achieve economies of scale in production
- The time spent on research and development (R&D) and marketing is shortened.

In each individual case the reasons why companies are involved in networking are different.

Broadly speaking, there are threefold reasons for corporate collaboration i.e., technological, market and organisational related (J. Tidd, J. Bessant and K. Pavitt, 2000, p. 198).

Reasons for corporate collaboration relating to developing new technology stem from the need to develop production technology and/or products. This is a time-consuming, costly process, particularly in cases when the technology is so complex that it is not possible for one company to develop it. In the wake of increasing competition in many industries, R&D has become an important precondition for increasing competitiveness of enterprises. At the same time the cost of increased innovation and R&D keeps rising and companies are forced to maximise its effectiveness.

Furthermore, managers are increasingly aware of the fact that part of the technology their company exploits is not its fundamental technology, while it may be fundamental to other companies. Consequently it is in the interest of the company to share the cost of developing its 'marginal technology', particularly in collaboration with those companies which use it as their fundamental technology. Technological development today is more rapid than ever before and often so complex that it is not possible for any one company to develop it entirely on their own 'in house'. For example, cars include a variety of computer controlled components, for example engine, transmission, brakes and suspension. Even large concerns in the automotive industry recognise that no company can be self-sufficient in technological development. For example, when Ford designed the Jaguar XK8 it established a partnership with the Japanese company Nippondenso to design the operating system for the engine and the German company ZF to develop an electrically operated drive (ibid., p. 198, see also R.B. Reich, 1992). It is also generally considered important for businesses to acquire new technology and knowledge from external sources in areas of fast scientific development; this is particularly advisable when development is rapid in traditional production areas of the corporations in question, or when technology development abroad is progressing at a swift pace.

Marketing-related partnerships result from answers to the question whether companies should buy technology rather than develop it themselves. Decisions in this field depend on evaluation of 'transaction costs' and the assessment of long term strategic implications. Analysis of transaction costs focuses on the assessment of productivity, particularly when uncertainty is high. Risk can be assessed in the light of a probability account when the state of uncertainty implies that the expected outcome is unknown. Innovation and development often involves significant uncertainty as to when outcomes or results are achieved, the success of the R&D plan itself and whether competitors will be the first to put a comparable new product on the market. In the case of marketing, uncertainty is often high, both due to lack of knowledge of the geographical and cultural context and insufficient information on the availability of comparable products. In such cases, companies are often willing to sacrifice high profit potential, preferring partnerships which reduce uncertainty. When companies choose to buy technology rather than developing it themselves, the disadvantage is that they depend on the good will of the supplying company and its price policy. The supplying company may be keen to use its monopoly position to maximise its rent. The smaller the market and the more sophisticated the technology, the more dependent companies are on the seller' terms. Transaction costs associated with obtaining attractive technology are highest in cases such as these, and the same applies if the buyer has little knowledge of the technology and finds it hard to assess its usefulness. The higher the transaction costs, the more likely the technology receiving company will be to establish partnerships with other firms in order to develop the new technology. However, what route is taken; that is, whether the technology is purchased or acquired in collaboration with other companies, is subject to various factors such as the stage of development of the technology in question (whether it is new or has been developed over a long period), whether the firm possesses superior technology compared to competitors and how important the technology is for the company's long term strategies and plans of development.

In practice, therefore, the transaction as such is not the most important factor when corporations decide to acquire technology from sources outside the company, but whether the technology will improve the competitive advantage of the company, increase its market share and/or differentiate its products. Thus, decisions are shaped by the companies' efforts to define and improve their long term strategies and opportunities (ibid., pp. 199–200).

Recent research of corporations has increasingly emphasised studies of their vision of future opportunities and its relation to their long term strategies. It has been revealed that companies seek to increase the knowledge and skills base of their employees in order to strengthen their own long term advantage. Cooperation with other companies is one way to promote the knowledge and skills base of businesses and bolster their long term business opportunities. Thus cooperation becomes a way to gain new knowledge and improve skills rather than simply remaining a tool to reduce costs. As companies seek external knowledge and technology they improve their capacity for in-house innovation activities. Improved innovation capacity is among the factors that are crucial for their competitiveness.

Having this in mind, it is apparent that when companies acquire external technology and knowledge they take transaction costs into account as well as maintaining a view of their long term strategic opportunities. For example, an examination of the factors managers consider when deciding on technology development partnerships with other companies showed that they take into consideration how important the technology concerned is for their long term business opportunities. They also consider the possibility of reduced risks associated with research and development to be among the most important factors (ibid., p. 200 and B.B. Tyler and H.K. Steensma, 1995). The choice of partners is obviously crucial in this context. The better both sides know each other, the lower their transaction costs are, the more trust exists between them and the more information and knowledge about the technology they share. Finally, social and personal relationships between the actors are important in this context, such as family or common background in schools and/or clubs. When companies acquire technology and knowledge from external sources they gain extra pay-off in many things that they otherwise could not access. There is a possibility to obtain professional evaluation of the R&D within their company by an investigator working for other companies and they acquire new ideas and perspectives from those employed by other companies. It can also be useful to collaborate with highly respected companies because this creates a positive view of the company among customers and governmental bodies.

Some risks, however, are associated with technology collaboration with other companies or organisations: information can leak, companies have to share the results of R&D with other corporations and objectives of other corporations in the alliance may be different which may lead to conflict (J. Tidd, J. Bessant and K. Pavitt, 2000, pp. 201–2).

Figure 4.1 depicts the main factors involved when decisions are made concerning technical cooperation with third parties.

Figure 4.1   Model of collaboration for innovation
Source: J. Tidd, J. Bessant and K. Pavitt, 2000, p. 199.

Above, we made a distinction between 'merger', 'acquisition' and 'networking' of companies. The term 'corporate network' refers to collaboration of companies on the basis of a frame of common goals without diminishing their independence; the companies remain as separate entities even though their collaboration ceases (OECD, 2001, p. 15). In recent years there has been a significant increase in various forms of corporate collaboration. The same is true of 'merger' and 'acquisition' of companies. The term 'corporate network' is different from the concepts of 'merger' and 'acquisition'. 'Merger' of companies involves two or more companies merging into one company. 'Acquisition' refers to a strategy according to which corporations buy shares in other companies in order to gain power in them. By way of mergers and acquisitions companies obtain, among other things, access to valuable R&D and know-how which is often limited to the corporations in question. The strategy of gaining external knowledge by way of mergers and acquisitions is in line with the 'closed model of innovation'. It presumes that innovation must be producer led and that it is best to keep knowledge internal to the firm in question. As we will discuss below, this model is very different from the more recent models of 'open innovation'.

Corporate mergers and acquisitions across countries and international business collaboration have increased considerably in the 1990s and early 2000s, as shown in the following figures. Figure 4.2 shows the scale of international integration and mergers of enterprises in the OECD countries, that is, development of mergers and acquisitions (M&As) of firms in countries other than the mother country of the relevant companies.

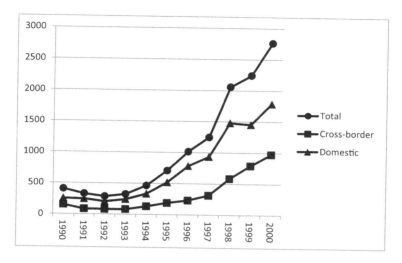

Figure 4.2   Trends in cross-border M&As in OECD countries, 1990–2000

Note: Deal value in billions of USD; Figures for 2000 refer to January to October.
Source: OECD, 2001: Annex Table 1.1., p. 123.

A report produced by UNCTAD shows a similar trend in the period 2000–2007. Table 4.1. indicates substantial global M&As in the years before the crisis of 2008 i.e., 780 billion US$ on average 2005–7. After the crisis M&As did not recover to the same level as before the crisis.

A similar development to that of mergers and acquisitions took place concerning strategic alliances. The number of alliances increased significantly among companies in OECD countries in the period 1989–95 and 1996–2000 i.e., judging by statistics on the number of new cooperation deals. This appears in Figure 4.3. As Figure 4.4 indicates, during 2000–2008 the pattern appears to have stabilised as information on US companies' that formed cross-border strategic alliances indicates.

Table 4.1   Selected indicators of FDI and cross-border M&Cs, 2013 and selected years and selected years

	1990	2005–2007 pre-crisis average	2011	1012	2013
FDI inflows	208	1493	1700	1330	1452
FDI outflows	241	1532	1712	1347	1411
FDI inward stock	2078	14790	21117	23304	25464
FDI outward stock	2088	15884	21913	23916	26313
Cross-border M&As	**111**	**780**	**556**	**332**	**349**

Note: Value at current prices (Billions of dollars).
Source: UNCTAD 2014, p. xviii.

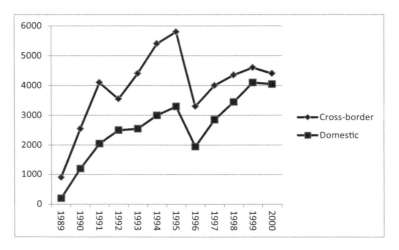

Figure 4.3   Cross-border and domestic strategic alliances (number of new deals 1989–2000)

Note: Figures for 2000 refer to January to October.
Source: OECD, 2001, p. 26.

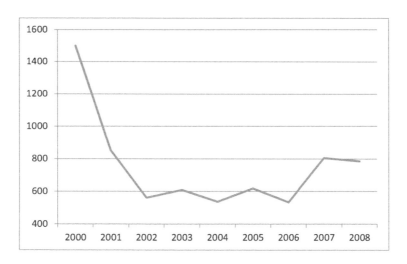

Figure 4.4   Cross-border strategic alliances by US corporations 2000–2008 (number of strategic alliances in terms of number of deals)

Source: S. Owen and A. Yawson, 2013, p. 3894.

4.3 Forms of Corporate Collaboration

As we observed above, the reasons for corporate alliances can be quite diverse. An example of such collaboration is Philips and Sony alliance to develop, produce and market a CD. Philips had developed a CD in 1978 after 6 years of development work, but realised that it would be difficult to make its CD into an international standard. Philips had previously developed a disk for films that turned to be a market failure. Therefore, Philips approached Sony in 1979. The aim was to work together on long term strategic alliance. Sony was chosen because it had the ability to do the necessary development work and had the required production capacity. Furthermore, it would open the way for Philips into the Japanese market. Like Philips, Sony had failed to market its Betamax technology for movies.

Philips had developed the prototype of copying technology for CDs, but the companies jointly designed a microprocessor to manage and correct digital signs. Sony also developed three integrated circuits, which reduced the number of components to 500 and, at the same time, made them small, more reliable and less costly to manufacture.

Philips and Sony then turned to making their technology into an international standard, through both official and unofficial channels. Their standard was adopted by the important institution Electronic Association of Japan, which prevented the standards of competing firms from gaining a foothold in the market. In addition, the corporations used their own publishing companies to ensure the availability of music CDs for their players. CBS/Sony in Japan and Philips/PolyGram in Germany were used for this purpose. Their CD technology was launched in Japan in 1982 and in Europe and the United States in 1983 (J. Tidd, J. Bessant and K. Pavitt, 2000, pp. 202–3).

Forms of collaboration vary, but six main types have been identified i.e., subcontracting, cross-licensing, consortia, strategic alliance, joint venture and, innovation network. Each form has its advantages and disadvantages. *Subcontracting* has the advantage of reducing risk and lead time while its disadvantage concerns search costs, reduced control of product performance and quality. While subcontracting arrangements are short term, *cross_licensing* is fixed term. Its advantage is better access to technology acquisition while the disadvantage is high contract cost and various constraints. *Consortia* arrangement presumes medium term duration, but has the advantage of providing access to external expertise, standards and funding is shared. The disadvantage concerns risk of knowledge leak and competitors may gain from product differentiation. The duration of *strategic alliance* is usually rather elastic. Its advantage is market access while its weakness is potential lock-in and knowledge leakage. *Joint venture* is typically long term arrangement. The partners benefit from complementary know-how and dedicated management. However, its shortcoming tends to be strategic drift and problems of cultural mismatch among the partners. Finally, *innovation networks* tend to be long term arrangements in which corporations benefit from their dynamic learning potential. However, their disadvantage is that they tend to be slow to respond to changing market situations and technical change (J. Tidd, J. Bessant and K. Pavitt, 2000, pp. 204–215).

Let us look more closely at the various forms of corporate collaboration, beginning with the *subcontracting* form. In recent years it has been popular among corporations and public bodies to let subcontractors take care of that part of their operation which is not regarded as core activity. In most cases, the goal of this measure is to reduce operational cost. Probably subcontractors are more competitive in relation to performing specific tasks at less cost because their overhead is comparatively lower. Furthermore, fixed cost and variable cost is lower and economies of scale are higher because contractors often serve more than one company. Contracts of this kind are in most cases limited to short term deals and subcontractors are rarely involved in the design and engineering work or R&D of the companies concerned. In Japan, however, this is different. There subcontracting is organised as long term collaboration and subcontractors are significantly involved in the R&D of enterprises. Such cooperation is well known in the automotive and electrical industries (ibid., pp. 204–5).

Cross-licencing allows companies to gain access to valuable technology or knowledge in the possession of other companies, but which would be too expensive for the firms in question to develop on their own. In this case, companies underwrite a contract that allows them to use the technology or knowledge for clearly defined purposes, specifying on which markets they have the right to sell products based on the technology or knowledge in question. Agreements on mutual exploitation rights reduce costs and risks related to research and development as well as marketing. They also shorten the amount of time spent on R&D and market entry. The disadvantages of such contracts mainly relate to restrictions the licence provider sets concerning usage of the technology or knowledge and the licence receiver cannot decide on the volume of the production covered by the licence. Transaction costs can also be high due to time consuming searches for partners and the lengthy process of consolidating agreements with them. A study of 200 industrial companies indicates that companies in the chemical, mechanical and pharmaceutical industries cooperate in terms of mutual exploitation of intellectual property rights because they obtain quicker access to the new technology rather than saving cost being the main reason. The same study showed that the main problem of this form of cooperation is the high cost of finding partners and the technology that fits the planned production of the companies in question. However, there are differences depending on type of industry. Searching for business partners, for instance, is harder for companies in the pharmaceutical industry than those in machinery industries. Enterprises in machinery industries focus more than pharmaceutical companies on reducing the cost of marketing products and speeding up this process (ibid., p. 205).

Consortia are established by many organisations and firms which agree to cooperate on a relatively clearly defined task. The purpose is to share costs and risks with other firms and gain access to rare expertise and equipment in order to conduct research and development necessary for reasons of competition and for the marketing of products. Furthermore, the aim is to determine and establish standards.

Consortia exist in many versions. The most centralised ones have joint research laboratories while the least centralised only coordinate the research activities of partner organisations. Each organisation performs its R&D in its own laboratories. European companies tend to generate highly centralised consortia, while American businesses prefer the decentralised type. Japanese companies often generate a mixture of centralised and decentralised consortia. The United States was slow to exploit this form of cooperation because of strict laws against monopoly and oligopoly markets. Early on the US gave birth to such large corporations that they required less corporate collaboration compared to European companies. A policy shift occurred in the United States with the 1984 National Cooperative Research Act which opened up the corporate consortia (ibid., pp. 206–7).

An example of a consortium is the Microelectronics and Computer Technology Corporation (MCC) consortium that US companies formed in 1982. This included Sperry, NCR, DEC, Honeywell, AMD and Motorola. MCC was founded to counteract the diminishing competitiveness of the US computer industry and due to fear of the Japanese plan to develop fifth generation computers. No foreign companies were allowed to participate in MCC. This consortium, however, violated the legislation against oligopoly in the US, so the government responded by passing the National Cooperative Research Act in 1984. Since then companies have been allowed to cooperate on basic research, given certain conditions and today more than 400 research consortia operate in the United States (ibid., p. 207).

A strategic alliance is created when two or more companies enter into an agreement to jointly develop a new technology or product. The partnership is not directed towards basic research, as with consortia, but aims at developing products which are immediately placed on the market. Unlike joint ventures, such strategic alliances narrowly define their objectives and operate according to a strict time schedule. Usually an independent company is not formally established to host the cooperation. The above example of the collaboration between Sony and Philips concerning the development of CD and CD player technology is an example of a strategic alliance.

A joint venture is launched when it becomes apparent that collaboration will last for a long time. In some cases, collaboration is established with the contribution of capital and a formally legal company is set up by the associated enterprises. In this case, the power relations of the parties are clearly defined in the firm. In other cases, cooperation is based on formal agreements of collaboration. A well-known example of a joint venture is Airbus Industries, a corporation established in 1969 in France by the German company MBB and the French Aerospatiale. In 1970 the Spanish company CASA joined the group and British Aerospace became a shareholder in 1979. The aim of the corporation was to undermine Boeing's dominant market position and respond to consistently shorter life-cycles of aircraft technology which increased the risk of investing in R&D. The first Airbus aircraft, A300, took to the skies in 1974 and was followed by A310 and A320 (ibid., p. 209).

Innovation networks are long term company partnerships for the purpose of research and development. The term 'network' has been prominent in the debate on the structure of companies in recent years and is considered by many to be an organisational form which undermines both the traditional structure of bureaucratic hierarchy and the market as a channel that distributes goods and money between firms and individuals. The term itself, 'networks', has various meanings, depending on the research tradition of the respective scholar or researcher. The terms 'network', 'web', 'cluster', 'alliance' have been used to describe different forms of business collaboration (J. Tidd, J. Bessant and K. Pavitt, 2000, p. 210). These words, however, have different meanings. Thus it can be broadly stated that French scholars focus on the geographical characteristics of networks of business collaboration; Anglo-Saxon studies, however, see networking as a synergistic system consisting of interdependent companies in terms of information, resources, production and sales of products. Although words such as *networks, webs* and *corporate alliances* have different meanings, it can be said that most researchers in this field assume that a network of companies is more than a bilateral business relationship and cooperation between different types of companies; the nature and content of the operation is in itself a prerequisite for increased efficiency and are thus inherently value-added (ibid., p. 210).

One could say that corporate networks are the intersection where companies, universities, institutions and customers, or other actors, are located and form the connection or relationship between the intersection points. Where a company is located in such networks can be crucial for its opportunities and provide significant information about its position of power and influence within a particular network. The power base of a company in a network may include special technology which it controls, its expertise, trust, economic strength and its positive reputation in the community in general. Furthermore, the relationship between firms in networks can be either strong or weak, depending on size and the nature of interaction between the companies. The links are permanent and need to be preserved by investing time and resources in them.

Innovation networks are developed for the needs of enterprises to develop production technology and processes, as well as products and services, and to provide information on new technology and market development. Such networks often develop locally or in areas that are relatively limited geographically. An example is Silicon Valley in California in the United States where the modern computer industry originated. Silicon Valley was/is based on formal and informal networks of individuals, companies, and universities, as well as cheap labour of immigrants and women. This context provided the dynamic flow of information and ideas which made the computer industry possible (R.D. Norton, 1999).

We will further discuss 'innovation networks' in the following chapter as we observe innovation clusters and social capital. It may improve our understanding of varieties of corporate collaboration if we draw a rough picture of collaborative business forms, on the one hand, with respect to duration of cooperation and, on the other, legal forms of collaboration.

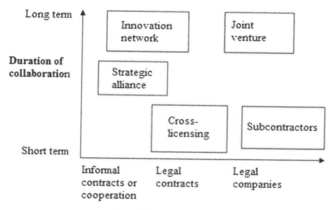

Figure 4.5   Organisational axes of corporate partnerships

4.4 Corporations and Open Innovation

As we have observed above, there was a rise in corporate innovation collaboration in the 1990s. Alongside this trend, multinational corporations increasingly located their R&D activities outside their headquarters and innovation became a 24/7 operation, sometimes on a global scale. Simultaneously, transaction cost relating to search for knowledge has decreased as knowledge has become more transparent. Web 2.0 tools such as wikis are being adapted by companies at the same time as it has become easier for them to find the knowledge they need and to approach information on professionals in social networking platforms such as LinkedIn and Facebook (S. Lindegaard, 2010, pp. 3–4). Around the turn of the century, a new phenomenon began to emerge on the scene of innovation activity; that is, open innovation. The consequent development has guided innovation strategies and research into new fields where the emphasis is on the role of the user in processes of innovation, rather than the producer alone, as has hitherto been the dominant view of innovation activity. We will now discuss this new development.

As Eric von Hippel (2014) claims, it was J.A. Schumpeter who was the founding father of the dominant 'producer's model' of innovation which presumes that the fundamental source of innovation is the producer. An alternative view is the 'open user model' of innovation, which assumes that

> … economically important innovations are developed by users and other agents who divide up the tasks and costs of innovation development and then *freely reveal* their results. Users obtain direct use benefits from the collaborative effort. Other participants obtain diverse benefits such as enjoyment, learning,

reputation, or an increased demand for complementary goods and services. (E. von Hippel, 2014)

Empirical studies, according to von Hippel, indicate that users are increasingly the first to develop substantial components of new industrial and consumer products. The reason for this is twofold: 1) design capabilities (innovation toolkits) resulting from advances in computer hardware and software make user innovations easier and; 2) new communication media such as the Internet help individual users to collaborate and coordinate their innovation related efforts. However, studies in the 1980s had already revealed that the role of users' innovation is important. We discussed B.Å Lundvall's studies of user-producer relations and theory of 'learning-by-interaction' in Chapter 2, which emphasises the role of users in developing new products. Eric von Hippel mentions C. Freeman's studies, who found that the most widely licensed chemical production processes were developed by user firms. Von Hippel's own research in the 1980s revealed that users were the developers of about 80 per cent of the most important scientific instrument innovations, as well as of most of the major innovations in semiconductor processing. Other studies found that the most commercially important equipment innovations in four sporting fields tended to be developed by individual users (ibid.).

Moreover, it has been known for a long time that firms which organised their own internal R&D experienced that their internal activity produced various ideas and results that the companies in question could not exploit. Such results were 'shelved' and kept internal to the firm without being commercialised (R. Nelson, 1959). This situation indicates that investment in internal R&D may not be as effective as one would presume. Consequently, one may ask why firms invest in apparently less than optimal R&D. One reason may be that internal R&D capacity helps firms to import and exploit external knowledge and hence strengthen their competitive advantage. This view was in accordance with research in the late 1980s into R&D of particular firms in the fields of scientific instruments, semiconductor process equipment and pultrusion process equipment, which found that users were the dominant sources of innovation (E. von Hippel, 1988). Cross-firm/competitor discussions between engineers on possible solutions to problems at hand were also an important source of knowledge. Furthermore, four external sources of useful knowledge were identified: a) suppliers and customers; b) university, government, and private laboratories; c) competitors and; d) other nations (Chesbrough, 2006, p. 6).

External sourcing of knowledge is, however, merely seen as a complement to internal R&D activities according to the 'producer model' of innovation. It is in this light that trends towards the growth of networks and innovation alliances must be seen; that is, they are complements to the dominant innovation model of corporations. We would claim that the relations of corporations to open innovation systems are also of this complementary type. Conversely, an open innovation model that optimises user initiatives in generating innovation evolves according to a different socioeconomic dynamic. We will now discuss forums of open innovation before we take note of corporate strategies in which firms exploit open innovation activities.

4.4.1 Forums of User and Open Collaborative Innovation

Scholars have become increasingly interested in innovation activity related to 'open source' means of developing and distributing new products of use-values. The late 1990s and early 2000s saw a particular focus on open source software. Nowadays, open source operating systems such as Linux and Android are commonplace, controlling millions of devices. Today, open source collaboration without payments or barter has developed far beyond software. There are user-to-user forums were individuals collaborate via the internet, sometimes with total strangers. Mailing lists and online communities are operated in different spheres of spontaneous and voluntary interest. People share, sometimes illegally, music, movies, TV series, software, etc. There are free services such as Skype and user developed products and services such as Wikipedia. Some firms have organised active collaboration with users, for example the internet retailer Amazon and TripAdvisor with its user generated content review site of hotels, restaurants allowing users' advice, photos and video clips. Within science, the Open Science movement has been established in order to reach out to disperse authority and expand collaboration (S.S. Levine and M.J. Prietula, 2014).

The extension of open source activity beyond the field of software has pressed researchers to use the wider concept of 'open collaboration innovation'. In the field of open sourcing researchers have used various concepts such as 'open collaborative innovation, 'peer production', 'community based innovation system', 'Wikinomics and mass collaboration', 'collaborative communities', 'transaction-free zones', 'crowdsourcing, 'collaborative consumption', 'electronic networks of practice or online communities' and simply 'open innovation' (ibid.).

The core of collaborative innovation projects is the involvement of users and others who share the work of generating a design for the creation of new products, Moreover, the participants reveal the outputs from their individual and collective design efforts openly for anyone to use.

> In such projects, some participants benefit from the design itself – directly in the case of users, indirectly in the case of suppliers or users of complements that are increased in value by that design. Each of these incurs the cost of doing some fraction of the work but obtains the value of the entire design, including additions and improvements generated by others. Other participants obtain private benefits such as learning, reputation, fun, etc. that are not related to the project's innovation outputs. (C. Baldwin and E. von Hippel, 2009, pp. 15–16)

Corporations have gradually realised that they can learn much from user and collaborative innovations, both in terms of forecasting market trends and reducing costs related to their own innovation activities. They have, therefore, increasingly developed corporate strategies in order to bridge the gap between their internal producer based innovation model and the open innovation model. We will now briefly discuss such attempts.

4.4.2 Corporate Strategies Aiming at Exploitation of Open Innovation

Briefly, we would claim that open corporate innovation concerns bridging internal and external resources throughout the entire innovation process to make innovation effective. This would require both changes in the way innovation processes are organised and who takes part in them, as well as accepting and developing new ways of thinking. Rather than being inward orientated and assuming that 'in our company, the brightest people in our field work for us', open innovation requires that one accepts that all the clever people work are not employed in our company. Hence, the company must find a way to get access to other external human resources. Furthermore, rather than presuming that companies can only profit from internal R&D, intramural inventions and developing their own products, as closed innovation assumes, in open innovation one accepts that other companies' R&D can provide significant added value. The company's own R&D is necessary but not sufficient in order to enhance added value to its products. Finally, closed innovation assumes that, in order to be the first to bring new products to the market, the company must itself invent products. In terms of open innovation thinking one presumes that research does not have to be solely internal in order to profit from it (J. Bloem, 2007, p. 24).

Open innovation procedures assume that corporations connect internal and external resources. The first step is often taken when corporations focus on soliciting ideas from outside. However, real open innovation goes deeper than merely involving other actors in the early phases of idea generation. As S. Lindegaard claims:

> The contribution from outside your company must be significant. It is also more than just a partnership which you pay for specific services. Everyone involved in an open innovation process focuses on problems, needs, and issues and works them out *together.* Furthermore, you can argue that closed innovation primarily focuses on the core products and services, whereas you are more likely to use open innovation to work with a broader range … . (S. Lindegaard, 2010, pp. 11–12)

H. Chesbrough's (2006, p. 11) has pointed at eight principles that differentiate strategies for open innovation compared to prior theories of innovation. These principles refer to: 1) giving equal importance to external knowledge andinternal knowledge; 2) working with flexible business models in converting R&D into commercial value; 3) evaluating R&D projects in terms of a non-reductionist business models; 4) realising purposive outbound flows of knowledge and technology; 5) utilising abundant external knowledge; 6) proactively managing intellectual property rights; 7) benefiting from the rise of innovation intermediaries and; 8) implementing new metrics for assessing innovation capability and performance.

The first principle assumes the corporation accepts that external knowledge is not merely supplementary, but plays an equal role to internal knowledge in the innovation activity of the firm.

Secondly, the business model must be flexible enough so that it will allow incentive outputs to go to the market through a variety of channels rather than the company's 'own' systematised marketing. This is in line with the firm's emphasis on reaching out and seeking people of genius, both from inside and outside the firm. In the closed innovation model the focus was on hiring 'the best and the brightest', and then trusting them for intramural work in order to internally come up with valuable new innovations for the market.

Thirdly, in the closed innovation model, one postulates a business model that reduces the number of possible products as much as possible as to be able to focus the innovation activity and make it as cost efficient as possible. This leads to a strategy which rates all anomalies harshly; that is, knowledge and innovations that do not appear directly applicable in relation to developing the kind of products the firm concentrates on. Consequently, the firm is neither capable of evaluating related future opportunities, nor is it able to identify potential new markets and business models that fit them.

Fourthly, while a closed innovation model would require firms to keep their technology to themselves, open innovation strategy enables outward flows of technologies, allowing firms to let technologies which lack a clear path to market internally seek such a path externally. By exporting the technology to other businesses, the firm now competes with these external channels in bringing new technologies to the market (such as licensing, ventures, and spin-offs that can generate additional value). The firm can now learn from the way the external parties further develop the technology and gain important evidence of emerging or neglected technical or market opportunities.

Fifthly, according to the closed model of innovation, in line with neoclassical economics, useful knowledge is assumed to be scarce and costly to find, and risky to rely upon. In open innovation, useful external knowledge is generally presumed to be widely distributed and largely of high quality. External sources of knowledge extend well beyond universities and national laboratories, to startup companies, specialised small companies, individual inventors, retired technical staff or graduate students, etc.

Sixthly, by proactively managing their intellectual property (IP), corporations are able to increase the value of their IP and enhance profitability by incorporating it in their corporate strategy. According to the closed innovation model, firms assume that the best way of using their IP is to suppress competition; that is by patenting the product, and thereby preventing potential rivals from offering customers an identical or similar product or service. It is presumed that this strategy will create market power which enables the firm to raise the prices of its own products or services and thus increase its profits. An open innovation strategy looks at other potential options such as selling (i.e., assigning) the IP right to another enterprise for which it would be more valuable; licensing the right, possibly to competitors; using the right as a vehicle to organise profit-enhancing collaborations with competitors, suppliers, customers, or the developers of complements; and even giving the right away (W.W. Fisher III and F. Oberholzer-Gee, 2013, p. 158).

The *seventh* principle refers to benefiting from the rise of innovation intermediaries (IIs) i.e., actors often called 'bridgers', 'change agents', 'brokers'. In recent years the number of firms and agents in this field has multiplied. Their function is 'matchmaking'; that is, finding suitable partners for innovation collaboration (T. Holtzman et al., 2014). These 'middlemen' facilitate innovation by providing the bridging, brokering and knowledge transfer necessary to bring together the range of different organisations and knowledge needed to create successful innovation. With open innovation involving complex networks of firms and users, external IIs play a central role in facilitating and coordinating

Chapter 5
Endogenous Conditions of Economic Growth

5.1 Introduction

In recent years, fruitful research has been conducted in the field of economic geography. This is presumably because trade has greatly increased within regions such as Europe, Asia and South-America and North-America. At the same time, globalisation has increased in particular branches of industry; that is, electronics and automobile industries and financial services (P. Dicken, 1992; R.B. Reich, 1992; L. Weiss, 1998, Chapter 6). In this chapter, we will discuss in brief research and theories of economic geography of innovation and the role of geographical factors in technological development. We will start by observing the development of theories in this field and show that institutional factors are increasingly emphasised. In the last two parts of this chapter we will discuss the role of 'social capital' and 'the creative class' in innovation and economic development.

5.2 Geography of Economic Growth

Traditionally, one of the main objects of study of economic geography was urbanisation, the development of cities and location of firms. The main aim of research of this kind is to explain urbanisation and location of firms with reference to local geographical conditions. Roughly three periods in the development of economic geographical theories can be observed; that is, the period of traditional theories, new institutional theories and institutional theories.

5.2.1 Traditional Theories of Economic Geography

Traditional theories of economic geography are based on neoclassical economics and the thought of Alfred Weber. These traditional theories assume that economies are characterised by a tendency towards equilibrium under perfect market conditions. Capital and investments flow to production sites where production cost is lowest. If this is correct, improvements in infrastructure like transport and communication systems would lead to the decentralised location of firms and corporations would move their production from cities to areas where land and labour is cheaper. In accordance with this argument, traditional economic geography presumes that knowledge and new technology spreads from cities and urban areas to less populated areas. The problem with theories of this kind is that they have not been sustained by empirical and statistical research (M. Storper and R. Walker, 1989, p. 21).

What is interesting in this respect and puzzles researchers is that many cities have been able to keep their advantageous position concerning average income per capita and new cities rise to advantageous position despite great transport costs. The traditional theories are unable to explain why some areas decline at the same time as other areas gain the upper hand and/or maintain their position. Some researchers have claimed that a kind of permanent hierarchy exists among cities and that the advantageous position of some of them endures, while others constantly lag behind. However, it has been difficult to confirm by empirical evidence that such a hierarchy exists; nevertheless it has been taken for granted in economic geography for decades (ibid., p. 29). Miscellaneous theories of hierarchies of cities have been developed despite this failing. As an example, the 'central-place' model presumes that different areas specialise in particular production and services. Small towns provide basic services and production to the surrounding areas. Larger cities develop, production and services which require large scale investments in order to reach larger markets. The 'central-place' model presupposes an equilibrium in which larger cities maintain their advantage over smaller towns. Cities grow with growing markets and the increased specialisation of cities.

Another group of theories of hierarchy of cities highlight division of labour between cities as an explanatory factor. According to these theories, a hierarchy is reproduced as leading cities host the headquarters of large corporations and jobs with high salaries are concentrated in these high value added headquarters. At the next level below are cities and related areas which host the offices of subdivisions of corporations, jobs in advertising and marketing and general engineering. At the third and lowest level are cities and related areas where the actual production is located. These theories postulate that the division of labour between cities and areas reflects the development of big corporations, but they miss the point that the hierarchy of cities existed long before the birth of large corporations (ibid., p. 31).

A third group of theories of hierarchical relations between cities take as their point of departure the fact that cities and regions vary with respect to level of productivity and this is presumed to be explainable in terms of different local conditions. These are similar to Gunnar Myrdal's ideas of a poverty trap (G. Myrdal, 1957). Externalities in different regions, such as human capital, a positive trade and business environment and easy access to inputs, generate the conditions for the high level of productivity needed to sustain a high level of income of employees and corporations. Generous incomes in these cities and regions leads to elevated demand for goods and services in the areas concerned. Consequently, there will be a gap between high-income areas and the areas that suffer from lower productivity and lower levels of income. Thus high-income areas enjoy an advantage which results in enhanced growth rates, making it easier for them to invest larger amounts in production and better exploit economies of scale which, in turn, lead to increased productivity and production and consequently services grow faster than in other areas. High-income areas are also quicker to specialise in high value added branches of industries. The export income of these areas resulting from trade with other regions leads to higher rates of economic multiplication and generates conditions for increased investment in their infrastructure. Advantages in terms of infrastructure reduce transport-related production costs and various other production expenses. High-income cities and centres of specialised knowledge gain advantage over other localities in terms of research and development and technical change. The location of headquarters and management departments of rich corporations further strengthens the growth of these cities and areas (M. Storper and R. Walker, 1989, pp. 31–2).

Although these last mentioned theories address important factors which explain why some cities and areas maintain their advantageous position, they do not account for the dynamics of their ability to secure advantage vis-à-vis other cities and areas. In order to explain their dynamic advantage one has to analyse the relationship between the corporations and factors in their environment that generate their growth potentialities. New institutionalist theories attempt to explain why cities are able to reproduce their advantage by observing the dynamics behind the relations between corporations. We will now discuss this approach.

5.2.2 New Institutionalist Theories in Economic Geography

New institutionalist theories find their grounding in the transaction cost theories of O.E. Williamson (1975) and R. Coase (1937), which, in short, aim at explaining why firms grow and develop their own production of inputs and hire new employees to take care of services that they previously bought from other firms. The reason is presumed to be that in many cases it makes sense to run intramural rather than extramural services and input production because it is costlier to reproduce business relations and search for new contractors that sell necessary inputs and services. The approach of the so called California School in geography (M. Storper, 1997, p. 9) is based on similar ideas, but in the opposite sense, when they explain why firms in certain branches of industry are concentrated in particular cities and regions and generate new high value added industries. The information technology based industries in the Silicon Valley in California and small scale industries in North-Italy constitute examples of this kind. The main idea of this school is that internal and external market relations, such as fluctuations in demand and technological development, generate uncertainty for businesses which firms reduce by collaborating with other companies. Through this collaboration they lessen the tendency to overinvest in their means of production, thus becoming more capable of maximising their specialisation without stagnating technologically. Geographical limits apply, however, because transaction cost rises following increasing geographical distances between the collaborating firms. Corporations tend to collaborate with other firms within their community or region as increasing geographical scales lead to higher transaction costs. Consequently, there is a strong tendency for the birth of regional clusters of collaborating firms.

Bearing Alfred Weber's theories in mind, we would claim that the theories of the California School explain phenomena that he as well as neoclassical theories based on the idea of general equilibrium cannot explain; that is, why firms tend to concentrate in clusters in particular cities and regions but are not evenly geographically dispersed. Besides reducing uncertainty, collaboration in clusters generates conditions for greater flexibility in their corporate operations. Consequently, it is easier for companies to respond to shifting demand for their products and adjust them to the needs of their customers.

In the late 1990s a certain self-critique emerged among the followers of the California School. Research into industrial clusters and industrial districts indicated that the sheer fact of firms belonging to clusters leads to increasing growth of production and makes it easier for them to exploit new technology and knowledge. Clusters appear to create a fruitful environment for dynamic innovation activity. It was particularly M. Piorter and C. Sabel's (1984) book, *The Second Industrial Divide,* that was path breaking and as a result students of innovation turned to Alfred Marshall's ideas of 'industrial districts' which he presented in his book, *Principles of Economics* (1890). Marshall spoke of something 'in the air' that makes industrial districts viable.[1] Many students of innovation turned their focus to such industrial districts and industrial clusters, but what they emphasised was different from what had been focused on until then. Instead of taking as their point of departure new institutionalist theories similar to those of the California School, the emphasis was more on institutionalist approaches which require a wider theoretical base. The emphasis became increasingly centred on cultural, social and political factors that would clarify the role of 'externalities' or features in the environment of firms. Followers of the California School began to highlight features such as 'evolution' and 'institutions'. Innovation theories of evolutionary economics influenced them, particularly the 'user-producer' theories of B.-Å Lundvall (1988) and the institutionalist approaches of M. Piore and C. Sabel. People felt that what was missing from the research and theories was explanations of the institutional preconditions for transactions in industrial clusters. Consequently, M. Storper (1997) started observing communication between firms in a new way. The communications and transactions between the actors were,

---

1   In Volume IV, Chapter X, paragraph 3 of *Principles of Economics* he wrote: 'When an industry has thus chosen a locality for itself, it is likely to stay there long: so great are the advantages which people following the same skilled trade get from near neighbourhood to one another. The mysteries of the trade become no mysteries; but are as it were in the air, and children learn many of them unconsciously. Good work is rightly appreciated, inventions and improvements in machinery, in processes and the general organization of the business have their merits promptly discussed: if one man starts a new idea, it is taken up by others and combined with suggestions of their own; and thus it becomes the source of further new ideas. And presently subsidiary trades grow up in the neighbourhood, supplying it with implements and materials, organizing its traffic, and in many ways conducing to the economy of its material'. http://www.econlib.org/library/Marshall/marP24.html#IV.X.7

according to him, characterised by 'interdependent' relations and not simply by 'transaction' relations in a narrow business sense as the California School had hitherto presumed. According to the new view, the actors depend on one another concerning buying and selling inputs and products; that is, their relations are based on 'traded interdependencies'. Besides such business relations, the actors are interdependent in relationships that are not of a business nature i.e., business relations presume 'untraded interdependencies'. This refers to informal contacts by which information and knowledge is communicated and which are useful for company operations. People communicate and mediate knowledge both in and outside of work. Informal communication generates trust between individuals which is a precondition for their business relations. Informal communication takes place in situations such as recreational activity, sport, conferences, seminars, family celebrations, etc. Let us have a closer look at the theories of M. Piore and C. Sabel and others that build on the foundations of institutionalist theories.

5.2.3 Institutionalist Theories in Economic Geography

Research in the 1970s of economic development in North-East Italy indicated that a viable alternative exists to Fordist mass production.[2] It became popular to talk about the developmental path of the 'Third-Italy' (M. Storper, 1997, p. 5). M. Piore and C. Sabel's book which we discussed above opened the eyes of English speaking scholars to the industrial rise of the Third-Italy. The book presented the concept of 'flexible specialisation' which presumes that small companies which collaborate in clusters and produce wide variety of products in small batches can be competitive and profitable. With small scale production and a large scope of products they are able to respond to ever changing demand in small market niches. Following the growth of information technology and automation of production in recent decades, the potential of flexible specialisation has become greater in most fields of production and services. At the same time, mass production has degenerated in many fields of industry.

M. Storper has summarised the main contribution of the Italian school and M. Piore and C. Sabel as follows (M. Storper, 1997, pp. 6–7):

Firstly, their research shows that no one particular kind of production technology or organisation of production is becoming dominant globally or is most

---

2   The concept of Fordism refers to production systems that are, on the one hand, based on mass production founded on assembly-line technology and Taylorist management. Taylorism is characterised by a clear hierarchy of power, exact labour measurement based on time study, incentive wage and highly specialised work functions and monotonous work of labourers. On the other hand, Fordism is characterised by mass-consumption, but a balance between mass-production and mass-consumption is created by means of Keynesian economic policies. This kind of economic policy secures general demand for goods with public investment in infrastructure and welfare state expenditure (I. Jonsson, 1989 and 1991a).

profitable in all industries. The choice of production technology and organisation is historically conditioned and depends on different market circumstances and the kind of technology at hand during the period in question. Decisions concerning these matters are determined by institutional contexts and therefore the results diverge in different countries.

Secondly, M. Piore and C. Sabel were basically right when they claimed that flexibility and specialisation were definite alternatives to mass production. Although the form of flexible specialisation varies in different industries and countries, the main ideas have diffused extensively both with regard to the organisation and operation of firms and in theories of management studies.

Thirdly, this research has brought to people's attention that the dynamics of capitalism today envisage highly advanced learning processes in technological development and innovation activity and that these learning processes are above all formed by local and regional, institutional conditions; that is, cultural, social and political circumstances.

Fourthly, in their studies, researchers of flexible specialisation place great emphasis on corporate networks of collaboration. This emphasis has had much impact on management studies, indeed the influence has been so strong that a new orthodoxy has emerged and established itself in this field of studies. This new orthodoxy presumes in an uncritical way that networks of firms must use this form of organisation as the best possible alternative, in a similar way as mass-production was supposed to be best-practice in the post Second World War era. But this perspective differs markedly from the general idea of flexible specialisation. According to the latter view, no particular form of organisation is optimal in all conditions and in all contexts. Furthermore, flexible specialisation does not emphasise maximisation as the sole aim of economic activity (ibid., p. 7).

The main shortcoming of the theories of flexible specialisation is that they do not take note of factors fundamental to the innovation activity of firms that participate in networks and alliances. They are unable to explain why some local networks of firms that build on flexible specialisation are leading in terms of innovation activity while others are not (ibid., p. 8). In order to further develop these theories scholars have turned to evolutionary economics, basing their work of, for example, Lundvall's theory of 'the learning economy' and theories of 'learning regions'.

Others have, in recent decades, worked with the catchphrase of 'Triple Helix' partnerships and attempt to explain differences in regional economic growth by analysing the conditions for industrial innovation in regional variations of 'Triple Helix' constellations; that is, in terms of systemic interrelations between three elements, namely university, industry and government. Approaches of this kind suffer from lack of understanding of how such constellations are generated. The fourth element is missing; that is to say, the role of actors and procedures in realising Triple Helix constellations. Consequently, a concept of Quatro Helix dynamics that involves the role of actors is needed in order to analyse the dynamics of structurisation of partnerships between the elements of Triple Helix constellations. We discuss Quadro Helix dynamics below as we discuss social innovations in Chapter 7.

In addition to the theories mentioned above, many students of innovation and regional development have emphasised institutional conditions of innovation activity and collaboration between firms, building their research on the concept of 'social capital' and 'the creative class'. Before discussing theories of social capital and the creative class, we should observe the relations between innovation activity and regional industrial clusters.

5.3 Innovation Activity and Regional Industrial Clusters

M. Porter (1990) was the first scholar to introduce the concept of 'cluster' in business studies i.e., 'clusters that lead to competitive advantage'. Porter used the concept to describe the relationship between branches of industry as he believed this relationship explains competitive advantage of nations (and regional economies). Scholars have made use of this concept in order to analyse innovation activity in a new way, to observe the role of innovation networks of firms in industrial development and to analyse regional economic development. The concept of industrial clusters has been used in the field of research on regional policy and on the role of networks of collaboration of firms in various branches of industries in different regions. This concept has also been applied in studies of support systems of businesses; that is, institutional knowledge infrastructure such as research institutions and developmental institutions which formalise collaboration between firms and public institutions. Policies based on this train of thought emphasise collaboration between firms, rather than public support for particular firms. Finally, the concept of cluster has been applied at a 'supranational' level such as in cases like the EU and OECD where cluster policy is an aspect of regional and innovation strategy (A. Lagendijk, 1999, p. 281).

It would appear from the discussion above that the concept of 'cluster' is ambiguous and this is indeed the case as scientists and politicians use the concept in a variety of contexts. Many formal definitions have appeared in recent years that outline the concept of 'regional cluster'. As an example, A. Isaksen and E. Hauge (2002, p. 13) define regional cluster as 'a geographically bounded concentration of *interdependent* firms'. S.A. Rosenfeld (1997) emphasises not only geographical concentration and bounded interdependence of firms in clusters, but furthermore highlights that a cluster constitutes active channels for business transactions, dialogue, and communications, and the firms collectively share common opportunities and threats. He claims that:

> active channels' are as important as 'concentration', and without active channels even a critical mass of related firms is not a local production or social system and therefore does not operate as a cluster. The dynamics of a cluster, not the size or

individual firm capabilities, are the key to synergy and thus its competitiveness. (ibid., p. 10)

Furthermore, firms in clusters use common technology and knowledge base or the same kind of raw material and labour is sought from the regional labour market. M. Porter (1998, p. 78) provides a wider definition of the concept of 'regional cluster' than Rosenfeld. According to Porter, a regional cluster is based on a geographical cluster of firms which are interdependent and often on the institutions of the branch of industry in question. Institutions here refer to formal institutions such as research institutions, knowledge and technology parks and various service organisations which are usually termed support systems. However, Porter's definition is blurred as a cluster may or may not include institutions.

In order to improve the definition of a regional cluster, A. Isaksen and E. Hauge (2002, p. 14) have proposed that a distinction should be made between 'regional cluster', 'regional innovation network' and 'regional innovation system'. To these three concepts we would add a fourth concept; that is, 'regional industrial district' which is a wider concept that observes both social capital and regional culture, besides covering some or all of the factors that the concepts above refer to.

Let us look closer at these definitions. 'Regional cluster' refers to a concentration of 'interdependent' *firms* within the same or adjacent industrial sectors in a small geographical area. 'Regional innovation network' is a more organised cooperation (agreement) between firms, stimulated by trust, norms and conventions, which encourages firms' innovation activity. Corporations in a regional innovation network work in a formal collaboration on particular innovation projects, such as collaboration between users and producers of particular goods, or develop products or technology to produce or sell them. 'Regional innovation system' includes a regional innovation network and formal innovation institutions that support it. These institutions participate in knowledge creation, technological development, import and implementation of new knowledge and technology in the firms. Universities and related research institutions are examples of support systems of this kind. Furthermore, various kinds of training centres, technology institutes, associations of branches of industry, industrial investment funds, etc. are also examples of elements of support systems. 'Regional industrial districts' are regions which enclose more than one regional cluster. These are characterised by regionally bound know-how which often has long historical roots and a strong tradition of collaboration between persons and firms; this constitutes grounds for the necessary trust to allow the industrial cluster to rise. The concept of 'social capital' has been developed in order to analyse conditions for such trust, as we will discuss later in this chapter. Let us now observe patterns of growth and development of industrial clusters.

A. Isaksen and E. Hauge (2002, pp. 14–15) have observed developmental stages of 'regional clusters' which appear to reflect many actual cases of such clusters. *Firstly*, the origin of clusters is often due to historical conditions that lead to the establishment of many firms in the same region. These are conditions such as when accessible raw materials, expertise of research institutions or traditional knowledge exists in the region. Furthermore, sometimes special needs of particular groups of people or firms exist in the region, or entrepreneurs and firms develop new technology which encourages the establishment of new firms in the area. An increased number of firms encourages competition among them leading to enhanced innovation activity. In the *second stage*, 'external economies' of firms are strengthened when a cluster has grown substantially and this growth increases productivity of the firms involved. At first, external economies are strengthened when new suppliers emerge, together with a growing specialised labour force with particular know-how and skills. The *third stage* appears when new institutions are established to serve the numerous firms of the growing cluster. These are institutions in the field of education, knowledge centres and associations of firms which stimulate collaboration among actors in the region, strengthen learning processes and encourage diffusion of technological know-how. Moreover, localised knowledge emerges among leading individuals in the regional industries. *Fourthly*, when external economies are ripe enough and the institutional environment has grown sufficiently the cluster becomes more visible; it acquires a reputation and external investors become interested in investment opportunities related to the cluster and local externalities. New firms and knowledge rise in the region, strengthening even further the reputation of the cluster and leading to the establishment of more new firms. In the *fifth stage* an environment emerges which fosters informal communication, which is important for diffusion of information and knowledge. Part of the knowledge needed for the development of goods and production technology is difficult to register in written form and sometimes the knowledge is so fresh that it has not been formalised and cannot, therefore, be mediated in reports or books, etc. This kind of knowledge is called 'tacit knowledge' which people acquire by watching how other people do things or through indirect information. Tacit knowledge is diffused in clusters via social events such as through discussion in workplace coffee breaks, company celebrations, workshops and seminars, expos, work-outs, when people play golf, or participate in other leisure activities, 'pub crawling', meeting of interest groups, family gatherings, recreation, etc. The *sixth and last stage*, concentrates on the declining phase of a regional cluster. The lifetime of a regional cluster can be counted in decades, but eventually they decline. Often this is due to an institutional, social and/or cultural 'lock-in' of the business community in question. The decline may be because the original competitive advantages of the region fade away or its conditions are not renewed or stagnate. These advantages may have comprised specific know-how of the labour force in the region, structural characteristics of the firms, knowledge centres and research institutions of the region, educational and vocational training institutions, close relationship between firms, employees and managers or powerful support of politicians and public officials in the area. Decline can also be caused by problems in recruiting the leadership of the business and political community of the region such as when recruitment is too socially constricted, involving family ties, membership of political parties, relatives and nepotism.

Research into regional clusters and industrial districts is still in its early stages with regard to research methods applying standardised criteria of measurement and definitions of concepts which scholars in the field agree on and use. 'Normal science' in this field of research has not been established (cf. T.S. Kuhn, 1970). Consequently, reasonably trustworthy international comparative research does not exist. However, some research has delivered results which give an indication of the state of the art. In a review written for the Commission of the EU (A. Isaksen and E. Hauge, 2002, pp. 21–26) the conclusions of various well-known reports on regional clusters and industrial districts are compared. It appears that there are 62 regional clusters in *Norway*, 55 of which are in manufacturing and they cover 22 per cent of jobs of Norwegian manufacture. Research indicates that between 1970 and 1994 profitability was slightly higher than the average of comparable branches of industry. Thirteen regional clusters have been analysed in *Denmark* and 16 so called 'national competition clusters'. Danish regional clusters exist both in traditional branches of industry like textiles and furniture and horticulture and in newer sectors like telecommunication and satellite communication. *The UK* hosts 154 regional clusters; this figure, however, is presumed to be too high as at times it refers to geographical aggregations rather than actual cluster relations between firms. Clusters in South-England compared to other countries are more often found in sectors like computer services, programming, corporate services and research and development. The clusters in the South are also 'thicker' than other clusters; that is, the institutional environment is more densely populated and more voluminous. Furthermore, job creation is much more substantial in the South-England clusters than in other countries. In *Germany* 11 regional clusters have been observed in North Rhine-Westphalia. These clusters are defined in terms of job creation by German authorities, or means of policy realisation rather than actual regional clusters. There are 142 'local industrial systems' in Spain most of which are in traditional labour intensive low technology industries. In Portugal, research on regional clusters for the authorities concentrated on export sectors. The aim of the authorities is to improve intercorporate collaboration and develop the technology and knowledge infrastructure to advance the competitiveness of corporations. There are 199 industrial districts in *Italy* employing 42 per cent of the Italian labour force in manufacturing. Profitability and productivity is higher in these districts than the average of comparative manufacturing branches (ibid., pp. 21–26).

The discussion above indicates that clusters in different countries have been researched in detail, but a consistent methodology for comparative research is lacking.

Since the 1990s scholars have been increasingly interested in researching the role of the social environment of firms in their innovation activities and observing the general role of social structures in industrial development. The concept of 'social capital' has played a central role in research in this field. We will conclude this chapter by considering the extensive theoretical discussion that has developed in this sphere of research in recent years.

5.4 Social Capital

It is often claimed that Pierre Bourdieu, James Coleman and Robert Putnam are the founding fathers of theories of 'social capital' (S. Baron, J. Field and T. Schuller, 2000, pp. 1–2). Putnam's theories are particularly important in relation to research into innovation activity.

Bourdieu developed theories of different forms of capital as a kind of ownership that people exploit in order to realise their social and economic interests. Bourdieu distinguished between 'economic capital', cultural capital', linguistic capital', 'scholastic capital' and 'social capital' but he never defined the different varieties of capital in detail, apart from the forms of cultural capital (ibid., p. 3). Cultural capital comprises the knowledge individuals have in the fields of art and science, as well as their competence in using symbols in discourse by which they identify themselves and are identified as belonging to particular social groups. Individuals acquire cultural capital in their socialisation; that is, in their family and peer groups such as in childhood and in kindergartens and schools. Bourdieu calls this social background 'habitus'. The competence individuals acquire in their socialisation, during which they learn how to use cultural symbols, is a key factor in their career in society. It also determines the kind of social groups they can join. It was as late as 1983 that Bourdieu defined the concept of 'social capital' (English translation first published in 1997) which he presumed to be one of three main forms of capital. The other two forms of capital are economic and cultural capital. Bourdieu's concept of social capital refers to real and potential means to access lasting networks of reciprocal acquaintance and respect that secure the support of shared capital for the benefit of the members of the network (P. Bourdieu, 1997, p. 51). Bourdieu's concept of cultural capital is unclear but he particularly concentrated on analysing the role of the educational system in reproducing class structure in capitalist society. The class system is reproduced as members of different social groups acquire uneven competence in using cultural capital. Hence, their ability to become members of the different classes of society is uneven. Or put differently, cultural capital is an important ingredient in mechanisms of social exclusion in modern society.

Bourdieu was French, but on the other side of Atlantic Ocean the American scholar of education, James Coleman (1994), presented ideas similar to Bourdieu's without referring to his work. Coleman particularly focused on social conditions of attainment of pupils and students and he was engaged in longitudinal research on university students and their achievement. Coleman defined 'social capital' as a set of resources inscribed in family relations and social institutions which are valuable to the child and young persons in their intellectual and social development (S. Baron, J. Field and T. Schuller, 2000, p. 6). Coleman presumed that social relations of individuals are useful in contexts in which agreement, expectations and trust are important. Such relationships are also important as a pathway for information, as well as being a framework for traditions and punishments that maintain and reproduce them (ibid., p. 6). Coleman particularly observed family relations and the social structures of the boroughs the children come from. In this respect, Coleman's approach was similar to that of Bourdieu concerning the concept of 'habitus'.

It is important to keep in mind, concerning Bourdieu and Coleman's theories, that their influence is crucial in directing the focus of research into innovation activity towards the social background of the actors and in pursuing the idea that this background influences interaction between individuals and actors in different fields, such as networks of collaboration of firms in the economy. The American social scientist Robert Putman (1993) follows this train of thought in his book *Making Democracy Work*. Like M. Piore and C. Sabel, Putnam focused on industrial development in Northern Italy. In order to explain the industrial success of regions in Northern Italy he focuses on the role of municipal and regional authorities, cultural tradition and patterns of interaction of individuals in local communities. In the wake of this research, he turned to analysis of American society and concentrated on participation of the general public in social movements and public institutions. The emphasis was on participatory democracy in the spirit of de Tocqueville. Putnam claims that social capital has constantly declined in USA, defining the concept in terms of 'norms of reciprocity and networks of civic engagement', as well as 'features of social organisation, such as trust, norms and networks, that can improve the efficiency of society by facilitating coordinated actions'. R.D. Putnam 1993, p. 167).

There are six factors in Putnam's definition that need to be scrutinised. *Firstly*, he mentions 'civic engagement'. This presupposition envisages active participation in the decision making process of society. The forms of participation can vary, for example being on the board of societies or committees in the respective communities. Participation of this kind is quantifiable and can be measured and used when comparing communities and indeed different countries as well.

Secondly, Putnam mentions the improved efficiency of society as social capital facilitates coordinated actions. Consequently he turns social capital into an instrument in the sense that networks, norms and trust become means to realise particular ends. In relation to this view Putnam has been criticised for making no distinction between means and ends. It is unclear whether a high level of social capital is an end in itself, as people behave in a mutually trustworthy way, or whether it is an instrument that can be used to realise a good society independently of how a good society is defined (S. Baron, J. Field and T. Schuller, 2000, p. 10).

The *third* factor in Putnam's definition is common aims implicit in 'coordinated actions' of society. This point has been criticised for being ideologically skewed; that is, for overemphasis on communitarianism and solidarity in communities which can lead to lack of tolerance towards social values that deviate from ruling values of the society in question. Following this critique Putnam has developed the concepts of 'bonding' and 'bridging' in order to deal with this defect in the concept of social capital. Bonding reflects homogeneity in society and like-mindedness that can lead both to problems of social exclusion and social degeneration. Bridging refers to processes that unify different values and different social groups in a heterogeneous society.

The *fourth* factor in Putnam's definition is 'trust' He has not defined the concept in detail (B. Fine, 2001, p. 95) and consequently a useful definition has to be sought elsewhere. D. Gambetta (1988) defines the concept of 'trust' in his analysis of cooperation and trust. He presumes that trust emerges through cooperation. Trust is, according to Gambetta, the likelihood that an individual can predict the behaviour of another person independent of whether he or she tries to influence the behaviour or not (D. Gambetta, 1988, p. 217). The precondition for trusting other people and the ability to predict their conduct is, accordingly, that the actors know the ruling norms and values of the society in question. Norms and social values develop in societies over long periods and belong to the cultural base of each society. Trust, in this sense, is not limited to individuals alone, but applies to firms as well. Trust between corporations takes a long time to develop and is rooted in norms and values of the respective business community which are taken for granted. Such trust is believed to have developed during decades of corporate collaboration in industrial districts such as in Northern Italy. In research of these districts, scholars usually distinguish between three kinds of trust i.e., 'contractual trust', 'competence trust' and 'goodwill trust' (M. Danson and Whittan, 1999, pp. 72–3). Contractual trust refers to the fact that firms learn from experience which corporations keep to their contracts and deliver their goods in time, and their goods will be of the required specification and agreed quantity and quality. Competence trust presumes that experience enables firms to predict in which fields and what kind of projects the corporations are competent and will fulfil particular tasks. Goodwill trust emerges in cases when corporate collaboration extends beyond the scope of contracts and new ideas and technology is transferred between actors. Goodwill trust plays a key role in creating conditions for vigorous innovation activity and development in industrial districts.

The *fifth* factor in Putnam's definition of social capital is the concept of 'network'. Workable definitions of this concept are not found in Putnam's vocabulary. Other scholars, such as Manuel Castells (2000), describe networks in a very abstract way: 'A network is a set of interconnected nodes. A node is the point at which a curve intersects itself ... The topology defined by networks determines that the distance ... between two points ... is shorter if both points are nodes in a network than if they do not belong to the same network'. (M. Castells, 2000, p. 501)

Castells provides examples of nodes in networks and mentions that they are:

> ... stock exchange markets, and their ancillary advanced service centres, in the network of global financial flows. They are national councils of ministers and European Commissioners in the political network that governs the European

Union. They are coca fields and poppy fields, clandestine laboratories, secret landing strips, street gangs, and money-laundering financial institutions in the network of drug traffic that penetrates economies, societies, and states throughout the world. They are television systems, entertainment studios, computer graphics milieux, news teams, and mobile devices generating, transmitting, and receiving signals in the global network and the new media at the roots of cultural expression and public opinion in the Information Age. (ibid., p. 501)

The concept of network has been familiar in social sciences in recent years and the core idea of the concept is that the relations between actors or 'nodes' in the respective network are pathways through which physical and non-physical resources move between the nodes of networks. The emphasis is on the relations themselves and it is thought to be impossible to reduce these relations to the characteristics of the actors in the networks (J. Scott, 1991, p. 3). Moreover, relations in networks appear in forms such as business transactions, information mediation, power relations of authorities, feelings, family relationships, etc.

The *sixth* main factor in the concept of social capital is norms. Norms, or rules of conduct, are one of two fundamental elements of the concept of culture in social sciences. The other main element is the values of the society concerned. Norms tell people what is considered right conduct and how people must not behave. They refer, as an example, to ideas of what is honest behaviour, whether one behaves truthfully, when people are bullying, what constitutes fairness, who is allowed to marry whom, etc. These issues are wide ranging and too general to be the basis for a concept of networks. However, scholars such as Francis Fukuyama have approached the problem in this way. He defines the concept of network as: ' ... a group of individual agents that share informal norms or values beyond those necessary for ordinary market transactions' (F. Fukuyama, 1997, p. 4). D. Cohen and L Prusak (2001, p. 57) have criticised Fukuyama's definition for being too broad and vague. Individuals who share no social relationships, as those who give high contributions to support thousands of victims of, for example, earthquakes in Turkey in 1999 and Haiti in 2010, respect the same norms although they have never met and have no knowledge of one another. What is needed here is a focus on interactive relationships between actors in a network. What is missing in Fukuyama's definition are mutual feelings and the fact that actors join networks in an active way.

The concept of network is well known to most of us because we all build our own networks and we know whom we know and the value of the relations we have with other participants of our networks (ibid., pp. 57–8). In terms of industrial districts and regional clusters it is clear that various norms have emerged from the collaboration of corporations and that these norms are part of the culture of the respective region. It is also clear that if individuals are to be able to work together they need to follow norms that they agree upon. However, it is not clear how one can prove that there is a relationship between these norms and the economic wellbeing of a regional cluster or industrial district. Research in this field is not advanced and comparison between regions and countries is difficult.

Despite the fact that research into social capital and its relation to innovation activity is not sophisticated, the topic has attracted considerable interest in recent years. The World Bank is of the opinion that social capital is an important means of development in the struggle against poverty and crime. The bank also assumes it plays a vital role in developing education systems and guiding policy formation in the fields of environmental policy, health, population control, urbanisation and the development of irrigation systems (S. Baron, J. Field and T. Schuller, 2000, p. 25). Further examples of empirical research on social capital relate to economic wellbeing of immigrant communities, salaries of directors of large corporations, comparative health levels of different communities and countries and preservation of intergenerational cultural capital (ibid., p. 25). The number of examples such as these constantly increases.

Moreover, the discussion above indicates that social capital is a fundamental precondition for collaboration between firms and social and political institutions. This applies to collaboration for the purpose of satisfying demand in markets and collaboration in relation to innovation activity. Consequently, social capital is considered to be fundamental for collaboration in the various forms of innovation activity. The core of social capital is trust between collaborators. However, trust is hardly possible without the necessary social tolerance which makes it possible for diverse actors to collaborate and generate new ideas and freely communicate. Richard Florida has developed a theory of regional growth which highlights the importance of social tolerance for innovation and regional growth. We will now discuss his contribution.

5.5 Innovation, Regional Growth and the Creative Class

In his influential book, *The Rise of the Creative Class,* Richard Florida (2002, pp. 8–9) works with the thesis that knowledge and creative activity has become so important in contemporary economies that it is transforming everyday life, work, leisure and community. Moreover, USA's geographic centre of gravity has shifted from traditional regions of industrial mass production towards new axes of creativity and innovation. The leading centres are Washington, D.C., Boston, the greater New York region, San Francisco Bay Area, Seattle and Austin. Florida also mentions smaller places like Boulder, Colorado and Santa Fe, New Mexico, Gainesville, Florida, Provo, Utah and Huntsville, Alabama (ibid., p. 11). According to R. Florida, the new creative class moves to and concentrates in these larger locations which are characterised by high tech, intensive innovation activity, strong academic and artistic communities and a high level of social tolerance. This kind of social context does not only breed creative activity but stimulates corporate localisation and investment in these regions which eventually leads to regional growth in terms of income and employment.

R. Florida's creative class that counts for 38 million Americans covers both the 'creative core' and a professional periphery consisting of 'creative professionals'. The former group involves people in science and engineering, architecture, and design, education, arts, music, and entertainment. They have the economic function of creating new ideas, new technology and/or new creative content. The latter group consists of professionals in business and finance, law, health care and related fields. 'These people engage in complex problem solving that involves a great deal of independent judgement and requires high levels of education or human capital' (R. Florida, 2002, p. 8). Furthermore, the creative class does not only have a particular position in the process of production, but is presumed to share a common identity; that is, they share a common ethos that values creativity, individuality, difference and merit (ibid., p. 8). Although not being a 'class for itself' in the sociological sense, Florida's definition of the creative class is close to M. Weber's (1978, pp. 305–6) definition of a status group that along with social class moulds society's structure of stratification.[3]

R. Florida's theory of the role of the creative class in regional development has been criticised for six shortcomings:

- *Firstly*, the concept of the creative class covers groups that are not necessarily creative but whose jobs are characterised by routine and repetition. Consequently, the concept of the creative class does not tackle the relationship between artistic activity and the capacity of scientists to create new knowledge and generate innovation (R. Root-Bernstein et al., 2013, pp. 97–8);
- *Secondly*, the theory is badly operationalised as empirically it concentrates on categories of human capital and educational degrees rather than indicators of creativity (E. Glaeser, 2005). Measures of creativity such as patents, copyrights, trademarks, designs, or new companies better assess originality than density of advanced educational degrees. Moreover, using advanced degrees as criteria of the creative class excludes most practicing artists, musicians, and craftspeople (R. Root-Bernstein et al., 2013, pp. 97–8);
- *Thirdly*, the concept of creative class does not take into consideration differences between various subgroups of that class. It appears that different subgroups are not all attracted to living in large creative centres, but smaller communities fit better the needs of families with children and those who prefer quieter surroundings than a metropolis does (K.V. Andersen et al., 2010);
- *Fourthly*, it does not take into account relationships of exploitation as corporations and professionals gain relatively more from creative activity than the creative individuals themselves (J. Peck 2005 and M. Bontje and

---

3   Max Weber refers to 'Status' (ständische Lage) as an effective claim to social esteem in terms of positive or negative privileges that is typically founded on style of life and formal education.

S. Musterd, 2009). Moreover, the problem of social and economic burnout of creative workers (under precarious labour market conditions) has been criticised. The societal consequences of the growth of the freelancing, non-unionised creative class constitute a potential long term decline of social welfare systems that will have negative effects for social reproduction, pensions, child care and other ancillary social programs (A.C. Pratt and T.A. Hutton, 2013, p. 94);

- *Fifthly*, it does not take into account social exclusion and social polarisation uneven income distribution leads to between existing groups of inhabitants and newcomers in the community i.e., the high income creative class (C.J.N. Yáñez, 2013);

- *Finally*, the claim of a correlation between economic growth and density of the creative class is not founded on adequate empirical evidence according to many critics of R. Florida's theory. As an example, E. Glaser maintains, on the basis of regression analysis of data for 242 metropolitan areas in USA, that neither Florida's super-creative core, tolerance (measured by the Gay-Index) nor the presence of artistic types (measured by the Bohemian-Index) explain regional (population) growth, but schooling does (i.e., percentage of adults with a college education) (E. Glaeser, 2005). However, recent research into the effects of human capital indicators on the economic efficiency of 257 regions belonging to the 27 member states of the EU shows different results. By distinguishing the various components of human capital into three non-overlapping categories – creative graduates, non-creative graduates and bohemians – and combining the information on educational attainments with that related to actual occupations, E. Marrocu and R. Paci (2012) showed that highly educated people working in creative occupations, the 'creative graduates',[4] are the most relevant component in explaining regional performance measured in total factor productivity[5] (TFP), 'non-creative graduates' exhibit a lower impact, while 'bohemians' do not show a significant effect on TFP. E. Marrocu and R. Paci conclude that R. Florida was correct, as their analysis confirms that talent matters: university graduates who work in 'non-creative' professions tend to be less

---

4   On the basis of the EC classification of the European Labour Force Survey (ELFS), they included in the category of 'creative graduates', those in scientific, life sciences, health, teaching, library and social sciences professional occupations (cf. R. Florida's "super creative core" or the "creative core" in the literature). The 'bohemians' consist of artistic, entertainment, and fashion professionals. 'Non-creative graduates' include senior governmental officials, directors and chief executives, general managers, nursing and midwifery professionals, business professionals, legal professionals, also technicians and associate professionals (see E. Marrocu and R. Paci, 2012, p. 375).

5   TFP refers to 'total factor productivity' that reflects how effectively capital and labour are used in production. TFP is by many economists presumed to be the most important factor that explains economic growth.

productive than do those who use their talents on actual jobs. However, Glaeser's hypothesis is also confirmed; that is, education is a crucial determinant of economic performance because the talent of graduates has a greater impact than does the talent of bohemians.

'In conclusion, our key result is that although higher education remains one of the most relevant factors in driving economic outcomes, it is important to acknowledge that its effectiveness varies according to the creativity content of the graduates' actual occupations'. (E. Marrocu and R. Paci 1912, p. 397).

Chapter 6
Entrepreneurs and Innovation Management

6.1 Introduction

In the previous chapters, we have discussed innovation and entrepreneurial activity in terms of macro and meso approaches. We have emphasised its role in long term social and economic aggregate development (macro). We have also observed innovation activity of firms and organisations in regional contexts (meso). In this chapter, we will focus on the micro-level; that is, on the dynamics of innovation activity within firms and institutions. We will, on the one hand, discuss P.F. Drucker's theories of innovation and entrepreneurship which he approaches from the point of view of strategic management. His main focus is on entrepreneurial management. On the other hand, we will observe an approach that emphasises the role of 'high-involvement' employees in organisations engaged in innovation activity. High-involvement innovation is an example of innovation management techniques.

6.2 Entrepreneurs and Entrepreneurship

In his book, *The Entrepreneur; An Economic Theory,* Mark Casson (1982) claimed that no real economic theory of entrepreneurship had been developed. The phenomenon of 'entrepreneur' has been researched by economists, sociologists, psychologists and political scientists and practically all disciplines have their own theories of entrepreneurship, except economics (Casson, 1982, p. 9). As we discussed in the chapters above, the situation is still the same i.e., economics has very little to add to research into entrepreneurship. In neoclassical economics, one presumes that information is accessible to everyone and decision making is simply reduced to the act of maximising the use of factors of production with the help of mathematical models (cf. the idea of 'production function'). The Austrian school of economics, rooted in the work of Böhm-Bawerk, von Mises and von Hayek, emphasised that the price of goods is determined by the degree of presumed utility, as estimated by individuals in the act of transaction, but not by the amount of labour that is needed for their production. The Austrian school shares this view of price formation with neoclassical economics. However, the main emphasis of the Austrian school was never on marginalism as is the case with neoclassical economics. Hayeks's opposition (1934 and 1935) to neoclassical economics became stronger as time went by and he turned against the overemphasis on mathematical models of equilibrium which characterise the work of neoclassical economists. In this respect, Hayek followed his mentor, von Mises, and was of the opinion that the dynamics of equilibrium formation in real economies is much more complicated than the mathematical models of neoclassical economics can explain. Hayek's view was that persons' ideas, experience and knowledge are first and foremost individual and dispersed. As a consequence, it is impossible to create indisputable knowledge of economic phenomena and generate the holistic overview that is necessary to establish general equilibrium in the economy, using the methods of a socialist command economy (Tieben and Keizer, 1997, pp. 8–11).

Hayek's idea of individualised knowledge is interesting as it may lead to analysis of the conditions that shape different individual entrepreneurs' ability to foresee innovation opportunities. Hayek's ideas might as well prove to be a valuable point of departure for the analysis of common features of entrepreneurs and their social background. However, as Casson points out in his book, Hayek and the Austrian school were unable to study the societal background of entrepreneurs because they were stuck in 'methodological individualism'. To Hayek's mind, knowledge is limited to the individual; it is diffused and difficult to access so that the best information one can obtain is prices of goods on markets. Presuppositions of this kind are far too narrow to analyse decision making in entrepreneurial contexts. Consequently, although this school has generated some valuable ideas in the field of economics, it has not contributed much to research into innovation and entrepreneurial activity (Casson, 1982, pp. 9–10 and 380).

Some theoretical discussion of entrepreneurship had developed in the first part of the 19th century. However, as neoclassical economics became the predominant version of economics in Western countries at the end of the century, the probability was bleak that substantive economic theories of innovation and entrepreneurship would develop. Richard Cantillon, an Irish businessman and banker in Paris during the first part of the eighteenth century, was the first political economist to use the term 'entrepreneur'. It was not until the beginning of the eighteenth century, however, that the concept of entrepreneur was analysed in a theoretical way by French economist Jean-Baptiste Say (1803) in his book, *A Treatise on Political Economy*, Book I, Chapter 1. The word 'entrepreneur' was translated into English as undertaker, adventurer or employer, but it was the Scottish political economist, John Stuart Mill, who made the word and concept of entrepreneur popular at the beginning of the nineteenth century. The concept disappeared from economic discourse following the triumph of neoclassical economics and its static view of economic development so that the concept was largely forgotten around 1900. As an example, the nineteenth century economist Alfred Marshall, one of the founding fathers of neoclassical economics, emphasised routine activities of management and superintendence in his economic works rather than the innovative activity of the entrepreneur (Casson, 1982, p. 19). Opposing this, contemporary research into innovation emphasises the behaviour of entrepreneurs rather than the administrative role of managers. The emphasis is, on the one hand, on methods that lead to positive performance concerning innovation activity in organisations and, on the other, interaction between employees of innovative organisations.

Consequently, research into innovation and entrepreneurship has increasingly focused on analysing entrepreneurial behaviour and searching for their success or failure in the context of the location of their activity. In the following paragraphs, we will look more closely at the matter and take note of theories and techniques of innovation management. It is necessary for entrepreneurs to be conscious of these matters as it helps in terms of minimising risk involved in engaging in innovation activity. The 'death rate' of new firms is high and the probability that they will survive is, therefore, low. Indeed, research in USA indicates that 24 per cent of new firms become bankrupt in the first two years of their life. Furthermore, 52 per cent are closed down within four years and around 63 per cent within six years. The main reasons are unrealistic business plans, overestimated income and insufficient financing. There are also indications that size matters. The smaller firms are, the more likely they are to be closed down. Life expectancy increases if venture capital funds are invested in the firms and their representatives are board members. In this context, the life expectancy of innovative firms is over 80 per cent (see J.A. Timmons, 2000, pp. 32–6).

6.3 The Theories of Peter F. Drucker

P.F. Drucker is one of the founding fathers of the school of strategic management (P.F. Drucker, 1964). In his book, *Innovation and Entrepreneurship: Practice and Principles*, published in 1985, he focuses on entrepreneurial management (P.F. Drucker, 2004). Drucker's ideas of innovation and entrepreneurship are influenced by J.A. Schumpeter; they were both Austrians immigrants in USA. Like Schumpeter, Drucker defines innovation activity as 'creative destruction'; that is, entrepreneurship generates new methods of production, new goods and needs that remove existing ones (ibid., p. 23). Both maintain that entrepreneurship implies more than establishing new firms, as entrepreneurs introduce novel methods of production and new products. Consequently, each and every new firm cannot be categorised as an entrepreneurial firm. However, although there are similarities in Drucker and Schumpeter's theories in this respect, there are differences in other areas. Drucker strongly emphasises the view that innovation activity results in goods and services which better satisfy the needs of customers and consumers than the existing goods and services. Moreover, innovation activity, according to Drucker, leads to creation of markets and generates a new kind of consumer. Although Schumpeter also emphasised that entrepreneurs often create new markets, his focus is on entrepreneurs' search for profits rather consumers' needs. Drucker's view clearly appears in his analysis of the hamburger company McDonald's:

> McDonald's ... did not invent anything, to be sure. Its final product was what a decent American restaurant had produced years ago. But by applying management concepts and management techniques (asking, What is 'value' to the customer?), standardising the 'product', designing process and tools, and by basing training

on the analysis of the work to be done and then setting the standards it required, McDonald's both drastically upgraded the yield from resources, and created a new market and a new customer. This is entrepreneurship. (ibid., p. 19)

McDonald's learnt that what is important to customers is the quality of the goods and knowing in advance what to expect. The speed of services is also important, as well as hygiene and friendly communication with staff. When these factors had become clear, McDonalds redefined all standards, employees were trained accordingly and wages and remuneration adjusted to the new standards (ibid., p. 15).

Drucker presumes that an entrepreneur is a person who is able to increase the efficiency of factors of production by using them in a new way (ibid., p. 25). He or she may be an employee, employer or public servant. As a consequence, only some capitalists, or investors, belong to the category of entrepreneurs; that is, those who generate conditions for increased productivity and profitability. The act of establishing a firm is not sufficient to be defined as an entrepreneur (ibid., pp. 22–3).

The core of Drucker's approach is the idea that the entrepreneur is a person who realises innovation. Innovation and entrepreneurship, according to Drucker, can be made more effective by exploiting the right kind of management methods based on the main principles of entrepreneurship. In this context, he highlights the conditions for effective entrepreneurship which he presumes to be 'the practice of innovation', 'the practice of entrepreneurship' and 'entrepreneurial strategies'. We will discuss these terms in detail below. It appears that Drucker emphasises the methodology of entrepreneurship. This is to be expected as he assumes it is impossible to prove a relationship between individuals' personality traits and their entrepreneurial ability.

We have summarised the relationship between Drucker's definition of the concepts of entrepreneur and entrepreneurship in Figure 6.1.

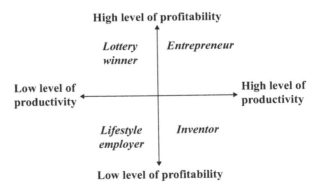

Figure 6.1   Drucker and entrepreneurship

The figure indicates that entrepreneurship leads to maximisation of productivity and profitability (or gains if the organisation is a non-profit organisation). Inventors increase productivity, but they are not always able to implement their inventions in a profitable enterprise. The aim of employers is not always to maximise productivity or profitability. Employers of this kind are called 'lifestyle employer'. Finally, there are persons who make large profits without increasing the productivity of their activity. In these cases, performance is due to luck or unusual or random market conditions. Hence, the persons in question have not done anything to increase the profitability of their ventures, but the gains are due to luck, as in the case of lotteries.

As we highlighted above, Drucker emphasises the role played by customers' or consumers' needs in entrepreneurial activity. In this respect, Drucker differs from many other students of entrepreneurship. Moreover, he diverged to certain extent from certain other theoreticians, especially Schumpeterians, insofar as he emphasised the role of innovation activity characterised by 'low technology'. As we discussed in Chapter 3, the existence of Kondratieff waves is explained by the emergence of basic innovations. Historical examples of this are the exploitation of steam power, electricity and oil as well as assembly-line technology and bio-technology. These different basic technologies are 'high-technology' of the respective periods in history. Drucker does not doubt the long term economic impact of these technologies, but he stressed that in periods during which these technologies are developing and have not generally diffused through the economies, low and medium level technology has been the basis of economic growth (ibid., pp. 12 and 238–9). In relation to this, he particularly refers to the service sector, as well as innovations in the management of organisations and education of the general public. Hence, what is at stake is innovation that meets consumers' needs rather than scientific and (high) technological excellence. In short, Drucker refers to the importance of various social and societal innovations for economic growth.

Drucker's conclusion is that innovation activity has to be systematic and its aims well- defined if it is to be effective. According to Drucker: 'Systematic innovation ... consists in the purposeful and organised search for changes, and in the systematic analysis of the opportunities such changes might offer for economic or social innovation'. (ibid., p. 31).

Let us have a closer look at what he is referring to when he claims that the precondition for effective entrepreneurship is a purposeful and organised search for change. The premise for this is threefold according to Drucker i.e., the practice of innovation; the practice of entrepreneurship and; entrepreneurial strategies.

6.3.1 The Practice of Innovation

Systematic innovation activity is based on well-defined aims. It is rooted in seven sources of innovation opportunities that Drucker refers to as *the unexpected; incongruities; process need; industry and market structures; demographics (population changes); changes in perception, mood, and meaning* and; *new knowledge.*

The first presumption, the unexpected, refers to unforeseen performance, mistakes or external events. Success in business is often unexpected, but despite, for example, increased productivity, managers sometimes hesitate to exploit new knowledge to enhance productivity. In cases like this, they may turn out to be conservative concerning implementing new production methods or they lack the nerve or resources to bring about necessary changes within the organisation. As an example of unexpected success, Drucker mentions the case of the American corporation MACE. This corporation had been a fashion store for a long time, but when it started selling housewares it appeared that 60 per cent of its sales were due to this product category. Although it turned out to be more profitable to sell housewares than fashion goods, the managers saw this as a problem because they believed 75 per cent of sales of corporations like MACE must be due to the retailing of fashion goods. It was not until after 1970, when new managers took over the business, that a new policy was introduced at MACE. (P.F. Drucker, 2004, pp. 33–4).

Incongruities are the second source of innovations that Drucker highlights. The theory presumes there is an incongruity between the real conditions of the business in question or its markets and, conversely, management's expectations or ideas of how conditions are or they want them to be. By analysing the incongruity, innovation opportunities emerge. Drucker brings up the development of the transport sector as an example of this. In the 1950s it was widely believed that cargo transport by ships was a dying form of transportation and airfreight would take over. Ship freight cost constantly increased and the response of the industry was to build larger and faster ships which consumed less energy. The solution, however, did not tackle the root of the problem; that is, how time consuming it was to load and unload the ships. Ships are capital intensive investments and it is expensive to pay interest on investment which remains idle over long periods. The solution did not appear until the innovation of containers diffused into the sector, reducing the time ships spent in harbours (ibid., pp. 56–7).

The third source of innovation opportunity is *process need*. This refers to productivity increase by making processes of production or services more effective and faster. This kind of innovation is based on deleting bottlenecks in processes, redesigning processes or speeding them up by the introduction of new knowledge or technology. Drucker refers to the birth of news magazines to exemplify his point. In the wake of the First World War it was clear to the public and newspaper publishers that there was a large market for worldwide and nationwide news. Local newspapers were unable to satisfy this need. Henry Luce came up with the solution, or specific innovation, based on analysis of hindrances in the production process of worldwide news. He established a special news journal which was not a local journal since local markets are too small and have too few advertisers for this type of news. The journal was not published daily as the news was not frequent enough. The result of all this was the journal *Time*, published as an international journal with international news (ibid., pp. 65–6).

The fourth source of innovation is *industry and market structures* that change little over long periods, but when change takes place, it tends to be swift. Markets are characterised by dominance of a few corporations which rule over them in terms of market share. As an example, the same American aluminium firms have dominated the world market of aluminium for more than a century; that is, corporations in Pittsburgh which generated the original patents in the industry. Alcan, a Canadian subsidiary of these corporations, is also dominant in this market (ibid., p. 69).

Various signs indicate that industry and market structures will change. As an example, if a particular branch of industry grows faster than the population of the respective economy, then it is almost certain that structural change will occur. When the size of the industry has become twice what it used to be, it is certain that a structural change has taken place. When this has happened, it is very probable that technology and production methods have become obsolete and new firms will emerge and implement new, more competitive methods. Consequently, relations between firms will change and the new firms come to dominate the industry. Signs that new technology is diffusing in the industry or existing technology is exploited in new way also suggest that structural change is taking place. An example of this occurred when the Bell Telephone Company lost its dominant market position for private branch exchange (PBX); that is, switchboards for offices and other large telephone users. Bell lost its position to the RALM company which introduced new technology based on computers and information technology (ibid., p. 77).

Innovation rooted in structural changes is particularly effective in branches of industry where oligopoly or monopoly persists. Dominant companies feel secure with their position and do not worry about threats from newcomers in their market. In this context, changes can be swift and profound. As an example of fast changes, the securities market is a case in point. In the 1950s, pension funds grew fast in USA, but no one was servicing this market to any extent. Around the middle of the decade, three young men realised that the funds were bound to become extremely large investors in the future economy. These young men established a company in 1959 that specialised in servicing pension funds' investment in securities. Five years later the new firm, Donaldson, Lufkin & Jenrette had become a major force on Wall Street (ibid., p. 74).

All of the four sources of innovation that we discussed above emerge within the business sector. In addition to these, Drucker highlights three sources external to this sector.

Firstly, in terms of external sources, Drucker highlights *demographics* or population changes such as fluctuations in size of population, its age distribution, level of employment of different social groups, education, income distribution, etc. Population changes are obvious and their impacts are easy to predict. As an example of foreseen population growth and related opportunities, Drucker mentions that in 1957 he forecast that the number of university students would increase substantially in 20 years. Specialists in the field of universities rejected his prediction, but failed miserably. A similar story can be told in relation to the growth in number of elderly citizens. In 1976 he predicted that retirement age in USA would have to be raised to 70 years or eliminated altogether within 10 years. So called experts – government economists, labour union economists, business economists, statisticians – dismissed the forecast as utterly absurd. However, in the following year the state of California abolished compulsory retirement and retirement before 70 for the rest of the country in 1978. In the corporate sector, some corporations realised what was happening concerning demographics. The Melville Company utilised knowledge of the baby boom following the Second World War. The company used to be a small chain of shoes shops, but turned to fashion wares for teenagers with 16 and 17 year olds as the main target group. Within a short time, Melville's new policy became a success story and the company was among the fastest growing and most profitable retailing firms (ibid., pp. 84–5).

Changes in perception, mood, and meaning are yet another source of innovation. How people experience their environment and related phenomena or their self-perception is often a source of demand for new goods and services. These changes are often based on social and economic trends or altered fashions which are difficult to explain. Developments in the field of health care constitute an example of what is at stake. Immense progress in this field in recent decades has led to an impressive fall in the infant death rate and increased life expectancy. However, the general public has never been as preoccupied with its health status as today. People are obsessed with youth-fetishism and terrified of not being physically 'fit'. They fear nothing more than long term sickness and age-related illnesses. Health perceptions of this kind are a rich source of innovation opportunities. Thus, large numbers of healthcare magazines have emerged, published with substantial profit margins, and the same goes for work-outs and health-centres. The health fervour has created markets for all kinds of specialised health foods and huge chains of shops concentrating on such products. The company Celestial Seasoning was established in Colorado in the 1960s by one of the 'flower children' of the decade picking herbs in the mountains, packing them, and peddling them in the street. Fifteen years later the sales of the company amounted to several hundred million dollars a year and it was sold for more than $20 million to a large food processing company (ibid., p. 91).

Finally, there is a source of innovation which Drucker calls '*new knowledge*'. This source leads to innovations which are not limited to technological change in the narrow sense, but social innovations as well, which are not less, but possibly more important than technological innovations according to Drucker (ibid., p. 99). Two elements distinguish innovations rooted in new knowledge from those originating from other sources of innovation characterised by the following: *Firstly*, a long time lag between the point at which the new knowledge in question emerges and the moment when the goods derived from it appear on the market. This usually it takes 25–35 years. *Secondly*, a synthesis of different kinds of knowledge which is not limited to science or technological expertise.

As an example of the length of time innovation of this kind can take, Drucker outlines how long it took the diesel motor to reach the market. Rudolf Diesel invented this motor in 1897 and it was generally believed that his invention would be an immediate turning point in the motor industry. It was not until 1935, however, that the American, Charles Kettering, redesigned the motor so that it could be installed in various types of vehicles such as ships, locomotives, trucks, buses and private cars (ibid., p. 99).

The history of computer technology is another example of innovation at hand. The first precondition of this technology is the mathematical theory of binary numbers, going back to the seventeenth century, which enables numeric values to be expressed by two numbers only, 1 and 0. It was not until the first half of the nineteenth century that Charles Babbage designed a calculating machine based on binary numbers. In 1890, Hermann Hollerith invented the punch card based on J.M. Jacquard's invention in 1801, the Jacquard loom. A punch card makes it possible to change numbers into 'instructions'. In 1906, Lee de Forest invented the audion tube, and with it created electronics. Between 1910 and 1913, Bertrand Russell and Alfred North Whitehead developed symbolic logic, in their *Principia Mathematica*, which makes it possible to express all logical concepts as numbers. Finally, the concepts of programming and feedback were developed during the First World War, primarily for the purposes of anti-aircraft gunnery. Consequently, all the knowledge needed to develop the computer was available by 1918. However, it was not until 1946 that the first operational computer materialised (ibid., p. 99).

Finally, in the sphere of service industries, an example from the banking sector is illuminating. The French aristocrat and socialist, Comte de Saint-Simon (1760–1825) who believed in the power of science and technology, prophesied a prosperous future society ruled by scientists and characterised by welfare and progress. Immediately after the Napoleonic wars, he developed a theory of an entrepreneurial bank that would focus on the purposeful use of capital to generate economic development. Until then, bankers lent against 'security' (i.e., the taxing power of a prince). Saint-Simon's bank was supposed to 'invest'; that is, to create a new wealth-producing capacity. He was an extraordinarily influential socialist, but it was not until 1852 that two of his disciples, the brothers Jacob and Isaac Pereire, established the first entrepreneurial bank, the Credit Mobilier, and with it ushered in what is now called finance capitalism (ibid., pp. 100–101).

Common to innovation is its reliance on new knowledge. If all the elements of the knowledge needed have not appeared, the innovation is doomed to fail. This is particularly applicable to innovation based on science and technology in the sense that it is riskier than other types of innovation because the uncertainty of success is much higher.

Besides the seven sources of innovation that Drucker mentions and we have discussed above, he adds the eighth source, namely '*bright idea*'. According to Drucker, this is the worst, riskiest and least likely source of successful innovations. He claims that only one out of every 500 bright ideas is likely to yield sufficient income to cover the costs of realising it. Consequently, entrepreneurs should not be advised to spend time or resources on bright ideas. However, there are of course many examples of successful innovations rooted in bright ideas such as the zippo lighter, the ball point pen, the aerosol spray can, the tab to open soft drinks or beer cans, etc. (ibid., pp. 119–20).

6.3.2 The Practice of Entrepreneurship

As we discussed above, according to Drucker, there are three preconditions for effective innovation activity; that is, 'the practice of innovation', 'the practice of entrepreneurship' and 'entrepreneurial strategies'. We have highlighted the first precondition. Let us discuss the second, 'the practice of entrepreneurship'.

Effective entrepreneurship requires purposeful practices. Entrepreneurial management is the means needed in this respect. It concentrates on four main managerial objectives: 1) building motivation for innovation among employees so that they do not fear changes, but experience innovations as opportunities; 2) using consistent measurements of performance and methods which indicate the relationship between intramural innovation activity and the organisation's performance; 3) optimising innovation by adapting organisational changes to it, as well as by changing the principles of hiring employees and systems of remuneration; 4) avoiding traps and failures which undermine innovation in the organisation (P.F. Drucker, 2004, p. 138). The three first mentioned objectives are highlighted in Table 6.1.

As we discussed above, Drucker claims it is important to avoid various traps in innovation management. Such traps undermine entrepreneurial activity in organisations. As an example of traps, he points out that innovation projects must never be put in the hands of managers who supervise already existing operations in the organisation. Entrepreneurial activity is also bound to fail if a consistent innovation policy is not implemented (cf. Table 6.1). Collaboration between the organisation and the external entrepreneur is also likely to fail. Because lack of agreement and opposing views as to how the innovation projects should be realised, failure is likely in case of innovation projects, which involve fields diverse from those in which the organisation or firm currently operates and where it has a competitive advantage due to intramural knowledge. It is safest for organisations to concentrate on innovation projects in areas where they have already established their specialties. Finally, Drucker points out that a takeover of entrepreneurial firms almost always fails unless, soon after the takeover, new innovation managers are hired to supervise the project. Many former managers usually quit soon after the takeover (ibid., pp. 160–1).

6.3.3 Entrepreneurial Strategies

Up to now, we have discussed innovation management in relation to intramural activities. It is necessary for all corporations and organisation to 'do their

Table 6.1 **Aims and means of innovation management**

Objectives of innovation management	Aims	Means
Entrepreneurial policies	Make innovation desirable in the organisation	Systematic elimination of all useless, obsolete and unproductive operations or management failures. This is done every three years by putting every single product, process, technology, market, distributive channel, internal staff activity on trial for its life. The question to be asked is 'would we *now* go into this product, this market, this distributive channel, this technology *today*?' If the answer is 'no' then it has to be decided which operations are wasteful and need to be closed down. At the same time productive operations have to be strengthened
	Make employees conscious that the lifetime of products is limited	Decisions concerning life expectancy of products based on detailed analysis and experience of the organisation's production of present goods or services, specificities of the markets, distribution channels, technological conditions and developmental tendencies
	Estimate the need for innovation	Define in detail the extent to which innovation is needed and when it is needed, concerning particular products or services. Their lifetime estimation and how fast the market will saturate. Following this estimation, the cost of innovation, production and distribution relating to the products or services is evaluated concerning their lifetime and the success of related innovation activity
	Organise the innovation activity in space and time	An innovation plan is developed to organise the objectives of innovation, costs, who will execute the job and when the work will be done
Entrepreneurial practices	Focusing managerial vision on opportunity	Operating reports must be goal orientated concerning the organisation's innovation activity. The report has to be twofold; with a traditional part that lists the problems and another part focusing on areas in which performance is better than expected. Typically, in companies managed for entrepreneurship, there are two meetings on operating results: one focusing on the problems and another focusing on the opportunities

Table 6.1   Continued

Objectives of innovation management	Aims	Means
	Generating entrepreneurial spirit among managers	Every half year, a two day meeting is organised that all managers of divisions, markets and major product lines attend. The first morning, three to four managers of units that have done exceptionally well in giving reports. They explain why innovation was successful and how the innovation opportunities emerged
	Top managers listen to ideas and goals of junior managers	Top management sits down with the junior people from research, engineering, manufacturing, marketing, accounting, etc. They declare that their role is to listen to juniors' aspirations, what opportunities they see and which threats are on the horizon. They search for juniors' ideas of new things, new products, market strategies, etc.
Measuring innovative performance	Develop methods to measure performance of individual innovative projects	The results of innovation plans are defined in detail. The next step is to define a realistic measurement unit in order to evaluate innovation performance. In addition, milestones are defined for each innovation project
	Develop a systematic review of all innovative efforts	Every few years, the innovation activity of the organisation is analysed and projects are evaluated in terms of whether they should receive further support and which projects open new opportunities. The evaluation identifies unsuccessful projects and whether to cancel them.
	Judge the organisation's total innovative performance against its innovative objectives	Roughly every five years, top management of the organisation analyses its performance. All major areas of the organisation are scrutinised in order to analyse which areas have turned out to be crucial for the organisation and to observe which are likely to become crucial in the next five years. The most important question in this respect is whether the organisation has captured a leading position in terms of innovation in a particular market and social or policy field

Table 6.1 *Concluded*

Organisational/structural changes	Organise the organisation's operations so that motivation for innovation activity is optimal	Clearly distinguish innovation projects from operations that already exist in the organisation. The best way to do this is to organise innovation projects as if they were independent firms within the organisation. Furthermore, one of the senior managers of the organisation has to be put in charge of future plans of the organisation and related innovation projects. This manager of innovation and development activity coordinates and supervises the innovation activity of the organisation. The managers of the different innovation projects should be promised part of the profit the project generates in order to make success probable. The successful manager could e.g., receive 25 per cent of shares in the project, but would have to sell her shares to the firm within a particular time limit. One should not require the same rate of returns from innovation projects as from other operations. As a rule of thumb, five years should be granted to develop a new product or service and market it. Sales will increase fast in the first year and in the second year in the market it should deliver large profits. Early in the third year, it should have delivered profits that cover research and developmental costs. It will reach sales peak in the fifth year
Staffing	Hiring the right people to manage the innovation activity	Hire persons who have miscellaneous experience of managing, marketing and finance. Middle aged people who have this sort of experience and have often worked for a long time with the organisation in question or with other organisations. They often start a new career by establishing their own entrepreneurial companies or they want to manage innovation projects in the organisation where they work. It is wiser to employ these persons rather than 'entrepreneurial personalities' because such personalities do not exist

homework'. It is just as crucial, however, to manage innovation with the aim of improving competitiveness and comparative advantage vis-à-vis other competing firms or organisations on the market in question. To put it differently, organisations must operate according to 'entrepreneurial strategies'. Drucker distinguishes between four entrepreneurial strategies: 1) 'being fustest with the mostest'; 2) 'hit them where they ain't'; 3) 'ecological niches'; and 4) 'changing values and characteristics' (P.F. Drucker, 2004, p. 193).

'Being fustest with the mostest' refers to attempts of firms or organisations to gain an advantage in developing particular goods or services or use their already existing advantage and cut the prices of their products so that competitors will find it hard to enter the market. An entrepreneurial strategy of this kind involves considerable risk and few corporations follow this path. As examples of firms that have used this strategy, Drucker brings to our attention the pharmaceutical corporations Hoffmann-LaRoche and the Dynamite Cartel established by Alfred Nobel.

The Swiss TNC Hoffmann-LaRoche, established in 1896, was a small company until the 1920s. This company produced textile dyes, but was totally overshadowed by the huge German dyestuff makers and big chemical firms. Hoffmann-LaRoche decided to bet on vitamin production, a potential which had recently been discovered but the scientific community had generally not accepted the existence of vitamins. Hoffmann-LaRoche acquired patents for vitamins while no other firm was interested in such patents. It hired the professors from Zürich University who discovered vitamins and paid them much higher salaries than the industry paid their colleagues. Moreover, it invested all its money and every loan it was able to obtain to finance its production and marketing of vitamins. Today, Hoffmann-LaRoche dominates more than half of the world's vitamin market although their patents are long outdated and its turnover in this market is billions of dollars every year. This company used the same strategy in the 1930s when it invested in production of new sulphonamides although most scientists were convinced that these drugs are ineffective against infections. The same story goes for its investment during the 1950s in production of muscle relaxing tranquillisers. Librium and Valium (ibid., pp. 194–5).

In the same year as Hoffmann-LaRoche was established, Alfred Nobel died, 63 years old. He had acquired 355 patents in his lifetime out of which the patent of dynamite was probably the most important one. Dynamite was a product of the research that the Nobel family had conducted into nitroglycerin. Emil, Alfred's younger brother, paid for this with his life in an explosion in one of their factories in 1864. Many other employees died as well. Alfred established the Dynamite Cartel that produced dynamite in many countries around the world. This cartel had a monopoly on the market until the First World War and indeed long after Nobel's patent was outdated. The cartel maintained its monopoly by lowering prices of dynamite by 10–20 per cent every time demand for dynamite increased. The subsidiaries of the cartel had long before written off the investment necessary for their surplus production. It was, therefore, not realistic for potential competitors to build new factories while the production of the cartel was profitable (ibid., p. 200).

Drucker also mentions an entrepreneurial strategy which he calls 'hit them where they ain't'. This strategy consists of 'creative imitation'; that is, the company in question knows better which market opportunities are at hand for the new product or service or is better equipped to sell it than the firm which created the product or service. An example of this strategy appears in the watches industry i.e., the Japanese Hittori company that gained an advantageous position in this market by way of imitation; namely, before Swiss watches producers realised what was going on, Seiko watches developed by Hittori had taken over the market. Swiss watches nearly disappeared from the market (ibid., pp. 204–5).

A similar story can be told about IBM. In 1945, the IBM company finished designing its first computer which was shown to the lay public in its showroom in midtown New York, where it attracted immense crowds. Shortly afterwards, IBM decided not to develop its computer further and concentrated instead on imitating the computer of its main competitor, ENIAC of the University of Pennsylvania. This computer was much better suited to firms than households when it came to handling, for example, payrolls. In 1953 IBM presented its version of the ENIAC computer which at once set the standard for commercial multipurpose, main-frame computers. Decades later, IBM took over the market for personal computers, the PC market, by using the creative imitation strategy. The Apple company created the idea of the PC. IBM started to produce computers which technically were a direct imitation of the Apple computer, but IBM exploited market opportunities that Apple failed to discover. From the start, IBM offered its customers a free operating system with their computers. Unlike Apple, which sold its computers in their own special stores, IBM also sold their computers in miscellaneous shops alongside their own stores. They were sold in big chains like Sears and Roebuck as well as in IBM stores (ibid., pp. 204 and 206).

The main characteristic of the creative imitation strategy is that market opportunities are exploited to their utmost and the needs of the customers are prioritised, rather than the products as such. Firms that follow this strategy are both market orientated and market driven. This strategy is the riskiest of the four strategies, because it concentrates on exploiting developmental work which other firms have already done and exploiting market opportunities that competitors are too conservative, narrow minded or arrogant to take advantage of.

The third entrepreneurial strategy is what Drucker calls 'ecological niches'. This strategy presumes that firms seek a practical monopoly position in a small market rather than gaining a dominant position in a large market or industry. Drucker identifies three strategies which belong the category of 'ecological niches': a) 'the toll-gate strategy'; b) 'the speciality skill strategy' and; c) 'the speciality market strategy'.

'The toll-gate strategy' consists of developing goods or services vital to a particular type of production or service, but which only constitute a small part of the overall cost of the respective production or service. The aim is to gain a monopoly advantage in a particular market niche. The Alcon Company is a case in point. It developed and obtained a patent for an enzyme necessary for eye-surgery in relation to cataract operations. No eye-surgeon would like to be without the enzyme, no matter what it costs. The market for the enzyme is so small, around 50 million dollars per year, that no one enters the market to compete with Alcon. If someone entered the market, prices would fall so that its production would not be profitable for anyone.

Another example of this strategy is a medium sized company, Cameron Iron Works, which had a 'toll-gate position' for more than 60 years with its blow-out protector for oil-wells. The cost of drilling an oil well may run into many millions and one blow-out will destroy the entire well. The market is too small for other companies to enter (ibid., p. 216).

The main disadvantage of this strategy is that opportunities to grow are slim, since the volume of production is entirely dependent on the growth of the market itself. There is also the risk that a new product which satisfies the same need might appear on the market.

'The speciality skill' strategy differs from the 'toll-gate position' strategy in the sense that the market niche is larger and the firms sustain their competitive advantage by constantly improving their knowledge and production capacity. As an example, only a few companies design and produce most of the electrical inputs in cars. Delco dominates the market in USA, Bosch in Germany and Lucas was dominant in the UK until TRW Automotive took over. For many decades only one company, A.O. Smith, produced almost every frame used in American passenger cars. The same goes for Bendix that produces brake systems for cars (ibid., pp. 218–19).

Companies that use this strategy are characterised by a successful, systematic search for potential goods or services to develop further. They succeed during periods when new branches of industry are being born and they can develop their speciality. Their advantageous specialised position can last for decades, although their growth depends on the expansion of the industry they produce their components for. When this industry is decaying, the companies' specialisation becomes an impediment to them as they cannot easily move into new fields of production.

The main difference between the 'speciality skill strategy' and the 'speciality market strategy' is that the former focuses on specialised goods or services, while the latter concentrates on specialisation in particular markets. As an example, specialised baking ovens for cookies and crackers are not technically complex and they can be manufactured by numerous producers. However, there are only two medium sized companies which dominate this market. One is English and the other is Danish. Their dominant market position is not due to engineering superiority but to specialised knowledge of the market for cookies and crackers and the needs of the producers in this market. The market for these ovens is not large enough for new competitors to enter (ibid., pp. 222–3).

Drucker's fourth main entrepreneurial strategy is 'changing values and characteristics' envisages that companies and/or organisations attempt to change their environment and its market, for example demand for goods and services, instead of adapting to the existing environment (as Darwinist evolutionary strategy would prefer). This category of entrepreneurial initiative appears in four types of strategies i.e., by creating utility, by pricing, by adapting to the customer's social and economic reality, and by delivering what represents true value to the customer.

'Creating utility', refers to analysing first what is actually useful to the customer and then developing the goods or services needed. As an example of this kind of innovation activity, Drucker cites the case of modern postal services which emerged in 1839 and Rowland Hill (1795–1879) who was the pioneer of this revolution (ibid., pp. 225–6). Ancient Rome had an excellent postal service with fast couriers carrying mail on regular schedules across the Empire. A millennium later, in 1521, the German emperor Charles V, following Renaissance fashion, looked back to Classical Rome and handed a mail-carrying monopoly in the imperial domains to the princely family of Thurn and Taxis. The family's monopoly lasted for 355 years. Hill's revolution was no technological transformation. Until then, the receiver of the post had to pay the costs that were calculated with reference to distance and weight of the item posted. Hill introduced a new method which required that postal deliveries should be paid in advance, independent of distance and carry a stamp similar to those people received when they paid taxes and public fees. He had originally written a secret report in 1837 on corruption in the postal services and argued why these services were too expensive and ineffective. In 1839, he was hired for two years to implement the new postal services. The core of Hill's innovation was the utility he created as his point of departure was what kind of postal service *would best satisfy the customers' needs*. Hill was originally a teacher and subsequently a public officer. He was the secretary to the Post Office from 1854 until 1864. In 1819, he established the Hazelwood School in Birmingham which was to provide a model for public education for the emerging middle classes, aiming for useful, pupil-centred education which would help the students to continue lifelong self-education after graduation. Moreover, after his retirement from teaching (1833), Hill invented a rotary printing press; that is, a printing press in which the images to be printed are curved around a cylinder.

'Pricing strategy' is another type of the strategy of 'changing values and characteristics'. An example of a pricing strategy is the case of Gillette shavers. The Gillette Company received large profits from pricing the shavers rather than from their design (ibid., pp. 227–8). King Camp Gillette established his company in 1901. It emphasised the fact that men wanted to have inexpensive and fast shaves and that it was too costly and time consuming for most men to go to a barbershop for a shave. At the end of the nineteenth century, there were many kinds of shavers on the market for men to use when shaving themselves. Gillette developed a shaver with changeable razor blades and acquired a patent for his razor. The company decided to sell its shavers at price that was only 20 per cent of their production cost. However, it sold the blades at a price that was fivefold their production cost. The company profited greatly from this pricing innovation and the utility to the customers was significant, as shaving was much cheaper with the Gillette razor than with other shavers. K.C. Gillette was a utopian socialist and wrote the book *The Human Drift*. He advocated that the entire manufacturing industry should be united in one communal company and that all Americans should live in a huge city he called Metropolis. The Gillette Company was sold to Proctor & Gamble in 2005 for 57 billion US dollars.

The third type of strategy which belongs to the category of 'changing values and characteristics' is 'adaptation to the customer's social and economic reality'. At times, the buyers of goods or services have too low an income to be able to buy them. Through time, various innovations have seen the light of day which aim at making it easier for customers to buy goods or services. It is a familiar procedure today that manufacturers sell their products by way of leasing. Around 1840, Cyrus McCormick developed a much needed harvesting machine. The machine earned back its own cost in two or three seasons, but the farmers did not have the purchasing power and were too poor to obtain necessary loans from the banks. McCormick solved the problem by offering instalments, to be paid out of the savings the harvester machine earned over the ensuing three years. The farmers could now pay for the machine (ibid., p. 230).

Finally, Drucker mentions the strategy of 'delivering what represents true value to the customer' as a type of the strategy of 'changing values and characteristics'. This is similar to the last mentioned strategy as it has its origin in the social and economic reality of potential customers. However, it is dissimilar in the sense that it focuses on what is of 'value' in the customer's mind rather than what the manufacturer can produce for the customer. The following example highlights what is at stake. The furniture manufacturer Herman Miller in Zeeland, Michigan, became known for manufacturing one of the early modern designs, the Earnes chair, which was marketed in 1956. When other manufacturers started selling 'design-chairs', Herman Miller turned to making and selling solutions for whole offices and work stations in hospitals, both with great success. When the 'office of the future' became popular, the company founded the Facilities Management Institute (FMI) in the late 1970s, which was influenced by the development of information technology. FMI does not even sell furniture or equipment, but advises companies on office layout and equipment needed for the best work flow, high productivity and high employee morale, all at low cost. In short, Herman Miller is *defining* 'value' for the customer. As Drucker puts it: 'It is telling the customer: "You may pay for furniture, but you are buying work, morale, productivity. And this is what you should, therefore, be paying for"'. (ibid., p. 232).

The theories of Drucker have had a significant impact on organisational and strategic management studies. However, his theories are first and foremost based on common sense and cases that he has studied himself or read about. In this sense, he is resembles American scholars of management and business studies who frequently apply methods of case studies rather than statistical and quantitative approaches in their research.[1]

6.4 High-Involvement Innovation and Innovation Management; the Theories of J. Bessant

Drucker's theories of innovation management reflect approaches which were influential in the 1980s. In this period, scholars agreed that the relationships between firms, institutions and markets are more complicated than presumed earlier. The emphasis was on customers' expectations and needs when goods are designed and developed rather than on focusing primarily on the role of engineering. The research of N. Rosenberg we highlighted in Chapter 3 is an example of this. In these years, theories of 'learning processes' in innovation activity emerged with their emphasis on incremental innovation (F. Malerba, 1992, pp. 846–7). Eventually, Peter Senge published, in 1990, his book, *The Fifth Discipline: The Art and Practice of the Learning Organization,* that knitted together human resource management and innovation in a consistent theory of 'learning organisations'; that is, a theory which describes how individuals and groups renew and further develop their knowledge and skills in organisations, as well as acquiring a better capacity to adapt the operations of their organisation to changing environments and markets.

In recent years, Senge's ideas have been expanded to the sphere of the whole economy and regions and scholars have accordingly developed the concepts of the 'knowledge economy', 'learning economies' and 'learning regions' which we discussed in Chapter 5. An example of this train of thought in the field of micro-level innovation activity is the techniques and methods of innovation management called 'high-involvement innovation' (J. Bessant, 2005). Let us have a close look at this approach.

Due to their emphasis on high-technology and technological revolutions, many students of innovation have been preoccupied with the role of science and engineering in technical change. This high-tech emphasis has been at the

---

1 The method of case study originates in Harvard Business School, but has its roots in German historicism in social sciences. Around 1900, many Americans studied in German universities and became acquainted with 'historicism' that emphasised the uniqueness of the culture of different nations which is presumed to be the foundation of their social and economic systems and explain their differences. Each nation is similar to a 'case'. Edwin Gay, Dean of Harvard Business School, was one of those who studied in Germany and was a disciple of Gustav Schmoller. Bruce Scott, Michael Porter and Thomas McCraw are examples of contemporary scholars of organizations and management who work in the spirit of the Harvard Business School's German historicism (E.S. Reinert, 2002, pp. 24 and 30–36).

expense of research into the role of incremental innovation in the development of production processes, products and marketing. Innovation management anchored in 'high-involvement innovation' (HII) focuses first and foremost on incremental innovation and has two main targets. One target is to create conditions for 'continuous innovation' (CI) of production methods applied in the production of goods and services. The other target is to focus on 'radical innovation' in organisations i.e., on fostering new production methods and 'doing somethings different' (ibid., p. 17).

'Continuous innovation' is a translation of the Japanese word 'kaizen'. This refers to Japanese management methods which activate all employees in organisations as a whole or in different departments and work groups, in a common search for ways of improving productivity and quality of production and services. Masaaki Imai (1986) analysed 'kaizen' which was introduced in Japan during the 1950s in his book, *Kaizen: The Key to Japan's Competitive Success*. These management methods were not implemented in Western industries until three decades later in relation to methods of 'quality control'. Similar management methods, the so called methods of 'human relations', had been applied before in both Volvo's factory in Kalmar and in Chrysler plants in the 1960s and 1970s. However, it was not until 'kaizen' and 'human relations' methods spread that this perspective became generally accepted in Western industries (J.H. Mendner, 1975). Theories and research into the importance of industrial democracy for the performance, innovation and development of firms are, however, much older than research of 'human relations'. The socialist, G.D.H. Cole, who was one of the main ideologists of guild-socialism and the Fabian Society which is related to the British Labour Party, wrote fundamental books in this field during the first two decades of the twentieth century (G.D.H. Cole, 1917 and 1920).

Radical innovation implies searching for new production methods or new products, but as in the case of kaizen, HII aims at activating all the employees in the organisation, or in a department, in the innovation work. The innovation activity is, therefore, not limited to the work of engineers or specialists in the R&D departments of the firms or organisations. Consequently, HII makes it possible to work across sciences and disciplines. Scientists and staff in different fields and layers in the organisation work together at particular, well-defined improvements and new ideas concerning production processes, goods, services and marketing strategies. In this way, 'innovation communities' emerge within the organisations. The results of HII are learning processes that create new knowledge necessary for improvements and innovation (J. Bessant, 2005, p. 13).

The method 'continuous improvement' aims at incremental innovation, which is indeed very important for value-added creation in the economy as a whole. It is also crucial for the competitiveness of corporations. In the 1980s, significant international research was conducted in the automobile industry in relation to the implementation of 'human relations' strategies and workers' self-control. At that time, it was clear to many that the Japanese car industry enjoyed a significant competitive advantage, compared to its European and American counterparts

(I. Jonsson, 1980). The research indicated that the best factories in this industry (most of them were Japanese) were twice as productive as the average factories, measured in working hours per car produced. The explanation for this difference was to be found in the active participation of the employees in innovation activity based on 'kaizen' – organisation (J. Bessant, 2005, p. 21).

More examples of HII tell a similar story. In 1997 the British Department of Trade and Industry funded research into the fourth part of British companies which were most profitable, 70 companies in all (ibid., pp. 21–2). The research indicated that:

- 90 per cent of them organised formal training of staff linked to the business plan;
- 90 per cent of them claimed that people management had become a higher priority in the past;
- 97 per cent thought training was critical for the success of the business;
- 100 per cent had a team structure;
- 60 per cent formally trained team leaders so that the team system became effective sooner;
- 65 per cent trained their employees to work in teams – it does not just happen.

Other British research indicates that HII is important for corporate performance. It shows that profit per employee is 76 per cent higher in firms which apply human resource management, compared to the average for all firms, that return on capital is 77 per cent and turnover/sales per employee is 33 per cent higher (ibid., p. 22).

Just before the turn of last century, research into 1000 corporations in 7 countries in Europe and Australia[2] indicated that HII had a highly positive impact on their business. The study concluded that, on average, productivity improved by 15 per cent, quality by 16 per cent, delivery performance by 16 per cent, lead-time performance by 15 per cent and product cost was reduced by 8 per cent (J. Bessant, 2005, p. 27).

However, only 10 per cent of firms emphasise this kind of management rather than marketing and finance, despite the indications highlighted above which suggest a significant impact of HII for corporate performance (ibid., p. 23).

The aim of HII is both to increase the productivity of existing technology and production methods and to create conditions for radical innovation leading to a new manufacturing technology, products and services. Briefly, we claim that HII is first and foremost an innovation technique consisting of 5 main steps to be taken in order to change firms and organisations from stagnated structures that 'do things as we have always done here' to organisations which 'do what we do better' and 'do something different'. Let us take a closer look at these five steps.

---

2   The European countries are Denmark, Finland, the Netherlands, Norway, Sweden and the UK.

Each step is more systematic than the previous step, better organised and more extensive. The first step in the transformation process, the *Precursors*, is characterised by 'natural' or background improvement, *ad hoc* and short term. The second step, the *Structured* step, comprises formal attempts to create and sustain HII. The third step, the *Goal oriented* step, presumes that HII is directed at company goals and objectives. The fourth step, the *Proactive* step, is characterised by the fact that HII is largely self-driven by individuals and groups. The fifth step, the step of *Strong innovation capability*, anticipates that HII has become the dominant culture in the organisation – 'the way we are doing things around here' (ibid., pp. 57–8).

An organisation which has embraced the culture of the fifth level emphasises values and attitudes that strengthen the close collaboration of its employees, tolerance and creativity. Values of this kind are reflected in attitudes such as:

- Everything can always be improved
- The best ideas on how to improve the company's processes and systems, including the process of continuous improvement itself, come from the people using them
- We need to learn from other people, other ideas, other processes
- Our people are trusted to have the desire and commitment to improve their work
- Innovation requires a blame-free culture
- The role of the manager in this 'continuous improvement' (CI) process is to enable people to express their ideas and to empower them to implement their proposed solutions (ibid., p. 203).

Successful embedding of culture and values of this kind in an organisation requires that employees be (re)trained i.e., both managers and other staff members, to tackle criticism and change. The biggest impediment to improvements is often managers who are afraid of critique or of losing their power position.

Briefly, we would claim that HII is an innovation technique which aims at improving employees' skills and capacity at the same time as the organisations' innovation performance is boosted. Before taking note of techniques which enhance the innovation ability of employees, we should discuss what this capacity consists of.

Mainly eight types of abilities are relevant in this respect. *Firstly*, there is the ability to understand CI; i.e., the ability to articulate its basic values. *Secondly*, there is the ability to generate sustained involvement in CI. *Thirdly*, there is the ability to focus and link CI activities to strategic goals of the company. *Fourthly*, there is the ability to lead, direct and support the creation and sustaining of CI behaviours. *Fifthly*, there is the ability to create consistency between CI values and behaviour and the organisational context (structures, procedures, etc.). *Sixthly*, there is the ability to move CI activity across organisational boundaries. *Seventhly*, there is the ability to strategically manage the development of

CI. *Eighthly*, there is, finally, the ability to enable learning to take place and be captured at all levels.

The fostering of these different competencies in organisations requires employees and the organisation as a whole to take on certain behaviour patterns which embed and reproduce the HII culture in the organisation. What is at stake is to enhance employees' ability to increase continuous innovation by fostering appropriate behaviours. *Firstly*, the ability to understand CI and to articulate its basic values has to be developed. Appropriate behaviour would presume that people at all levels would demonstrate a shared belief that assumes that everyone can contribute by being actively involved in making and recognising incremental improvements. Furthermore, when something goes wrong, people at all levels would look for reasons why it happened rather than to blaming the individual(s).

Secondly, CI has to become a habit so that involvement in CI will be sustained. That would require behaviour patterns according to which employees make use of a formal problem finding and solving cycle. Hence, they use appropriate tools and techniques to support CI. Furthermore, employees use consistent measurement tools that help shaping the improvement process and (as individuals and/or groups) initiate and carry through CI activities.

Thirdly, the ability to focus CI and link it to the strategic goals of the company has to be fostered. In this case, individuals and groups use the organisation's strategic goals and objectives to focus and prioritise improvements. Individuals and groups (such as departments and CI teams) assess their proposed changes against departmental or company objectives so that they are consistent with them. Furthermore, individuals and groups monitor the results of their improvement activity and the impact it has on strategic or departmental goals.

Fourthly, the ability to lead and support the creation and sustaining of CI behaviours must be fostered. In order to do that, behaviours should be introduced according to which managers support the CI process through allocation of time, money, space and other resources. Managers recognise in formal ways the contribution of employees to CI and lead by example. By so doing they become actively involved in the design and implementation of CI. Managers do not punish employees for mistakes, but support experiments by encouraging learning from them.

Fifthly, the ability to align CI and create consistency between CI values, behaviour and the organisational structures and procedures, etc. should be fostered. Behaviour practices should be introduced that secure ongoing assessment and organisational changes that ensure that, on the one hand, the organisation's structure and infrastructure and, on the other hand, the CI system consistently support and reinforce each other. Furthermore, individuals responsible for particular processes/systems in the organisation, organise continuous reviews in order to assess the compatibility of these processes/systems and the CI system. In similar way, it is ensured that the CI system is assessed and adjusted to planned organisational changes.

Sixthly, the ability of the employees to take part in shared problem solving and moving CI activity across organisational boundaries, must be fostered. Fostering this ability requires that people learn to cooperate across internal divisions in the organisation and they must as well learn work in cross-functional groups besides working in their specific areas. Furthermore, the employees must learn to share a holistic view of the organisation and become oriented towards internal and external customers in their CI activity. Hence, they learn to cooperate with customers, suppliers and others.

Seventhly, employees' ability should be fostered to improve constantly procedures of continuous improvements and strategically manage the development of CI. That would require adoption of behaviour in which it becomes natural to continually monitor and develop the CI system. In this case a particular individual or group monitors the CI system and measures the CI activity in the organisation and its results. The CI system is regularly reviewed and, if necessary, amended (single-loop learning). Furthermore, a periodic review of the CI system is performed in relation to the organisation as a whole, which may bring about a major regeneration of the CI system and the organisation (double-loop learning). For this purpose, senior management makes sufficient resources available, such as time, money, personnel to support the continuous development of the CI system.

Eighthly, the ability to enable learning to take place and develop a 'learning organisation' at all levels of the organisation must be fostered. In order to do that, employees need to be able to learn from their positive as well as negative experiences. Each individual learns how to seek out opportunities for learning and personal development and set their own learning objectives. It must become natural for all individuals and groups at all levels to share their learning from all work experiences. Furthermore, the organisation must consistently articulate, share and spread the learning of individuals and groups. Hence, mechanisms must be provided to ensure that what individuals and teams learn is captured and spread. Finally, designated individual(s) diffuse the learning that is captured across the organisation with the help of relevant and effective organisational mechanisms (J. Bessant, 2005, pp. 227–8).

Keeping in mind the five steps highlighted above and the extent to which the innovation ability of employees is optimised as they take on the behaviour patterns discussed above, the organisation can develop itself from one step to another. Let us analyse these steps in relation to behaviour patterns that characterise each level. These differ concerning the scope and depth of HII.

According to J. Bessant, *the first step*, the pre-CI step, refers to the point in time when interest in the concept of CI awakens. The interest may come about following a crisis, by attendance at a seminar, by a visit to another organisation, etc., but in the pre-CI step implementation is on an ad hoc basis. This step is accompanied by behaviour patterns that are characterised by solving problems randomly. No formal efforts or structure exist for improving the organisation and improvement efforts are scattered. Solutions tend to realise short term benefits and no measurable targets are defined related to their strategic impact on human resources, finance etc. Moreover, CI as a process is not known to staff and management.

The second step, referred to by J. Bessant as structured CI, is characterised by the fact that formal commitment has been introduced to build a system that will develop CI across the organisation. Furthermore, the organisation has initiated CI or equivalent improvement measures. Staff behaviour is characterised by use of structured problem-solving processes and high proportion of employees participate in CI activities. In this step, employees are trained in using basic CI tools and structured idea-management system is in place. Recognition system has been introduced, but CI activities have not been integrated into day-to-day operations.

Taking *the third step*, the step of goal-orientated CI, the organisation is committed to linking CI behaviour, established at 'local' level, to the wider strategic concerns of the organisation. Besides having introduced all the behaviour patterns mentioned in the steps above, the organisation has now started formal deployment of strategic goals. Furthermore, CI is monitored and measured against these goals and CI activities become part of the main (business) activities of the organisation. The focus is now on cross-boundary and even cross-enterprise problem solving.

In *the fifth step*, the proactive CI, attempts are made to introduce principles of autonomy and to empower individuals and groups to manage and direct their own processes. In addition to the behaviour patterns mentioned above, CI responsibilities are now devolved to problem-solving unit and high levels of experimentation prevails.

In *the final step*, the step of full CI capability, the organisation reaches the stage of 'learning organisation'. Besides the behaviour patterns mentioned above, the organisation is now characterised by a culture of extensive and widely distributed learning behaviour. Problems are systematically searched for and solutions are found at the same time as experience is captured and learning is shared across the organisation. Experimentation in the organisation is widespread, autonomous and controlled (J. Bessant, 2005, pp. 229).[3]

The above analysis of the relationship between HII, different categories of innovation abilities and behavioural patterns constitutes the framework that shapes techniques and methods of innovation management. The technique itself and the methods differ depending on the kind of organisation they are applied to. Examples of tools employed are brainstorming meetings, boxes to collect ideas, newsletters, blackboards for suggestions, statistics on the number of ideas of improvement over a particular period, success of improvements etc.

---

3 As we will learn from the discussion on social innovations in Chapter 7, the steps described above have many similarities to Benjamin Franklin's eighteenth century organisation of the activities of his Junto club.

Chapter 7
Social Innovation and Entrepreneurship

The half-wit does not know that gold
Makes apes of many men:
One is rich, one is poor
There is no blame in that.
Cattle die, kindred die,
Every man is mortal:
But the good name never dies
Of one who has done well.
From *Hávamál* (more than a thousand year old Norse poem)

7.1 Introduction

It is claimed in Havamal that ' … gold makes apes of many men'. The meaning of this claim is that accumulation of wealth may diminish a person's intelligence. People are not evaluated in terms of their wealth, but in terms of their reputation which is eternal. It is well to keep this in mind when we observe social innovation and entrepreneurship. Motivations behind social innovations do not concern accumulation of wealth and maximisation of profits. In this chapter, we will discuss innovation activity that aims at social improvements. First we will discuss mainstream definitions of social innovation and offer a wider alternative definition that covers different levels of this kind of activity; that is, micro-, meso- and macro-levels of social innovation. Finally, we will observe the cases of Lord Nelson, Benjamin Franklin and Margaret Thatcher in order to illustrate processes at these different levels of social innovations.

7.2 The Concept of Social Innovation

Researchers of social innovation usually limit this concept to innovation that takes place in the social economy.[1] However, although the bulk of social innovation

---

1   Non-profit activity and activity that aims at social reforms has been variously labelled in scholarly discussion. Terms have been used like 'social economy', 'the third sector', 'the voluntary sector', 'civil society', 'the independent sector', 'the third economy' and 'non-profit sector'. The last mentioned term, 'the non-profit sector' is traditionally used by US scholars, referring to particular subsector of the 'third sector'. In Europe the term 'social economy' is traditionally applied to non-profit activity and activity aiming at social reforms. A common feature of these concepts is the idea that there exists in

may occur in this area, it is not confined to the social economy since it is not limited to organisations as such. Individuals are often important social innovators who initiate social improvement. The concept of social innovation may be defined as innovation activity leading to social improvements. This is a definition common to many studies of this subject.[2] A more substantive definition is to be found in the work of M.D. Mumford (2002, p. 253) who emphasises that social innovation refers to creation and implementation of new ideas about how people should organise interpersonal activities, or social interactions, to meet one or more common goals. At first glance this definition appears to focus on activities at the micro-level of social life, but by referring to common goals the concept of social innovation may be developed further so that it covers social organisation at micro-, meso- and macro-level. At the micro-level social innovation refers to developing and implementing social relations which lead to new ways of interaction between individuals. Micro-social innovation would affect internal relations between individuals in groups and social interaction within organisations. Meso-social innovations refer to interactions between organisations such as stakeholder associations, organised interests and the state. Macro-social innovations imply changes in social relations and interactions between individuals and organisations at a societal scale, referring long term structural changes in the way society as a whole is organised. Let us elaborate further on this concept of social innovation.

Social innovation, involves the generation and implementation of new ideas about social relationships and social organisation as well as developing ways and means to realise them. A distinction should be made between scope and levels of social innovations. *The scope of social innovations* may range from rearranging interpersonal or inter-organisational relations in the name of altruistic aims to the ambition of maximising profit. As for levels of social innovations, they may be realised and implemented on micro-, meso- and/or macro-level. *Micro-level social innovation* refers to developing and implementing social relations which lead to new ways of interaction between individuals. Micro-social innovation would affect internal relations between individuals in groups and social interaction within social institutions and organisations. Hence, at micro-level, social innovation may rearrange interpersonal relations in such intimate institutions as the family or

---

capitalist societies a separate sphere of activity alongside the market and the state. This kind of activity is characterised by a social or economic calling which appears in altruism independent of claims for profit (L.M. Salamon, 1999, p. 3; OECD, 2003, p. 10). Some basic characteristics of this kind of activity have been highlighted, such as: It takes place in the form of organisations; they are private, as opposed to governmental; non-profit-distributing; self-governing; voluntary; and aim at public benefit (L.M. Salamon, 1999, p. 10). A recent UN report (L.M. Salamon et al., 2012, p. 2) shows that in 13 developed and developing countries the size of this sector in terms of percentage of total work force is 7.4 per cent. Out of this figure, 5.2 per cent are paid workers while 2.2 per cent is voluntary work. However, large sectors are not included in these figures, such as cooperative movements and mutuals.

2   For an overview of this kind of definitions, see C. Crepaldi et al., 2012, pp. 20–22.

more or less formalised interrelations between workers in the production unit of a workplace. In the case of Benjamin Franklin, his partnership with his apprentices in printing would be an example at hand. *Meso-level social innovations* refer to interactions between organisations such as stakeholder associations, organised interests and the state. Hence, at meso-level, social innovation may generate various forms of partnerships and collaboration at regional level such as the organisation of provincial innovation clusters or corporate alliances at national and global level, etc. In the case of Franklin, the establishment of the University of Pennsylvania is an example of this, when he arranged collaboration between various religious sects and stakeholders. *Macro-level social innovations* imply changes in social relations and interactions between individuals and organisations at a societal scale since they relate to long term structural change in the way society as a whole is organised. Social innovation at this level suggests societal structural transformations which encompass social, political, economic and technological developments such as the transformation of feudal society to capitalism, the transformation of Japanese society in the Meji period (D.E. Westney, 1987), the Nazi regime in Germany, varieties of post war welfare capitalism (P.A. Hall and D.W. Soskice, 2001) and the recent neoliberal revolution (I. Jonsson, 2012). In this context it would be sensible to refer to the formation and implementation of 'societal paradigms' that define the various forms societies take and their trajectories of development. Such societal paradigms are composed of 'techno-economic paradigms', 'power-political paradigms', 'reproduction-social paradigms' and 'ethical-prescriptive paradigms' (for a more detailed discussion, see I. Jonsson, 2001, pp. 331–2).[3] Figure 7.1. highlights the different dimensions of social innovation with some examples.

Social innovation is basically an activity involving processes of structurisation in which actors or agents engage in structuring social relations at different levels of society. The agents may rearrange elements of existing social structures and relations or they may introduce elements based on novel ideas and create new social relations and social structures. However, the acts of (re)structuring often lead to unforeseen results which require new ideas and strategies to be developed. Consequently, social innovation as a process of (re)structurisation is largely an experimental, non-teleological enterprise. Let us discuss the ontological implications accompanying this approach.

---

3 'Societal paradigms' concern fundamental principles upon which societal development is to be based. These principles refer to basic ideas as to how society is best organised, and when they become dominant they shape societal development over long periods. These paradigms are mediated through hegemonic politics (I. Jonsson, 1995, pp. 32–44) in which organised socio-economic forces struggle for their interests within the framework of alternatives that structural conditions allow.

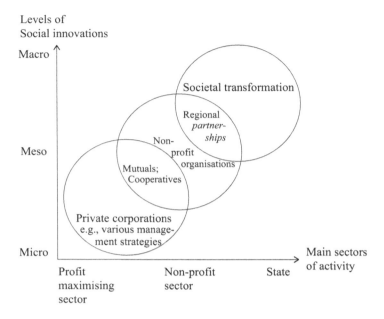

Figure 7.1   Levels of social innovation and main sectors of activity

7.3 On the Ontology of Social Innovations

From the point of view of ontology, in order to explain the occurrence of particular social relations (or social formations) in certain space and time (the explanandum), one has to observe the structure and powers that characterise the agents, social institutions and organisations (the explanans) that led to the social relations (or social formations) in question. One has to examine the specific propensities of the explanans that leads to certain kinds of change; that is, their causal and potential powers. Thus propensities comprise, on the one hand, causal powers of the explanans; that is, their capacities to behave in particular ways leading to actual results, or the explanandum. On the other hand, propensities involve potential powers which may be activated and lead to different results in different contexts. The same objects, or explanantia, may, therefore, lead to more than one result, depending on the propensities of the phenomena they encounter and the contexts in which the encounter takes place (I. Jonsson, 2012, p. 7).

Causal relations of this kind occur in 'open systems' (A. Sayer, 2000, p. 15) such as in everyday social contexts in which agents' interrelations are characterised by strategic intentions, norms and values and in which the agents attempt to change or reproduce the social contexts, norms and values, behavioural patterns, operations of institutions and power relations between agents and institutions. In short, social agents are engaged in processes of social construction and transformation of social contexts.

However, social construction is not voluntary by nature because social agents reflectively 'interiorise' existing norms and values in their processes of socialisation,[4] but at the same time they are faced with social contexts of 'sticky' structures of social relations. Social structures, like other structures, are composed of internally related elements whose causal powers, when combined, are emergent from those of their constituents. On the basis of this view of scientific explanation, we would claim that analysis of social innovation and 'social windows of opportunity' must concentrate on social innovators as agents of structurisation. These are always bounded in particular contexts of balances of power or power structures which determine their alternatives in forming the aims and scope of their social innovation, as well as the means to realise them. The balance of power refers to the distribution of power resources among actors such as stakeholders and interest groups in particular societal fields. The power resources relate to means such as organisational strength, ideological apparatuses, universities and research institutions, lobbyism, framing, dominant culture etc. (I. Jonsson, 2012). Let us concretise this rather abstract approach and focus on activities of social innovation.

In Chapter 5 we mentioned that researchers of innovation focus on partnerships of actors that affect the conditions for innovation. We discussed theories of 'Triple Helix' (H. Etzkowitz, 2008) which explain differences in regional economic growth by analysing the conditions for industrial innovations within regional variations of 'Triple Helix' constellations; that is, in terms of systemic interrelations between three elements, namely university, industry and government. Approaches of this kind tend to be rather taxonomical and suffer from lack of understanding of how such constellations are generated. The fourth element is missing; that is to say, the role actors and procedures play in realising Triple Helix constellations. Consequently, we would claim that a concept of 'Quatro Helix dynamics' is needed which involves the role of actors in order to analyse the dynamics of structurisation of partnerships between the elements of Triple Helix constellations. We will now attempt to explain what is at stake by concentrating on social innovation and highlight processes of structurisation of social innovations, since it appears that such innovations progress through certain steps or stages.

We would claim that stages of social innovation start with the 'associative' steps of searching for social problems to be defined and generating solutions. These starting phases proceed to the stage of implementing solutions as social

---

4 The process is not to be considered in terms of 'internalization' as it is active and not mechanistic. The individuals in question are both marked by the socialisation they went through in their social background, or 'habitus' (cf. P. Bourdieu, 1993, pp. 78–9) and the constant process of 'interiorisation', but not mechanistic 'internalisation', in which they reflect on their present and past 'situations' and develop their 'horizons' and world views that affect possible puzzle definitions and imagined solutions (cf. J.P. Sartre, 1972; I. Craib, 1976, p. 28; H.-G. Gadamer, 1977).

innovations. Implemented social modifications subsequently enter a stage of transforming the innovations as a response to experience of how they actually work in reality. Figure 7.2 highlights the main features of the social innovation processes.

In order to illustrate social innovations as processes of structurisation and in terms of levels, scopes and stages, we would prefer to highlight historical cases such as the leadership of Vice Admiral Lord Horatio Nelson as an example of micro-level social innovation (J.F. Callo, 1999). Benjamin Franklin introduced many new ideas and projects for social improvement and activated many independent stakeholders in order to realise ideas for the betterment of society and formulate common goals (M.D. Mumford, 2002). Franklin's social innovations are good examples of meso-level innovations. Macro-level social innovations refer to societal transformation and often arise from extreme social struggle or are implemented in the shadow of totalitarian regimes. As examples of such macro-social innovations we would mention the transformation of Japanese society in the Meji period (D.E. Westney, 1987), varieties of post war welfare capitalism (P.A. Hall and D.W. Soskice, 2001) and the recent neoliberal revolution (I. Jonsson, 2012). Below we will observe the case of M. Thatcher's macro-social innovation.

7.4 Lord Horatio Nelson's Micro-level Social Innovation

Vice Admiral Lord Horatio Nelson (1758–1805) is considered by many to be one of the few persons that had a profound impact on history. He marked his place in

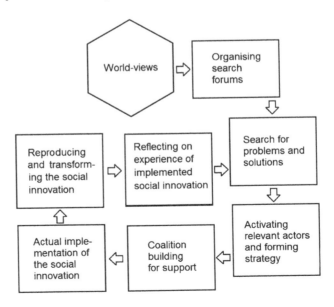

Figure 7.2   **General model of social innovation processes**

history with his innovations in military tactics and victorious battles of the Nile, Copenhagen and Trafalgar in the Napoleonic Wars. He is particularly famous for his combat tactics and victory in the Battle of Trafalgar in 1805, which was fundamental for England's global military dominance at sea and the growth of the British Empire.

Lord Nelson was a highly religious person, being a son of a clergyman in Burnham Thorpe in Norfolk, England. He was the fifth son and sixth child of Edmund Nelson and his wife, Catherine's, 11 children (A.T. Mahan, 1897). Catherine's maiden name was Suckling. His mother died when he was 9 years old which must have been a great shock to a child at this age. Many biographies of Horatio Nelson indicate that he was a highly sensitive person and attribute that to the loss of his mother.

Horatio was attached to the sea early on as he grew up in Burnham Thorpe, in Norfolk, a county which lies along the eastern coast of England, bordering the North Sea. With the help of his uncle, Captain Maurice Suckling, Nelson became an ordinary seaman and coxswain only 12 years old on Suckling's ship *HMS Raisonnable*. Shortly after boarding, Nelson was appointed a midshipman and began officer training. Suckling was a highly respected gentleman and influential in the British Admiralty. He became Controller of the Navy in 1775 and was able to enhance Nelson's career. Nelson became a lieutenant 19 years old and was appointed captain at the age of 20. Eighteen years later, he entered yet another stage in his career as he became Commander in 1796 and Vice-Admiral in 1801. Finally, in 1803, he became Chief Commander over the Mediterranean fleet. During his long career, he served on various ships and world oceans. What is interesting and important for our case is the fact that Lord Nelson's career indicates he worked on and had practical experience or insight into the actual work and working conditions at all levels of the hierarchy on board ships of the Royal Navy.

7.4.1 Nelson's Personality

Nelson's personality was probably a necessary, although not sufficient, condition for his success as an innovative and victorious commander. He is said to have been a sensitive person because he lost his mother at an early age. This experience may have made him a more understanding person who was able to interiorise other persons' feelings and points of view. This is a particularly valuable capacity for a leader who needs to build trust and motivation among his shipmates and to develop teams and a culture of collaboration on board.

Sensitiveness was not his only personality trait. He showed physical courage and mental toughness as well as aggressiveness (J.F. Callo, 1999, pp. 14 and 20). His physical courage was notorious as he was recurrently in the frontline in his battles at sea and was unafraid of risking his life. As examples of this, one may refer to night action off Cadiz when his boat crew was greatly outnumbered by the enemy. Nelson led a successful and desperate hand-to-hand struggle. This incident is among the most enduring examples which have kept his fame alive in for more than two centuries. Another occurrence of a similar nature took place at the beginning of the Battle of Trafalgar. Nelson refused to conceal his identity by covering his conspicuous medals and awards. He was exposed to French sharpshooters and this appears to have contributed to his death in combat at Trafalgar.

Perhaps Lord Nelson's best known example of physical courage, however, is his part in the siege of Calvi and the assault on Santa Cruz. Indeed, as is well known, he lost the sight in his right eye at the siege of Calvi 1794 (A.T. Mahan, 1897, pp. 2299–2304 and 4594–4605).

Lord Nelson's personality was characterised by mental toughness and a strong belief in his convictions. He was a persuasive person who would not easily yield, not even to orders from his commanders, for example when he believed concrete battle situations required. In 1799 he disobeyed orders from Admiral Keith to join his fleet and sail for Minorca. Nelson decided to defend the Kingdom of Naples instead of Minorca. As it turned out, Nelson could not have accompanied Admiral Keith's fleet nor in the event did any harm come to Minorca. However, Nelson had no information in his possession indicating that an encounter between the two great fleets was impossible (A.T. Mahan, 1897, pp. 6619–6620).

This was not the only instance in which he would risk his professional and political career. This was demonstrated in the Battle of Cape St. Vincent in 1797. At the early, critical stage of the battle he turned his ship out of formation and, by so doing, precipitated the close combat desired by his commander-in-chief, Jervis. Due to Nelson's quick and bold action, the Spanish were entirely defeated (ibid., pp. 4137–4140).

The Battle of Copenhagen in 1801 was another example of Lord Nelson's willingness to follow his own battle tactics in preference to orders. Nelson's response to his Commander-in-Chief's flagged signal to break off the fight is famous. Nelson ignored orders to leave off action, put his telescope to his blind eye and declared: 'I have only one eye. I have a right to be blind sometimes. I really do not see the signal'. Again, he secured victory out of a lost battle situation with his bold decisions, choosing boldness over a safer course (J.F. Callo, 1999, pp. 22–3). Here he showed his ability to adapt to changing circumstances under fire, similar to today's manoeuvre warfare. But, the battle was costly. In total the British lost 350 killed, and the Danes 6,000 killed, wounded, or prisoner. The story became part of the Nelson's myth, although the battle turned out to have been unnecessary,[5] it fell apart and would have done so without the bloodshed of April 2 (J. Wilson, 2001, pp. 14–15).

---

5   On March 24, even before the battle was fought, the mad Czar Paul I of Russia was assassinated. He was the force behind the Second League of Armed Neutrality, or the League of the North, which was an alliance of the north European naval powers Denmark – Norway, Prussia, Sweden, and Russia and had the goal of securing free shipping of goods to the First Republic of France, against the Royal Navy's wartime policy.

An additional character trait of Lord Nelson was his aggressiveness. His aggressiveness clearly appeared in his battle tactics and in the act of battle. When he received the order to retire from his fleet commander, Sir Hyde Parker, at the Battle of Copenhagen, Nelson's reaction was emphatic, 'Leave off action! Now, damn me if I do'. In the Battle of Trafalgar he used an aggressive tactic which directly opposed the conservative doctrines of the Royal Navy. One of his famous phrases was 'the boldest measures are the safest'. Rather than following the traditional tactic of lining up the battle ships in two opposing lines, he broke up the British line into two groups of ships that opposed the Spanish and French fleet and cut through the lines of the enemy (J.F. Callo, 1999, p. 23).[6]

Lord Nelson was a patriotic and religious person. These are important factors for his unusual and strong motivation to do his duty for his country and his willingness to do his best in his service. His patriotism and religion legitimised his readiness to sacrifice himself and let God decide his fate. He was fighting for a higher cause. His motivation for fighting against French was not only due to his hatred of that country which biographers contribute to his mother's attitude, but apparently had its roots in his belief in monarchy and the defence of his religion. He presumed monarchy was the ideal political system and that the French republic did not only threaten that form of government, but was also a threat to Christian religion in general (ibid., pp. 19 and 24). Lord Nelson's advice to his Midshipmen (1793) somewhat reflects his way of thinking: ' … you must consider every man your enemy who speaks ill of your king; and … you must hate a Frenchman, as you do the devil'. (T.J. Pettigrew, 1849, p. 580).

As outlined above, it appears that Lord Nelson himself was not a conformist and did not follow orders blindly. He had started his career at the age of 12 and worked himself up the ranks in the fleet. He had, therefore, profound knowledge of seamanship and work in the Navy. His experience of the varied duties to be undertaken in a warship made it easier for him to identify himself with the crew on board and helped the crew to identify themselves with him. This is a human relations resource which helped Lord Nelson to contribute to an interesting micro-social innovation in relation to leadership style and the work motivation of his subordinates.

7.4.2 Lord Nelson, the Micro-level Social Innovator

Lord Nelson introduced relations with his subordinates that were quite unusual in the late eighteenth and early nineteenth century. He was famous for his engagement in the work conditions and personal problems of the seamen in his ships and he showed great consideration for their health and wellbeing. He discussed their

---

6   Nelson did not 'invent' this tactic, but implemented it as tactical innovation in sea battle. This tactic was already used by Admiral Jervis at the Battle of Cape St Vincent, 14th of February 1797 and the same year by Admiral Duncan at the Battle of Camperdown, 11th October, 1797 (P. Padfield, 2000, p. 99).

problems with them in person, independent of their position in the hierarchy on board. This created mutual respect and led to strong motivation among the sailors to fight and do their duty. Lord Nelson also discussed his strategic plans and war tactics with his subordinates and encouraged them to comment and present their own ideas. In this sense, he introduced processes of team building which fostered an atmosphere where obedience enforced by discipline and punishment was minimised. The sailors were, therefore, self-motivated. Indeed, Lord Nelson reduced the use of severe physical punishment and his leadership was characterised by mild punishment which was unusual in his era (J.F. Callo, 1999, pp. 27–8).

However, Horatio Nelson was not only a successful team builder in terms of involving his subordinates in mutual information exchange and 'brain-storming' procedures. He also introduced an organisational principle which superseded linguistic information exchanges by a mode of tacit knowledge learning. This he did in relation to his innovation of 'combat doctrine' as it is called today.

Very briefly, a combat doctrine refers to battlefield operations that aim at streamlining the movement of units on the field to achieve unit cohesion and strategic/tactical victory, while attempting to keep losses due to enemy action to a minimum. In this context 'doctrine' refers to principles by which military forces guide their actions in support of objectives. It is authoritative, but requires judgement in application (SA Navy, 2006, p. 106).

Combat doctrine is enduring and contextual and evolves in response to changes in the political or strategic environment, in the light of experience, or as a result of new technology. In turn, it influences the way in which policy and plans are developed, forces organised and trained, and equipment procured. Sailors' understanding of a combat doctrine provides a common approach and way of thinking, which is not bound by prescriptive rules. This leads, through training, to consistent behaviour, mutual confidence and properly orchestrated collective action that allows for individual initiative (ibid., p 5).

Lord Nelson's work with combat doctrine is interesting in relation to both leadership of organisation and organisation of leadership. In short, Lord Nelson broke with the paradigm of centralised control which had developed in the eighteenth century in the Royal and European navies. Following the expansion of European colonial powers and their navies in the sixteenth and seventeenth centuries, sailing navies evolved into complex organisations, and systems of command developed accordingly, while bureaucracies expanded ashore. In order to secure better control, ship types were reduced and standardised, a naval officer corps developed and large fleets were broken up into divisions. Each division would have its own flag officer. Finally, the line ahead formation became the accepted order in battle (M.A. Palmer, 1988, pp. 105–6).

Curiously enough, despite the professionalization, standardisation and divisional organisation, the fleets were not easily manoeuvrable and slow in acute battle situations. A doctrine was developed to provide a shared philosophy, such as the *Fighting instructions* of the Royal Navy, so that all parties would act in a coordinated manner. But, despite a common doctrine, chaos prevailed in immediate battles due to the primitive communications systems available at that time in history. This situation called for improvements in communication and in the last quarter of the eighteenth century, visual signalling underwent remarkable development in an effort to bring order to naval engagements. Increasingly detailed signalling made direct control possible by a commander in chief. *The Fighting instructions* gave way to the signal book as commanders' main resource of instruction. However, enhanced centralised control over fleets did not do the trick in actual battles where swiftness and independent decisions of ship captains are more effective than waiting for signals from commanders.

This appears from comparing famous battles of Admiral Sir George Rodney, Earl Howe and Lord Nelson. In the Battle of Saintes in 1782, Rodney intended to exercise nearly full centralised control with 40 flags and 7 pendants. His fleet won the battle with 5 of the 30 French ships captured. Earl Howe's, 'Black Dick's' Glorious First of June Battle in 1794 which took place west of Usher, France, was also tightly centralised. Earl Howe used 14 signals; 8 general to the fleet and 6 to individual ships. His fleet destroyed 7 out of the 26 ships it faced (ibid., p. 106). These victories were presumed to be exceptionally successful due to the superior performance of centralised control and signalling. However, Lord Nelson rejected the view that centralised control and signalling would produce a decisive victory. His experience led him towards the decentralised philosophy of command which suited his character traits better; that is, almost ceaseless activity, personal sacrifice, heroism and a sense of duty (ibid., p. 107). This is the soil out of which Lord Nelson's social innovation grew i.e., the 'Band of Brothers' and the 'Nelson Touch' as he called it (ibid., pp. 111 and 110).

The decisive technique developed during the preparations for the Battle of Nile in 1798 and proved crucial in 1805 in the Battle of Trafalgar. Rather than believing in a technological revolution of communication and centralised control, Nelson provided a coherent battle doctrine and trusted his subordinates to act at the hour of battle with independent initiative within the frame of the doctrine. His stand was that the best way to win a battle was to bring the enemy as quickly as possible to close combat and give his subordinates a thorough indoctrination before the engagement, and near complete initiative once it had begun (ibid., p. 110). One of the cornerstones of this strategy was, therefore, self-confidence building among the subordinates and their trust in each other as well as in Lord Nelson himself.[7]

Two months before the Battle of the Nile at Aboukir Bay on the first of August 1798, while Nelson was searching for the French fleet in the Mediterranean, he ordered his captains to the flagship *Vanguard* where all became acquainted with his ideas 'ideas and intentions ... by which means signals became almost unnecessary ... ' noted his flag captain Edward Berry (cited in M.A. Palmer, 1988,

---

7 This way of preparing battle and leaning on individual initiative closely resembles how Inuits 'organised' their hunting i.e., a culture that developed centuries before Nelson was born. See I. Jonsson, 1996 and R. Petersen, 1992.

p. 111). Earl Howe told Berry after the Nile that 'It stood unparalleled and singular in this instance, that every captain distinguished himself'. (ibid., p. 111).

At the Nile, Nelson's 13 of the line captured 9 of the 13 French liners and burned 2. The victory was complete.

'The Band of Brotherhood' was more than a forum for information in which Lord Nelson briefed his ideas of possible scenarios in future battles. "The Nelson Touch", as he called it himself in a letter of first of October 1805 to Lady Hamilton, was crucial. However, he never explained what he meant by this concept, but it appears that he was referring to his personal charismatic leadership and subordinates' strong belief in his doctrine (N.H. Nicolas, 1846, p. 60). However, Nelson would strongly emphasise the importance of the independence of his subordinates and their own judgement in the act of battle. This and the intimacy and communion he had with his subordinates clearly appears in his letter to Vice admiral Collingwood before the Battle of Trafalgar. Twelve days before the Battle, on the ninth of October 1805, he communicated in writing his celebrated Plan of Attack to every captain under his command. The plan is an 830 word secret Memorandum (ibid., pp. 89–92). In his letter to Collingwood he wrote:

> The reception I met with on joining the Fleet caused the sweetest sensation of my life. The Officers who came on board to welcome my return, forgot my rank as Commander-in-Chief, in the enthusiasm with which they greeted me. As soon as these emotions were past, I laid before them the Plan I had previously arranged for attacking the Enemy; and it was not only my pleasure to find it generally approved, but clearly perceived and understood. (Published in N.H. Nicolas, 1846, pp. 66–7)

His attitude towards his subordinates and trust in them is reflected in his letter to Vice-Admiral Collingwood:

> I send you my Plan of Attack, as far as a man dare venture to guess at the very uncertain position the Enemy may be found in. But, my dear friend, it is to place you perfectly at ease respecting my intentions and to give full scope to your judgment for carrying them into effect. (Published in N.H. Nicolas, 1846, p. 95)

At Trafalgar, the British fleet was outnumbered and outgunned. The allied fleet had 33 ships of the line and nearly 30,000 men and 2568 guns, but the British had 27 ships of the line and 17,000 men and 2148 guns. However, the British victory was colossal as they took 22 vessels of the Franco-Spanish fleet and lost none.

7.4.3 The legacy of Nelson as a Micro Social Innovator

As M.A. Palmer highlights, Lord Nelson's skills as naval commander can best be understood within the framework of a modern term, C3 – command, control and communication. Nelson's colleagues, Rodney, Howe and others overemphasised the technological innovations in signalling and exaggerated the use of centralised control. Hence, in practice they skewed the balance of the C3 equation (M.A. Palmer, 1988, pp. 105 and 106). They failed to realise the importance of vivid communication and decentralised control which emphasises diffusing responsibility downwards to subordinates.

Consequently, we would claim that the legacy of Lord Nelson is foremost his micro-level social innovations; that is, his practice of fostering what today is called 'human relations' and various motivation theories, ranging from A. Maslow's (1943) hierarchy of needs[8] to observations of reward management (M.A. Murlis and H. Murlis, 2004), emphasising the importance of intrinsic as opposed to extrinsic rewards.[9] In relation to Lord Nelson, Maslow's emphasis on everyone's need for love and belonging was satisfied to some extent by Nelson's practice of fostering friendship relations with his subordinates by showing interest in their health and personal situation. Furthermore, Maslow highlights the importance of everyone's need for esteem. Nelson showed great respect and strengthened his subordinates' self-esteem and confidence by demonstrating his respect for and interest in their work. Esteem is also fostered by satisfying the need to be respected by others. Nelson fulfilled that need by his heroism and by being generally respected as one of Britain's most successful commanders. Finally, self-actualisation is one of the fundamental human needs that Maslow emphasises. This would refer to the human need for morality, creativity, spontaneity and problem solving. Nelson appears to have given his subordinates the opportunity for morality with his repeated emphasis on doing one's duty, cf. his patriotic signal sent from his flagship HMS Victory as the Battle of Trafalgar was about to commence: 'England expects every man will do his duty'. Lastly, his strategy of decentralising control, which required optimal trust in his subordinates' initiative and individual responsibility in battle, well satisfied the need for creativity, spontaneity and problem solving.

Along with Lord Nelson's human relations related legacy, is his way of fostering trust with regard to management. Students of leadership accept the importance of trust in the relationship between leaders and subordinates. In an organisational context, the focus is on leadership-style as being the art of finding a balance between using power and trust. In the field of leadership style studies, a distinction is often made between authoritarian and democratic styles. Douglas McGregor's (1960) Theory X and Theory Y developed in the 1960s at MIT Sloan School of Management, reflects this train of thought. He presumed that managers who adhere to Theory Y way of thinking are open to interaction with subordinates and their ideas and views. Such managers are likely to develop the climate of

---

8 Maslow referred to needs such as physiological, safety, belongingness and love, esteem, self-actualization and self-transcendence to describe the pattern that moulds human motivations generally.

9 Extrinsic rewards refer to monetary and tangible rewards, while intrinsic rewards give personal satisfaction through individual information/feedback, recognition, trust, relationship and empowerment.

trust with employees required for the human resource development which is a crucial aspect of any organisation. Hence, managers would communicate openly with subordinates and minimise the difference between superior-subordinate relationships. A comfortable environment would be created in which subordinates can develop and use their abilities. This climate encourages participatory decision making so that subordinates have a say in decisions and influence them. Furthermore, such an attitude is important for developing leadership styles that enhance learning organisations. It appears that Lord Nelson practiced such a Y-type of leadership.

We have seen how capable Lord Nelson was of creating a team spirit and strengthen his subordinates' self-motivation. In so doing, he was able to involve his subordinates in his combat doctrine and let them take part in a process of seeking concrete and workable solutions to acute problems. This assimilates what Benjamin Franklin did when he organised the Junto club. We will discuss that in the following part.

7.5 Benjamin Franklin's Meso-Level Social Innovations

Benjamin Franklin is among the most famous persons in the history of USA. He is well known for his role in the American Revolution and his career as diplomat. Moreover, he is particularly famous for his inventions such as the lightning rod, bifocals, the Franklin stove, a carriage odometer, and the glass 'armonica'. Besides his technological inventions and contributions to natural science or 'natural philosophy' as it was called in his days, he was very active member of his local community. He was driven to working on social improvements and implementing social innovations. Furthermore, he was active in his local civil society and organised a club, the Junto, one of the main aims of which was to generate and discuss ideas of social improvements. Moreover, he activated different stakeholders in order to build civil support for various social innovations.

7.5.1 Benjamin Franklin's Personality

Like Lord Nelson, he came from a humble but not poor family and both had relatively old parents. Benjamin Franklin was born in 1706 into the family of the English immigrant, Josiah Franklin, who had his own business in Boston and produced candles and soaps. Benjamin's father was 49 years old when his 39 year old second wife, Abiah Folger, gave birth to Benjamin. She was Josiah's second wife with whom he had 10 children. His late first wife was Anne Child Franklin who died in 1689 of complications while giving birth to her seventh child. Josiah and Anne's family was big; Benjamin had nine brothers and seven sisters.

Benjamin received two years of education in a grammar school and a school for writing and arithmetic. He was 8 years old when he started his studies and was a good pupil, but failed in arithmetic (B. Franklin, 2006, p. 345). Afterwards he became an apprentice in his older brother, James', printing office. However, Benjamin was a keen book reader and became a well self-educated man, accumulating knowledge from a wide range of fields such as literature, science, politics, satire, polemics and rhetoric. When he was scarcely 17 years old he read such major works of the enlightenment era as John Locke's *Essay on Human Understanding* and *The Art of Thinking* on rhetoric by Messieurs du Port-Royal (ibid., pp. 496–7).

Benjamin's personality was characterised by stubbornness, self-confidence and self-control. This appears from his conflicts with his older brother, James, which led Benjamin to leave his print office as he ran off to New York 17 years old. The same goes for his becoming a vegetarian at the age of 16, having read a book on the matter by the British vegetarian Thomas Tryon. As Franklin describes:

> I determined to go into it. My brother, being yet unmarried, did not keep house, but boarded himself and his apprentices in another family. My refusing to eat flesh occasioned an inconveniency, and I was frequently chid for my singularity. I ... proposed to my brother, that if he would give me, weekly, half the money he paid for my board, I would board myself. He instantly agreed to it, and I presently found that I could save half what he paid me. This was an additional fund for buying books. But I had another advantage in it. My brother and the rest going from the printing house to their meals, I remained there alone, ... for study, in which I made the greater progress, from that greater clearness of head and quicker apprehension which usually attend temperance in eating and drinking. (B. Franklin, 2006)

Being moulded by the era of the enlightenment in which the ideas of science or natural philosophy reflected the works of Isaac Newton and John Locke, Benjamin Franklin adhered to empirical experimentation as the ideal way of creating reliable knowledge. This way of thinking emerges in his work on social innovations. Moreover, he was preoccupied with morals and virtue, being influenced by his reading of John Bunyan's *The Pilgrim's Progress*. While staying in London from 24th December 1724 to 23rd July 1726, he became acquainted with the satirist Bernard Mandeville. Mandeville wrote the satire *The Fable of The Bees: or, Private Vices, Public Benefits* in which he claimed that self-interest or the self-love of individuals is the prime motor of economic progress. Their vicious greed and desire for personal gain leads to inventions and invisible cooperation that stimulates both production and consumption. However, self-love may develop into extreme greed which undermines public benefit. Hence, politicians must ensure that the passions of man result in public benefit.[10] Benjamin Franklin appears to be influenced by Mandeville, in so far as many of his social innovations are organised around the idea of the self-interest of stakeholders as we will discuss below.

---

10 Mandeville's conclusion here opposes Adam Smith's conclusion that only Laissez-faire and his 'invisible hand' secures spontaneous order and cooperation in society.

Benjamin Franklin was apparently under strong influence from the puritan Dr Cotton Mather of Boston. Franklin's 'admirable style was in part modelled on that of the famous Massachusetts divine, Cotton Mather, whom he had known and whose books he had read in his boyhood'. (S.G. Fisher, 1903, p. 2011). Mather was a socially and politically influential New England Puritan minister. Moreover, he was the first American fellow of the Royal Society and an enthusiast of natural science, much as Franklin himself was to become.

Mather was a preacher of philanthropy and an important source for Franklin's higher values, as expressed through philanthropy. Franklin mentions in his *Autobiography* that a book by De Foe's, called an *Essay on Projects*, and Dr Mather's book, *Bonifacius: Essays to Do Good*, ' ... perhaps gave me a turn of thinking that had an influence on some of the principal future events of my life' (B. Franklin, 2006, p. 436). He claimed that this book ' ... gave me such a turn of thinking, as to have an influence on my conduct through life; for I have always set a greater value on the character of a doer of good, than on any other kind of reputation; and if I have been, as you seem to think, a useful citizen, the public owes the advantage of it to that book' (quoted in P.D. Hall, 2003). Cotton Mather preached the importance of forming voluntary associations to benefit society, a charitable notion which Franklin picked up from him. Indeed, there were many such societies in Boston when Franklin was growing up. The movement of establishing benefit societies had started in Boston and was soon to spread to the main cities of Massachusetts (V. Bernhard, 1976, p. 237).

It appears from the above discussion that Benjamin Franklin's world view was that of the era of enlightenment i.e., the view that the world is impregnated with natural laws which can be researched, established empirically and put to the use of Mankind. Furthermore, the world can be improved in terms of Mankind, society and nature.

7.5.2 Benjamin Franklin as a Meso Social Innovator

Creativity is a social process and as such involves similar stages as those discussed above. As M.D. Mumford (2002) highlights in his studies of the social innovations of Benjamin Franklin (1706–1790), a creative process can be organised as team-work focusing on problem definition and searching for solutions. Being a very active member of his local community, Franklin was inspired to working on social improvements and developing and implementing social innovations. Moreover, in 1732 he organised a progressive, reformist gentlemen's club, Junto, which had as one of its main aims to generate and discuss ideas of social improvements. He also activated different stakeholders in order to build support for various social innovations.[11]

---

11   Besides Junto, Franklin's social innovations involved a subscription library; public police force financed by property tax; volunteer fire departments; paper currency; paving and lighting streets; subscription hospital; partnerships of establishing printing houses

On the basis of his studies of Benjamin Franklin's social innovations, Mumford draws up 8 tentative propositions concerning basic characteristics of social innovations (M.D. Mumford, 2002, pp. 263–4):

1. *Identifying and defining a problem* is the first stage in a social innovation process. Such identifications may result from an experimentally based search for solutions to concrete day-to day problems. The establishment of the Junto club and subscription libraries are examples of this. These innovations emerged as a response to problems related to Franklin's printing enterprises; that is, collecting information, writing articles, producing newspapers and publishing. The innovation of a subscription hospital was an experiment which resulted from recognising a good idea emerging in the course of day-to-day interactions. The Junto club was organised in such a way that members were obliged to present social, intellectual and academic problems and the club members would collectively analyse the essentials of the problem and possible solutions.

2. *The scope of experience* an entrepreneur has is likely to affect the scope and scale of the variety of new ideas and problem solutions. Individuals who have unique life experiences, or rather who have more experiences than the ordinary person, are likely to have larger *conceptual fluidity* and memory procedures characterised by *flat associative hierarchies* (L.M. Gabora, 2000 & 2002). Franklin was a talented person who pursued somewhat unique paths through life. Thus, he had singular patterns of experience due to his social advocacy, characteristic of publishers and politicians and his, at that time rare, analytic, experimental approach of the scientist. His unusual interests resulted in a rather original view of the value of education and social relationships which resulted both in the founding of the Junto and the University of Pennsylvania.

3. *Analysis of cause and effect.* Social innovation, like the *evaluative analytic mode* of creative acts, requires a focus on relationships of cause and effect (ibid.). Ideas and solutions must be based on identifying a limited a number of manageable key causes or essential elements of the situation that one can do something about. As an example, when founding the fire department, Franklin considered many causes but chose to focus on one central issue: the 'want of regulation'. Another example is the case of paper currency where Franklin's success appears tied to a single intervention – linking it to land as the medium of exchange.

4. *Innovation trajectory implementation.* A social innovation does not necessarily have to be fully developed before it is implemented. Its role

with his apprentices; non-denominational university with a balanced power structure of representatives of all main religious sects on the board and; the Albany Plan of Union of 1754, which was an initial attempt to unify the American Colonies under one government (M.D. Mumford, 2002).

is often to set the stage for further improvements or solutions that seed changes likely to encourage yet other refinements. Franklin's project on paving and lighting streets is an example. Initially it was incomplete, but successful and spurred further social and technical developments.

5. *Demonstrative capacity to show practicality* of innovation is important to secure support for an original idea. It is important to be able to show an example or prototypes in order "to sell" the idea of a particular social innovation or to obtain financial support or assistance in the form of voluntary work. This kind of strategy proved important in relation to Franklin's innovation of subscription libraries and paving and lighting of the streets of Philadelphia.

6. *Organizing financing of a social innovation.* Besides creating popular support for a particular idea or social innovation, the innovator needs to find ways to motivate the public so that they will be willing to finance the project. Franklin, presumably under the influence of B. Mandeville, activated people's egoism in order to finance projects. His principle was that stakeholders; that is, those who had the largest use of the innovation in question would be willing to pay for it. The subscription library, the police force, the paving and lighting, the university, the hospital, and the Junto are good examples of this strategy.

7. *Persuasion beyond recognition.* New ideas of social innovation are often heavily criticised. Persuasion is often necessary to convince sceptical stakeholders that the new idea or social innovation is important enough to develop and/or implement. Persuasion, however, may undermine the innovators' recognition in society or make them unpopular. To be persuasive despite unpopularity and risking self-promotion is an important personality trait for an innovator. Moreover, self-promotion is not a critical requirement for social innovation. The examples of the organisation of police force and the University of Pennsylvania showed Franklin's willingness to take such risks.

8. *Social innovation encompasses a readiness to rearrange or restructure existing social relationships.* Rearranging social relationships may involve interpersonal relations and even changing societal structures. Franklin's willingness in this respect is evident in the founding of the police force, management of his printing business, and the formation of the Plan of Union. In the case of the police force innovation, Franklin managed to have the police force changed into a public institution with public employees and the activity was financed by public tax. The wealthiest paid the highest tax as they had the greatest risk in case of fire or burglary. Before, the safety of people and property was the responsibility of the city watch. Constables of the watch could require homeowners in their ward to serve as watchmen. However, homeowners could pay the constable for not doing the watch. In that case, the constable would get the money to hire other men cheaply to do the job. Often criminals or outcasts would be hired. This system was

risky for the homeowners but gave the constable extra income. Franklin also rearranged social relations when he invested in the printing houses of his apprentices who then became his partners rather than students. His Plan of Union was a project of even more profound rearrangement of social relationships as it aimed at building a new society of union of the American Colonies, a forerunner of the American constitution and revolution.

7.5.3 The legacy of Benjamin Franklin as a Meso Social Innovator

The legacy of Franklin is not only that he gave examples for others to follow concerning how to organise processes of social innovation. He is also one of the founding fathers of the 'voluntary sector' and communitarianism in USA. As a world famous person at his own time, he helped spread ideas of this sector far beyond USA. The cases of Benjamin Franklin's social innovations outlined above provide a brief idea of social innovation as a process of defining social problems, analysing key problem factors, developing possible solutions, experimenting with implementation of reforms, generating support and creating a trajectory of innovation for future development. These main elements of the process also characterise social innovations on a greater scale, such as the neo-liberal macro social innovation of the Thatcher regime in the UK. We will now analyse the case of Margaret Thatcher.

7.6 Margaret Thatcher as a Macro Social Innovator

Margaret Thatcher (1925–2013) is one of the most famous and influential politicians of contemporary history. She was the leader of the UK Conservative Party in 1975–1990 and prime minister in 1979–1990. As UK prime minister, she implemented neoliberal policies and led a regime in the UK which fundamentally changed industrial relations and the role and nature of economic policies in Britain. In short, she implemented a macro-level social innovation that fostered a societal paradigm shift in British politics.

Neoliberalism as an ideology shares some features with other ideologies. It takes for granted a set of ideas which provide pictures of how the world is and how it should be. They also provide guidance as to what actions are necessary in order to realise the promised ideals. Furthermore, these ideas are based on knowledge considered to be trustworthy, such as 'scientific' theories or religious doxa. Ideologies are realised by force or by way of persuasion and they are actively institutionalised in a context of existing social structures which the agents of the respective ideology transform by way of gaining hegemony over existing social and political organisations and by implementing new ones. Once institutionalised, they become naturalised as a taken-for-granted way of doing things. As ideologies have materialised in consequent institutions, cultures and social and economic relations, they form constellations of institutions and relations that prevail, often for long periods, as ideological regimes which determine the distribution of resources, production and wealth among members of a society or blocs of countries.

The process of realisation of ideologies is essentially a morphogenetic process of agency in which collective and individual agents reflect on the opportunities for transforming structural hindrances in the existing material context and organise resources. The objective is to realise the opportunities identified for transforming the material context in question and create the ideologically preferred state of affairs. Although agency may be presumed to be the 'efficient cause' of change, its efficiency depends on the emergent properties allowed by existing social structures. Causality can, therefore, neither be reduced to agents' intentions, voluntary actions and/or discourse nor to determination of their actions by structures. Structures of social relations usually comprise properties that can lead to different results in terms of transformed social relations (Archer, 1995, pp. 90 and 153; Lewis, 2000, pp. 260 and 264).

Although different ideologies are based on a core of taken-for-granted ideas of how the world is, or should be, the meaning and/or interpretation of the ideas varies among the followers of the ideology in question. Hence, they adhere to some and not necessarily to all core ideas and beliefs of the respective ideology. Furthermore, interpretations and emphases of different adherents change through time, due to experience of how implementation of the ideology works in reality and as a result of external historical factors. The domination of one interpretation over other(s) will depend on the structure of ideological struggle that is pre given, as the different agents' access to and power over different ideological apparatuses, such as media, universities, art, etc., are unevenly distributed. Ideological concepts are malleable in this sense; the intentions and discourse of the agents are influenced by power relations of ideological struggle. In short, structure has an important role together with agents in the realisation processes of ideologies.

Thus neoliberalism is pliable in this respect and not reducible to one and only one interpretation, as I now briefly illustrate. Neoliberalism spread in the context of the crisis of Keynesian policies in the 1970s following the problem of 'stagflation'. Neoliberal ideas diffused in the 1970s and had their breakthrough in Western societies when Margaret Thatcher became the British Prime Minister in 1979 and Ronald Reagan the US President in 1980. The main roots of neoliberalism and the critique of Keynesian policies were Milton Friedman's 'monetarism' and the critique of state involvement in the economy associated with the Austrian school and in particular Friedrich von Hayek's critique of social democratic state interventionism (Gamble, 2001, pp. 127–8 and 2009, pp. 73–4).

The main concern of Friedman's monetarism was to make sound money once more the cornerstone of economic policy, requiring governments to follow strict monetary targets concerning growth of the money supply (Friedman, 1968, pp. 16–17). This also meant that governments had to give up the Keynesian objective of full employment. Moreover, public expenditure on welfare and infrastructure had to be reduced. It was presumed that public services 'crowd out' private investment opportunities and low interest rate regimes limit the role markets play in eliminating 'mal-investments'. Hayek emphasised that the problem of inflation was a matter of political balance of power. He was particularly critical of the 'coercive power' of trade unions that leads both to too high real wages and the expansion of public services due to their grip on political parties (von Hayek, 2009, pp. 72–3 and 93–6).

The idea of a strong state which is able to secure necessary institutional conditions for free market competition is among the core ideas of neoliberalism. However, the public sector and regulation of the economy must be minimal as it is presumed that private investment and competition are best suited to optimising economic rationality, output and individual freedom.[12] Neoliberal policies differ across countries but have typically appeared in programmes of privatisation of public services and public property; deregulation of trade, financial markets, investment and labour markets; undermining of progressive tax systems and corporate taxes; and introduction of monetary systems with independent central banks.

Despite these similarities in neoliberal programmes, emphases on their different aspects have varied with different strands of neoliberalism. There are three main strands emphasising: anarcho-capitalist; laissez-faire; and social market. The anarcho-capitalist strand is more extreme than the other two. It seeks privatisation of all state functions, including defence, law enforcement and all forms of economic and financial regulation. The laissez-faire strand, or 'market fundamentalism' as it is sometimes called, maintains that markets should be endorsed to function with as few obstacles as possible and with absolute minimal interference from governments. The role of the state should be primarily limited to removing obstacles to market competition. The social market strand accepts this role of the state, but requires more. It presumes that the state must intervene with a wide range of measures in order to create the right institutional framework for the market economy to work and adjust to changing circumstances. It promotes structural adjustment, social capital and good governance in developing economies as well as welfare safety nets, investment in human capital, corporate social responsibility and limited forms of redistribution (Gamble, 2009, pp. 71–2).

Margaret Thatcher's neoliberalism or 'Thatcherism' was of the 'laissez-faire 'kind, but with a strong element of 'authoritarian populism' (S. Hall and M. Jacques, 1983, p. 30). Out of the two fundamental pillars of neoliberalism; that is, monetarism and von Hayek's emphasis on breaking down the 'coercive power' of trade unions, only the latter remained. The Thatcher government gave up its monetarism already in its first term of office, from 1982–3 onward. (E.J. Evans, 1997, p. 33). Geoffrey Howe, Chancellor of the Exchequer, and Thatcher met revolt among Tory backbenchers and part of Thatcher's cabinet in the wake of

---

12   Hayek, however, was not a dogmatic advocate of laissez-faire as he claimed that where free market competition cannot be made effective the state must exercise a wide range of activity (Hayek, 2008, pp. 85 and 88).

Howe's new budget plans in 1979, involving severe cuts in welfare and social policy. Gradually Howe and his successor as Chancellor of the Exchequer, Nigel Lawson, with the acceptance of practical politician Thatcher, focused more on election results than on keeping the money supply tight. By the 1987 election monetary targets had been almost forgotten. (ibid., pp. 30 and 33).

Thatcher was more successful in undermining the power of the trade unions, by implementing the Employment Act of 1982 which restricted the definition of a lawful strike and which made striking in sympathy with other workers virtually illegal. Furthermore, the Trade Union and Employment Acts of 1988 which made a union's legal immunity from prosecution for damages sustained during strike contingent upon a secret ballot of its members having been held, and having provided a majority for strike action (ibid., pp. 37–8). Her greatest success was probably her symbolic victory in the coal miners' strike 1984/5 and the defeat of the print workers' strike which was a major piece of industrial action in 1986. The mine workers' union lost 72 per cent of its members in the years 1979–86, while the number of trade unionists as a whole shrank from 13.5 million in 1979 to 10.5 million in 1986, and had fallen below 10 million by the time Thatcher left office in 1990 (ibid., pp. 38–9). How the government treated the trade union question made it popular and so did its anti-tax rhetoric, although the fact is that the Tories did not succeed in cutting the overall tax burden as taxation accounted for 38.5 per cent of GDP in 1979 and 40.75 per cent 1990 (ibid., p. 31). The government was also popular for its privatisation policies. The compulsory sale of local authority houses to sitting tenants had increased the proportion of owner occupied homes and helped boost owner occupation from 55 per cent to 63 per cent in the decade after 1979. Privatisation of public companies was also a popular policy, particularly within the Conservative Party. It is estimated that this raised almost £19 billion in the years 1979–87 and helped reduce government debt (ibid., p. 34). Revenues from North Sea oil, which were increasing substantially in the early 1980s, enabled the government to offer inducements to voters (ibid., p. 33).

7.6.1 Margaret Thatcher's Personality

Margaret Thatcher was the daughter of Alfred Roberts and Beatrice Ethel Roberts. Her father owned two grocery shops in Grantham, where Margaret spent her childhood. Her father was active in local politics and the Methodist church, serving as an alderman and a local preacher. Margaret was brought up as a strict Wesleyan Methodist attending the Finkin Street Methodist Church. Alfred stood as an independent in council elections and became Mayor of Grantham in 1945–6.

Margaret Thatcher was an active member of her church and already from the age of 12, played the piano accompaniment to smaller children's singing of hymns (M. Thatcher, 2013, p. 157). Thatcher appears to have been significantly influenced by her father and accords him great respect in her autobiography. She describes him as a man who stuck to his principles, but 'adopting a utilitarian rather than a dogmatic approach' and 'These upright qualities, which entailed a refusal to alter your convictions just because others disagreed or because you became unpopular, were instilled into me from the earliest days'. (ibid., pp. 174 and 179–180). Thatcher was an incisive personality. In an ICI personnel department assessment that rejected her job application, she was described as follows 'This woman is headstrong, obstinate and dangerously self-opinionated' (BBC, 2013). Brought up in Methodist spirit, she was a hard-working person, or as she puts it: 'In my family we were never idle – partly because idleness was a sin, partly because there was so much work to be done, and partly, no doubt, because we were just that sort of people'. (M. Thatcher, 2013, pp. 255–256).

It is interesting to note that the fathers of social innovators, Lord Nelson, and Margaret Thatcher, were protestant preachers and Benjamin Franklin was under strong influence from the puritan minister and preacher Cotton Mather. All three of them were described as obstinate and highly independent personalities. However, Nelson was a great team builder, while Thatcher did not do well in team work as demonstrated by her relationship with her cabinet. Unlike Benjamin Franklin, Thatcher was an authoritarian leader. As S. Buckley (2006, pp. 160–61) highlights, Thatcher made major policy decisions without first consulting her cabinet and kept major issues off the cabinet agenda altogether. She would also appoint weak ministers who could then be easily controlled. Moreover, she had a distinct approach to cabinet meetings which would begin by her stating her own views rather than first listening to her ministers' contributions. Furthermore, Thatcher had an odd relationship with the convention of collective cabinet responsibility as she was prepared to leak and brief against ministers when it suited her. Significant use of the 'kitchen cabinet' and ad hoc committees characterised her leadership style.

7.6.2 Margaret Thatcher as a Macro Social Innovator and the Social Innovation Process of Neoliberalism

Having briefly discussed Thatcherism and Thatcher's personality and leadership style, we will now observe the neoliberal, macro-level, social innovation process as it appears in the case of Thatcherism. Figure 7.3 summarises the main features.

The first stage in the process is the formulation of a world view on which the neoliberal ideology is founded. The intellectual promoters of the neoliberal worldview and puzzle/problem analysers are the founding intellectuals. These are first generation academic authorities such as Friedrich A. von Hayek, von Mises, Karl Popper, John Clapham, Rose Wilder Lane, Isabel Paterson, Ayn Rand and Milton Friedman. Besides them are the second tier academics such as James M. Buchanan, Gordon Tullock, Peter Bauer, Charles Murray and Stanley Dennison. These academics created the philosophical and scientific framework that moulded the work of neoliberal think-tanks, journalists and politicians who cook, implement and legitimise concrete governmental policies in various areas.

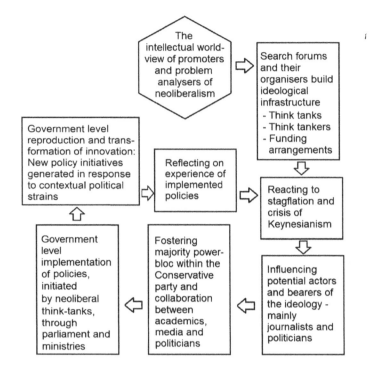

Figure 7.3   Social innovation process of neoliberalism

The second stage in the neoliberal process of social innovation is reached when search forums and ideological infrastructures are built. The ideological infrastructure consists of think-tanks, think-tankers and arrangements for funding the activity.[13] We will now briefly discuss the neoliberal infrastructure.

a) Think-tanks. The history of think-tanks that fostered and advocated the neoliberal ideology goes back to the early part of the twentieth century. The first wave of such think-tanks started in the late 1930s in USA, while a second wave took off in the 1970s. Figure 7.4. shows the most important think-tanks of neoliberalism.

It is not easy to locate the direct influence of think-tanks on particular government policies (A. Denham, 1997, pp. 144–8). However, we know their task is to bring politicians and businessmen into contact with ideas and thinkers through conferences and media. It is also difficult to demonstrate a direct influence of the

---

13   The following analysis of the neoliberal ideological infrastructure is mostly built on Jones, Daniel Stedman (2012). Other sources are: Edwards, Lee (2002); Abowd, Paul (2013); ParenteBeard (2013); WhoFundsYou and; http://www.sourcewatch.org/index.php/ SourceWatch; Wikipedia.org

publications by think-tanks on general public opinion. Our aim is not to prove such direct causal links, but to demonstrate how think-tanks play a role in searching and framing problems in the process of social innovations. The role of think-tanks today is similar to that of the Junto club at the time of Benjamin Franklin's social innovations and the 'Nelson Touch' in the case of Lord Nelson. For decades the neoliberal ideological infrastructure and think-tanks created various networks and spread their message without a direct relationship with governments. However, in the case of Thatcherism, the think-tanks' Centre of Policy Studies and the Adam Smith Institute had the role of feeding the neoliberal Tories with ideological arguments in their struggle within the Conservative Party so that they could form solutions to a twofold problem: *Firstly*, the political and ideological crises of the Conservative Party following the defeat of Heath's government in the 1970s and *secondly*, the need for alternative policies to Keynesianism and the deepening economic crisis of stagflation.

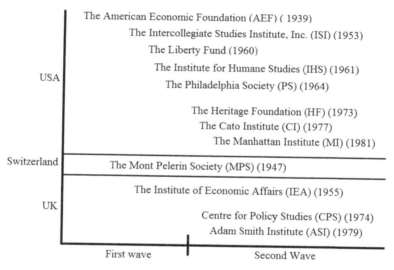

Figure 7.4   Anglo-Saxon neoliberal think-tanks[14]

Think-tanks work on different levels of opinion building and thus affect governmental policy formation. A broad definition of think-tanks has been suggested by Hames and Feasey (1994, p. 216) as 'a non-profit public policy research institution with substantial organisational autonomy'. They admit, however, that this definition reveals but little about the character and nature of think-tanks. In the British context, the term was first used in relation to Prime Minister Edward Heath's Central Policy Review Staff (CPRS), established in the

---

14   See Appendix for an overview of the neoliberal think-tanks.

Cabinet Office in 1970–1 (A. Denham, 1998, p. 8). Thatcher abolished the CPRS in 1983 and think-tanks became increasingly referred to as ideologically charged, free-market bodies outside government (ibid., p. 9).

Andrew Denham (1997) claims there are three kinds of think-tanks; that is, 'universities without students', 'contract research institutions' and 'advocacy tanks'. The first type concentrates on substantive policy issues and policy processes. They focus on research relevant to current policy issues rather than theoretical matters of scientific disciplines. The second kind of think-tanks are institutes which serve government agencies and/or private sponsors on a contractual basis. Their choice of subjects is strongly influenced by their clients and their life depends on adjusting research results so that they will not lose their market share to competitors. Hence, their objectivity is much more disputed than is the case of 'universities without students'. According to A. Denham, there are no think-tanks in the UK that fit the first category and only a few in USA, such as The Brookings Institution and the American Enterprise Institute for Public Policy Research (AEI). The Policy Studies Institute (PSI) and the Institute of Economic Affairs (IEA) aspired to be of this type but did not succeed. In Britain, several think-tanks fit the category of 'contract research organisation' such as Political and Economic Planning (PEP) which later became the PSI and the National Institute for Economic and Social Research (NIESR). As for 'advocacy tanks' the Centre for Policy Studies (CPS) and the Adam Smith Institute (ASI) belong to this category in the UK (ibid., pp. 10–11).

b) Think-tankers. Think-tankers are thinkers who present a serious intellectual cutting edge. They popularise ideas and make them both accessible and applicable to policy and politics (D.S. Jones, 2012, p. 167). Some persons played a particularly important role in shaping the concept of neoliberal social innovation. These were individuals such as Arthur Seldon, editorial director of the Institute of Economic Affairs (IEA). Charles Murray was also important with his book on post-war social policy, *Losing Ground,* which suggested that growth of the welfare state had led to a culture of dependency among the poor and indigent. Stuart Butler at the Heritage Foundation made important contributions such as building on British socialist urban planner and geographer Peter Hall's idea for enterprise zones, which subsequently became the centrepiece of the Reagan administration's urban policy. Arthur Sherman of Centre for Policy Studies helped promote the concept, as did John Leigh Austin Hungerford Hoskyns with his influential *Stepping Stones Report,* analysing what he considered to be wrong with the UK and presenting a strategic guide for the implementation of neoliberal policies and political take over.

c) Funding arrangements. These refer to foundations and funders that finance the activities of think-tanks and think-tankers. Let us highlight some examples of this kind of actors that have been important in funding the decades' long neoliberal ideological struggle. We will first look at examples of foundations and then contributions by free market scholars and institutes.

i. Foundations:

i.a. *The Earhart Foundation* (EF) was founded in 1929 by the oil executive Harry Boyd Earhart with the fortune he made with White Star Oil Company. Among the foundation's early beneficiaries was Friedrich von Hayek. The British-based American conservative philosopher Shirley Letwin, for example, was nominated by Hayek in 1955 to receive funding from the Earhart Foundation. EF was a regular supporter of meetings of the Mont Pelerin Society throughout the 1950s and 1960s.

i.b. *Relm Foundation* (RF) was also established in 1930 by Harry Boyd Earhart. RF funded institutions devoted to furthering economic freedom, like the London based Institute for Economic Affairs, and the Mont Pelerin Society. It also supported individual scholars like Leo Strauss, Eric Voegelin, and Peter Bauer. RF was a regular supporter of meetings of the Mont Pelerin Society throughout the 1950s and 1960s. In 1977, RF was closed and all of its remaining assets went to the Earhart Foundation. Among those supported by the Relm-Earhart foundations over the decades were nine Nobel laureates in economics: Gary Becker, James M. Buchanan, Ronald Coase, Milton Friedman, Friedrich A. von Hayek, Robert Lucas, Daniel McFadden, Vernon L. Smith, and George Stigler. Since the early 1950s, over 2500 graduate students have received assistance from the foundation as H.B. Earhart fellows. In 1964, the Relm Foundation joined the Intercollegiate Studies Institute in creating the Richard M. Weaver Fellowships which has awarded well over 300 fellowships. One of those who received an Earhart fellowship in 1960 was Thomas Sowell, today an influential conservative black intellectual in America.

i.c. *The William Volker Fund* (WVF) was founded in 1932 by businessman and home-furnishings mogul William Volker. The WVF was instrumental in bringing Hayek to Chicago from the LSE in 1950. Its leadership was assumed by Harold Luhnow in 1944. Luhnow was also responsible for helping Hayek to establish the Mont Pelerin Society. Furthermore, WVF funded von Mises' salary at New York University and Hayek's salary at the University of Chicago. Milton Friedman put forward a suggestion that the British economist Stanley Dennison received a grant from the WVF in 1958. At the time, Dennison was one of the few anti-Keynesian voices at Cambridge University. Moreover, Murray Rothbard, the founder and leading theoretician of anarcho-capitalism was supported by the WVF.

i.d. *The Atlas Economic Research Foundation* (the Atlas Network) was founded in 1981 in USA by Antony Fisher who founded the IEA, and helped establish the Fraser Institute, the Manhattan Institute and the Pacific Research Institute in the 1970s. Atlas provides seed funding to new think-tanks on a case-by-case basis. Grants are usually given for specific projects and range between $2,000 and $5,000. Both Friedman and Hayek were regularly consulted in the 1950s and 1960s about who should receive scholarships and grants from these large foundations.

ii. Funders of free market scholars and institutes:

Examples:

ii.a. Joseph Coors of Coors Brewing Company, who was a founding member and board member of the Heritage Foundation (HF). Coors provided $250,000 to HF to cover its first year budget in 1973. He was involved in founding the conservative think-tank called The Free Congress Foundation. He was also involved in founding The Council for National Policy in 1981 which is an umbrella organisation and networking group for social conservative activists in the United States. It has been described by *The New York Times* as 'a little-known club of a few hundred of the most powerful conservatives in the country';

ii.b. Charles Koch of Koch Industries was a member of the Mont Pelerin Society. He funded a scholarship in his name at the Institute for Humane Studies. Charles and his brother David have for decades funded various neoliberal, free market projects. In 2011, they donated through their foundations $24 million with much of the money going to support free-market and libertarian think-tanks and academic centres. The George Mason University Foundation received $4.4 million and the Institute for Humane Studies received $3.7 million. Eight other think-tanks received over $1.4 million;

ii.c. Richard Mellon Scaife was a major, early supporter of the Heritage Foundation. As a billionaire in Banking and oil and aluminium industries, he and the Scaife foundations had by 2002 donated $340 million to various conservative and libertarian organisations (SourceWatch, 2015).

It is not our aim, to prove direct causal links between, on the one hand, think-tanks and government policies and, on the other, think-tanks and general public opinion. Rather, we are preoccupied with think-tanks' function of searching and framing of problems and solutions in the process of social innovations. As we highlighted above, the role of think-tanks is similar to that of the Junto club in the case of Benjamin Franklin's social innovations and the "Nelson Touch" in the case of Lord Nelson. The neoliberal ideological infrastructure and think-tanks for decades developed various networks and spread the message without direct relations with governments. However, in the case of Thatcherism, the think-tanks Centre of Policy Studies and the Adam Smith Institute had the role of feeding the neoliberal Tories with ideological arguments in their struggle within the Conservative Party and contributing alternative policies to Keynesianism and the deepening economic crisis of stagflation.

Now we will now move to *the third stage* of the neoliberal social innovation process; that is, reactions to the societal problem of stagflation and the crisis of Keynesianism.

It is not as if a group of neoliberalists suddenly appeared on the political scene in the UK and made a political paradigm shift or the so-called neoliberal revolution. Instead, particular societal and historical conditions made it possible to define and actively introduce a different trajectory of development from what hitherto had existed. This trajectory shift emerged gradually and had its setbacks. As we have seen, the neoliberal world view and ideological infrastructure already existed before the 1970s. What was needed, besides this infrastructure, was both a feasible policy to solve the problem of stagflation and a reshuffle of the balance power between different factions within the Conservative Party. Furthermore, there was a need for a new party leader who was respected and influential enough to gather the political resources to start a process of defining the fundamental causal relations that determine the challenging problems at hand and the apparently logical solution or policies to solve the problem.

After the defeat of the Conservative Party in two parliamentary elections in 1974, party leader and former Prime Minister, Edward Heath, lost much of his support among party members and Tory MPs. In the following year, his former Education Secretary Margaret Thatcher, challenged and defeated Heath as leader of the party. Inflation was a severe problem following rising unemployment in 1972 and Heath's reflating of the economy. Two miners' strikes, in 1972 and another one in 1974, forced Heath to give in which proved damaging to the government. The oil crisis of 1973 and increases in prices of domestic and imported goods made the problem of inflation even more severe.

Thatcher, the new party leader, joined Keith Joseph in founding the Centre for Policy Studies in 1974. He had been Trade Spokesman and Secretary of State for Social Services in Heath's governments. Joseph had already, in the run-up to the 1970 election, made a series of speeches under the title 'civilised capitalism', in which he hinted at cuts in public spending. Now was the time to formulate a 'scientific' analysis of the causes of the crisis of British capitalism and present the observations in a form understandable to the Tory MPs, party members and the general public. Joseph, who gradually became the main philosopher of the neoliberal Tories, at first attempted to find explanations for the crisis of British capitalism by making comparative studies of European economies with particular focus on the so called 'social market economy' as practised in West-Germany (M. Thatcher, 2013, pp. 3015–16). This was a variety of neoliberalism which differed from the laissez-fair version that the Conservative Party eventually promoted. As Thatcher puts it: 'The original proposed social market approach did not prove particularly fruitful and was eventually quietly forgotten, though a pamphlet called *Why Britain Needs a Social Market Economy* was published'. (M. Thatcher, 2013, pp. 3023–3025).[15]

The search went on for analysis that would be adequate as well as producing acceptable and promising policies in the view of the neoliberal Tories. The next step was to adjust the theories of Milton Friedman and F. von Hayek to the British political context. Rather than following the path of German neoliberalism and the social market economy, monetarism, deregulation, cuts in the welfare state and state enterprises and curbing the power of trade unions became the essence of the analysis and political solutions that would transform British capitalism from post-war social-democratic hegemony to the new trajectory of laissez-faire neoliberalism.

The fourth stage in the process of neoliberal social innovation consisted of influencing potential actors and bearers of the ideology – mainly journalists and politicians. The think-tanks played a crucial role in this respect. The Centre for Policy Studies and the Adam Smith Institute had a certain division of labour between them. CPS was particularly important in framing, or influencing, what journalists and politicians would consider to be the core problems of British capitalism. The ASI had the role of feeding Thatcher and her government with policy proposals and ideas after Thatcher had become Prime Minister. Peter Jay, the economic editor of the *Times* and at the BBC, was one such receptive journalist. He was under strong influence from the Chicago school and CPS in the 1970s and used his column in the Times to promote the monetarist ideology in Britain. He was son-in-law of and adviser to the Labour Party's Prime Minister, James Callaghan, in the 1970s and wrote parts of his famous speech given at the party's conference in 1976 (D.S. Jones, 2012, p. 174). That speech marked the first steps of the long lasting march of neoliberal ideology in British politics. Jay wrote the following neoliberal formulation in Callaghan's speech:

---

15   The German 'social market economy' approach was a compromise between the main factions within the German Christian Democratic Party (CDU); that is, Christian socialists who were powerful in the German labour movement and the market orientated faction led by Konrad Adenauer and Ludwig Erhard. In the era of the Cold War, influenced by the Ordoliberalism of the Freiburg school of economics and having learnt from the experience of Nazi Germany and the societal power of oligopolistic companies, an ideology emerged which was directed against both the liberal laissez-faire doctrine and the doctrine of the planned economy. The compromise culminated in the *Düsseldorfer Leitsätze* platform of the Christian democrats in 1949 that advocated a new societal order based on social justice, socially responsible freedom and real human dignity. A comprehensive social policy for all economically and socially dependent groups was emphasised and the family was to be protected. Furthermore, the value of the working person was confirmed as well as the right to co-determination. The idea of free market competition was the cornerstone of the German neoliberalism, but it emphasised the powerful role of the state in terms of legal control of monopoly and oligopoly in the economy. This last mentioned emphasis is missing in the Anglo-Saxon version of neoliberalism. See K. van Kersbergen (1995, pp. 73–6).

We used to think that you could spend your way out of a recession and increase employment by cutting taxes and boosting government spending. I tell you in all candour that that option no longer exists, and in so far as it ever did exist, it only worked on each occasion since the war by injecting a bigger dose of inflation into the economy, followed by a higher level of unemployment as the next step. (cited in Powerbase, 2014)

Callaghan was also swayed by the IMF as Britain received their loan with an accompanying austerity policy package, requiring cuts in public expenditure. He approached the IMF for a loan in September, the same month he gave his speech at the Labour Party conference.

The story of Peter Jay and James Callaghan is not to be understood as a one directional top-down path in which the neoliberal ideology is passively internalised by receiving journalists and politicians; rather, the process is mutual with journalists and politicians actively seeking an alternative to the Keynesian policies which had proved outdated in the era of stagflation.[16] The neoliberal think-tanks and ideological infrastructure were at hand, providing the fuel needed.

The fifth stage in the process of neoliberal macro-social innovation involves a process of fostering a majority power-bloc within the Conservative party and collaboration between academics, media and politicians. It turned out be Thatcher's role to build a successful neoliberal power-bloc within the Conservative party and prepare a shift from the post-war Keynesian regime of E. Heath to a neoliberal regime.

As R. Mulé has highlighted, conflicts between fractions within the Conservative Party were both more frequent and more overt in the 1970s than they had been before. Overt conflicts fostered the formation of more stable alignments and fractions of ideological groups in the party (R. Mulé, 2001, pp. 95–96). There are four main pillars of Conservative ideology which determine the formation of fractions within the Conservative Party; that is, progressive and traditional Tories on the one hand, and liberal and corporate Whigs on the other. *Progressive Toryism* had paternalistic roots and rejected laissez-faire while it favoured the welfare state and programmes for reducing the extremes of poverty and wealth. It envisioned the state as trustee for the community. *Traditional Tories* were sceptical about the virtues of social progress and social planning. Strong government and leadership was their primary concern. Liberal and corporate Whigs saw preserving private property as the most effective means to achieve economic welfare. *Liberal Whigs* were against government intervention as it would distort the role of market forces and undermine economic growth, while *corporate Whigs* believed that a close partnership among government, trade unions and business would enhance economic welfare. From the early 1950s to 1974, the dominant power bloc within the Conservative Party comprised corporate Whigs and progressive Tories. Following Edward Heath's failure to deal with inflation and the trade unions and

---

16   See I. Jonsson, 1991.

the defeat of the Conservative Party in 1974, the rule of the post war power bloc began to crack.

Thatcher led the process of building a new power-bloc, which connected liberal, free enterprise Whiggery with traditional, authoritarian Toryism (Crewe and Searing, 1988). Table 7.1 highlights the eras of shifting power-blocs in the post-war history of the Conservative Party.

Table 7.1   Ruling power blocs in the Conservative Party

Pillars of Conservative ideology	Tories	
Progressive – paternalistic	Traditional – authoritarian	
Whigs Liberal		1976 + Thatcher era
Corporate	Early 1950s to 1974	

It took Thatcher and her associates within the party, in particular Keith Joseph and Geoffrey Howe, some five years to lead the Conservative Party from Heath's corporate, progressive paternalism to their monetarist neoliberalism. This process culminated in the Conservative Party's Manifesto of 1979 (M. Thatcher, 2013, pp. 4559 and 4579). On the way, Thatcher reshuffled her shadow cabinet several times. Heath's paternalism was characterised by emphasis on voluntary price and income policies and, if necessary, moves to a statutory policy if voluntary support was not achieved. Thatcher's stand was quite different as she presumed that a realistic strategy to bring down inflation must be based on control of the money supply and government borrowing (ibid., pp. 3545–3546 and 3550–3551). According to Thatcher, this could only be achieved by curbing the power of trade unions that stood in the way of cuts in public expenditure and closing down non-profitable state owned industries such as the coal industry.

The sixth stage in the process of neoliberal macro-social innovation presumes implementation of government policies initiated by neoliberal think-tanks. The implementation takes place through parliament, ministries and governments which usually reformulate the initial policy initiatives. The effect on legislature is mostly indirect as policy initiatives rarely pass unchanged through the policy formation process. Hence, think-tanks work on different levels of opinion building that affect governmental policy formation. How and to what extent think-tanks influence policy formation and concrete policies is an underdeveloped research area, however, and it is difficult to empirically prove such influences. Thatcher, Howe, Ridley and Lawson did not mention in their autobiographies how think-tanks, such as CPS or ASI, affected implemented policies, (A. Denham, p. 166). IEA's activity focused mainly on popularising free-market ideas by publishing pamphlets, papers and organising lectures, lunches and seminars targeted at intellectuals who spread Hayek's ideas or on those 'opinion-formers' (journalists, academics, writers, broadcasters and commentators) who are considered to determine the political thinking of the nation as a whole. Conversely, the ASI's target is the future priorities of government. It uses media, informal contacts or its own publications to provide blueprints for concrete reform which can be readily translated into legislation (ibid., p. 163).

Despite difficulties in proving empirically the influence of advocacy think-tanks on government policy (D.E. Abelson, 2009, pp. 86–7), we would expect both direct and indirect influences depending on how close are the relationships of ministers and politicians with different think-tanks. After 1975, Thatcher participated in events sponsored by IEA since 1975 and regularly attended 'lunches at the Institute of Economic Affairs where Ralph Harris, Arthur Seldon, Alan Walters and others – in other words all those who had been right when we in Government had gone so badly wrong – were busy marking out a new non-socialist economic and social path for Britain'. (M. Thatcher, 2013, p. 3041). Ralph Harris described IEA's direct impact on Thatcher in *National Review*: 'Margaret Thatcher's central reform of trade unions, state industries, monetary policy, and much else owed a great deal to the advisors and members of Parliament directly instructed in market analysis by IEA publications ... ' (cited in N. Hoplin, 2008, p. 162). After becoming the leader of the Conservative Party in February 1975, Thatcher had a meeting at the party's Conservative Research Department to discuss a paper on the family policy of the German Christian Democrats. In her authoritarian way Thatcher set the ideological line for the party at the meeting. John Ranelagh has described this important incident:

> 'Another colleague had also prepared a paper arguing that the middle way was the pragmatic path for the Conservative party to take ... Before he had finished his paper, the new Party Leader ... reached into her briefcase and took out a book. It was Friedrich von Hayek's *The Constitution of Liberty*. Interrupting [the speaker], she held the book up for all of us to see. "This", she said sternly, "is what we believe", and banged Hayek down on the table'. (John Ranelagh, 1991, p. ix)

In 1977, Thatcher gave the message a workable formulation in her and J.L.A.H. Hoskyns' CPS report '*Stepping Stones*'. It echoed Friedman's monetarism and Hayek's anti-trade unionism. The report demanded, among other things, that secret ballots should take place before trade unions went on strike. Furthermore, it formulated various concrete directives for the ideology the Conservative Party promoted in the upcoming parliamentary elections. After the 'winter of discontent' in 1978, Thatcher's shadow cabinet and MPs finally aligned under Thatcher.

ASI may have had a more direct influence on the policy formation of Thatcher's government. In the Institute's pamphlet, *The First Hundred*, produced for internal use, it is claimed that ASI was successful in steering the government towards various policy implementations such as privatisation, contracting out and deregulation, as well as replacing rates with the notorious poll tax that Thatcher later publicly apologised for having implemented.[17]

The seventh and the last stage in the process of neoliberal macro-social innovation presumes government level reproduction and transformation of innovation which involves responding to political strains contextually contingent upon new policy initiatives. In the case of the Thatcher regime, the implementing of monetarism was among its main objectives. It required cutting public expenditure in order to control public debt and inflation. However, monetary targets were not realised and control over the monetary supply was not as easy as originally presumed. Economic policy changed significantly from 1982–3 onwards as fiscal targets was repeatedly loosened, partly due to increasing unemployment-related expenditure. This was very much unwelcomed by academic monetarists who preached the need to maintain the tightest of controls on the money supply. But populism was required and pure monetarism was sacrificed for the sake of maintaining longer term political support for the government and securing Thatcher's leadership (E.J. Evans, 1997, p. 33; R. Mulé, 2001, p. 105). The 1981 Budget had envisaged severe cuts in welfare state expenditure, but led to fierce reactions among cabinet members. Thatcher's response was a cabinet reshuffle in 1982: Out went the 'wets', Ian Gilmour, Christopher Soames and Mark Carlisle, and in came 'dries'; that is, hardliners, Norman Tebbit, Nigel Lawson and Norman Fowler (R. Mulé, 2001, p. 106). Meanwhile, Thatcher's monetarism was a dominant media theme and distracted public attention from a major shift that was taking place as social security veered towards a residual system and means testing i.e., away from Beveridge's welfare state universalism (R. Mulé, 2001, pp. 86 and 95). This was a shift that marked the reintroduction of a pre-World War II mode of tackling welfare issues.

Restructuring the tax system and cutting taxes was an important part of the monetarist ideology. The Thatcher regime, however, was only partly successful in implementing its monetary policy and contractual fiscal policy. The government did not succeed in cutting the overall tax burden as taxation accounted for 38.5 per cent of GDP in 1979 and 40.75 per cent of GDP in 1990. However, a qualitative

---

17   Among the first hundred are items such as: introduction of school boards; abolition of the Greater London Council; phasing out student grants in favour of loans; privatisation of local government and NHS services; splitting the DHSS into two departments; curbing council spending for political purposes; phasing out stamp duty on house purchases; scrapping school catchment areas; establishing City Technology Colleges; selling British Rail subsidiaries and the privatisation of BR itself; bus service deregulation; selling off British airports; encouraging private investment in new roads; ITV regional franchises being auctioned to highest bidder; privatising the water industry, Rolls-Royce, British Leyland, British Gas and, to come, the electricity supply industry and the National Coal Board; cutting tax rates; closing Job Centres; scrapping the Wages Council; scrapping agricultural price support grants; phasing out SERPS; privatising prison services; introducing electronic tags for offenders; removing imposed separation of barristers and solicitors; establishing the NHS 'internal market'; introduction of indicative drug budgets for GPs; tax relief on private health insurance for elderly (D. Douglas, 1989).

shift took place as the existing progressive tax system was undermined and a regressive system introduced. As E.J. Evans puts it:

> ... in March 1988 ... Lawson announced an income tax structure comprising only two rates: the standard rate at 25 per cent and a single higher rate of 40 per cent. Tax cuts served their turn as propaganda in the 1987 election as they have in many others, enabling the Conservatives to present themselves as the party of low taxation. Lawson's rationalisation was also very astute politically. Since a low top rate affects a large number of only modestly wealthy people as well as the far smaller number of the genuinely rich, any proposal to tinker with the higher rate is open to the charge that it would penalise the middle classes as a whole. (E.J. Evans, 1997, p. 31)

The government initially cut the top marginal tax rate on earned income from 83 to 60 per cent, and later reduced it to 40 per cent. It also lowered the basic rate of income tax from 33 per cent to 25 per cent. At the same time, the Thatcherite tax policy marked a shift from direct taxes to indirect taxes as Value Added Tax was raised to 15 per cent (R. Mulé, 2001, p. 88). The tax policies led to increased inequality in British society. This was a trend towards greater inequality which had begun in 1977 under the Callaghan government. The bottom quintile's income share (adjusted household post-tax-post-transfer income) fell from 9.2 per cent in 1979 to 7.2 per cent in 1991, while the top quintile's share shifted from 36.5 per cent to 42.0 per cent in the same period (ibid., p. 108).

Despite setbacks on the monetarist side, the Thatcher regime was successful in terms of privatisation, deregulation and curbing the power of trade unions. With the Employment Act of 1982 the definition of a lawful strike was limited to one between workers and their own employers. Strikes in sympathy with other workers became illegal. Furthermore, the Act contained clauses which made 'closed shops' of exclusively unionised labour more difficult to sustain. Individuals who were dismissed for not joining a union were entitled to high rates of compensation. The Trade Union Act of 1984 made postal ballots compulsory at least every five years for all union offices and provided subsidies for holding them. Finally, the Trade Union and Employment Act of 1988 gave individual union members greater powers against their unions. They could no longer be disciplined for working during an official strike. Crucially, a union's legal immunity from prosecution for damages sustained during strikes was available only if a secret ballot of its members had been held and had provided a majority for strike action (E.J. Evans, 1997, pp. 37–8). Among the long lasting policies of the Thatcher regime was the implementation of New Public Management in public sector institutions and services that endorses flexibility and authoritarian rule by managers over employees (G. Gruening, 2001, p. 2).

7.6.3 The Legacy of Margaret Thatcher as a Macro-Social Innovator

Despite some setbacks involving the legacy of the Thatcher regime, its introduction of macro-level social innovation is a societal trajectory that shifted not only the Conservative Party's ideology towards neoliberalism, but that of the left as well. Consequently, the Labour Party adjusted its ideology and implemented 'New Labour's' 'Third Way'. There was 'no turning back' as hardliner Thatcherites called it (A. Denham, 1997, p.165). Moreover, European social democratic parties gradually followed suit. Deregulation was accepted and theoretically transformed into the more convenient rhetoric of 'globalisation' (A. Oakley, 2011, pp. 4–5). Tony Blair's Labour government gave the Bank of England independence in 1997. Although this independence is one of the cornerstones of monetarism, it was not the work of M. Thatcher's government. Indeed, Labour leader and Prime Minister Tony Blair proudly claims that it was his idea and not the idea of his Chancellor of the Exchequer, Gordon Brown (T. Blair, 2011, p. 114).[18] The Labour government neither renationalised any industries or public services nor did it abandon the policy of contracting out or wind down the New Public Management strategies in the public sector. Concerning trade union issues, the New Labour government did not undo the Labour Acts of the Thatcher government. However, the government introduced a national minimum wage and increased public expenditure. Income inequality which had sharply increased in the 1980s became even higher under New Labour in 2007 when the GINI-coefficient, based on net income, reached about 36 per cent. This was the highest level of inequality in 50 years (J. Hills et al., 2010, p. 9). The reasons for the rising inequalities were that New Labour policy stuck to Thatcher's tax regime, but did not raise income tax or the burden of taxation on the better off. Nor did it seek to restrain the excessive bonus culture of top management (P. Gregg, 2011,p. 29). Instead of tackling inequality, New Labour attempted to reduce poverty by focusing on relative income poverty among families with children and among pensioners. The redistribution policy emphasised targeted social benefits and tax credits. The combined tax and redistributive policies of the government in 1997–2008 led to increases of 16 per cent, 14 per cent and 10 per cent in the income of the three poorest deciles of the UK population, while the top decile became 2 per cent worse off, the 9th lost 1 per cent and the 8th decile was on average unaffected (P. Johnson, 2008, p. 73).

This redistribution policy was, however, economically unsound as it was built on revenues from indirect taxation and failed when economic growth slackened in the late 2000s and measures against poverty were cut. Even after the crisis in 2008–9 Labour did not 'undertake a fundamental rethink of the model of British capitalism within

---

18   The independence of the Bank of England meant that the Bank decided the level of interest rates. As Tony Blair puts it: 'I had talked about it often with Roy Jenkins. Gavyn Davies – at that time with Goldman Sachs, and someone I often turned to for economic advice – had been immensely persuasive on the merits. I knew Nigel Lawson – a Chancellor I really admired – had wanted to do it' (T. Blair, 2011, p. 113).

which United Kingdom policy makers had operated. This remains a significant lacuna of the New Labour years'. (P. Gregg, 2011, p. 29). It clearly appears that New Labour followed the neoliberal trajectory set by the Thatcher regime: There was, indeed, 'no turning back' as the most passionate supporters of Thatcher in the Conservative Party had claimed and founded a group of activists with this name.

7.7 Summary

In this chapter we have discussed social innovations in terms of being an active search for the definition, solutions and processes of implementation. We have seen that social innovations concern social improvements realised by agents who actively influence the contexts in which social innovation takes place. We have highlighted common features of processes of social innovation in rather dissimilar contexts and at different levels of social transformation i.e., micro-, meso- and macro-levels. It appears that processes of social innovation are non-teleological, but at the same time moulded by the particular societal contexts in which social innovators structure and actively transform social relations in a social constructivist way.

Appendix:
Anglo-Saxon Neoliberal Think-Tanks

First Wave Think-tanks:

i. *The American Economic Foundation (AEF)* was founded in Cleveland in 1939 by Fred G. Clark to promote free market ideas. By 1963, important neoliberal academics such as Hayek and Antony Fisher, the British economist Graham Hutton, and the British advertising executive John Rodgers (then head of J. Walter Thompson) had all served on its board. They were accompanied from the United States by Friedman, von Mises, Russell Kirk, Richard Mellon Scaife, William F. Buckley jr., and Henry Hazlitt. The AEF ceased to exist in 2003.

ii. Another fundamental institution was *The Mont Pelerin Society (MPS)*, which is an international organisation established in 1947 in Switzerland. It has for decades been a leading forum for international cooperation of the neoliberal elite. Its founders included Friedrich Hayek, Karl Popper, Ludwig von Mises, George Stigler, and Milton Friedman. MPS's revenue was $136,740 in 2012.

iii. *The Intercollegiate Studies Institute, Inc. (ISI)* was founded in USA in 1953 by journalist Frank Chodorov, William F. Buckley jr. and E. Victor Milione. The ISI supports limited government, individual liberty, personal responsibility, the rule of law, a free-market economy, and traditional values (especially in the Judeo-Christian tradition). It focuses on educating students in the ideas behind the free market, the American founding, and Western civilization. It aims to educate future leaders who will shape American culture through academia, journalism, politics, business, law, and other areas. It provides an integrated programme of campus speakers, intensive conferences and seminars, student-led newspapers and clubs, fellowships and scholarships, books and magazines, and online resources. Revenue in 2013 was $6.9 million.

iv. *The Institute of Economic Affairs (IEA)* was founded in 1955 in the UK by Antony Fisher and encouraged by F.A. Hayek. The IEA is a free market think-tank whose mission is 'to improve understanding of the fundamental institutions of a free society by analysing and expounding the role of markets in solving economic and social problems'. The IEA has mainly been funded by tobacco companies, including British American Tobacco, Philip Morris and Japan Tobacco International since 1963. The Social Affairs Unit was established in 1980 as an offshoot of the IEA in order to carry IEA's economic ideas onto the battleground of sociology. Within a few years the Social Affairs Unit became independent from the IEA. The IEA's annual income was £1,059,000 in 2012.

v. *The Liberty Fund*, was established in Indianapolis, USA, in 1960 by businessman Pierre Goodrich to spread libertarian ideas through publications, events, courses, and the sponsorship of students and scholars. Its aim is to fund libertarians' academic study and institutional bases. It offers two online libraries, yearly publishes over 20 books and conducts over 150 conferences every year throughout the United States, Canada, Latin America, and Europe.

vi. *The Institute for Humane Studies (IHS)* is a neoliberal think-tank founded in California, USA in 1961 by F.A. Harper who was a member of Mont Pelerin Society. Its aim is to fund libertarians' academic study and institutional bases. The IHS received revenue amounting to $10.5 million in 2012.

vii. *The Philadelphia Society (PS)* was founded in 1964 by Edwin J. Feulner. It is a membership organisation whose mission is 'to sponsor the interchange of ideas through discussion and writing, in the interest of deepening the intellectual foundation of a free and ordered society, and of broadening the understanding of its basic principles and traditions'. Among its distinguished deceased members are Milton Friedman and F.A. von Hayek. The PS's revenue amounted to $259 thousand in 2012.

Second Wave Think-tanks:

i. *The Heritage Foundation (HF)* was founded in USA in 1973 by Paul Weyrich and Edwin J. Feulner. Feulner studied at the LSE in the 1960s and was also an intern at the IEA. From the start, the HF had tight links to the Republican Party, despite claiming to have a nonpartisan aim; that is, to provide briefings and policy advice to congressmen, executive branch staffers, academics, and journalists. Its mission is to 'formulate and promote conservative public policies based on the principles of free enterprise, limited government, individual freedom, traditional American values, and a strong national defense'. Feulner is former President of the Heritage Foundation, the Mont Pelerin Society, the Intercollegiate Studies Institute and the Philadelphia Society. The HF's revenue amounted to $86 million in 2012.

ii. *Centre for Policy Studies (CPS)*. Founded in the UK in 1974 by Keith Joseph and Margaret Thatcher. Unlike most of the other think-tanks, which regarded themselves as independent of political parties, CPS was explicitly tasked with the exploration and development of new ideas for the Tory leadership. CPS, like the IEA, was crucial in bringing the thought of Hayek and Friedman to wider public attention in Britain. Their work provided a 'public platform' for neoliberal 'academic dissenters' and influenced important journalists. CPS's annual income was £573,567 in 2012.

iii. *The Cato Institute (CI)*, founded in USA in 1977 by a young businessman Ed Crane, Charles Koch and Murray Newton Rothbard. Crane was recruited by billionaire businessman and philanthropist, Charles Koch, of the energy conglomerate Koch Industries. Koch was a major member of the Mont Pelerin Society and a supporter of neoliberal causes. The CI is different from the Heritage Foundation. It is libertarian rather than conservative. It works very closely with The Atlas Economic Research Foundation, the international umbrella organisation of neoliberal think-tanks. Crane was ideologically mainly influenced by Hayek, Friedman, and the American libertarian women authors, Isabel Patterson.

Chapter 8
General Theory of
Collective Entrepreneurship

8.1 Introduction

It is clear from the discussion in this book concerning the wide range of research and theories developed in the field of innovation and entrepreneurship, that it is inadequate to reduce the studies to one factor such as characteristics of entrepreneurs or the intramural organisation of firms. Approaches like that do not generate a substantive explanation of the dynamics of innovation and entrepreneurship. Innovation activity is driven by collaboration between individuals within firms and institutions, as well as between firms and/or institutions. The collaboration generates groups or social units which become autonomous and collectively form their aims and strategies. Innovation activity is, therefore, usually a process of collaboration evolving on the basis of interactive and purposeful thought of the participants of the innovation activity. Furthermore, it is part of the societal processes and cultural context in which it takes place. Thus, it is reasonable to regard innovation and entrepreneurship as being 'collective' (see I. Jonsson, 1991c, p. 109, 1994b and 1995).

Managers of firms and institutions, organised interests and public authorities have in recent years systematically searched for ways to increase collaboration between actors in the field of innovation and entrepreneurship. At the same time, they have emphasised the collective nature of innovation activity. Firms and institutions have increasingly implemented management strategies that boost the participation of employees in creative innovation activities, as we discussed in chapter 6. In this context, human resource management and formation of group identity is of great importance in motivating employees to take part in innovation activity. Measures are taken in order to make risk and remuneration increasingly collective, such as implementing bonuses, profit sharing systems and helping employees to own shares in the corporation in question. Furthermore, the company's future vision is presented to employees and they are supposed to identify with it. They are also empowered by increasing their participation in decision making in the company or institution in question. A liberal and relaxed atmosphere and health issues are emphasised and the work place is developed so as to have more in common with an academic institution. Fairness is highlighted when staff is hired and an applicant's work-related career is taken into consideration. Fairness is also a priority when the outcomes of production periods and management plans are evaluated and when conflicts are solved. In short, measures are taken to create a corporate culture characterised by a high level of trust among employees (P. Mourdoukoutas, 1999, pp. 105–112).

8.2 Principles of Collective Entrepreneurship

The figure below shows the main elements of collective entrepreneurship. Corporate culture is only one among many factors which affect innovation activity. Figure 8.1 highlights some common forms of organising innovation and participants or actors of collective innovation.

Innovation projects financed and executed by the public sector are examples of well- known organisational forms of innovation activity. Projects of this kind are of various types, such as the development of space technology (e.g., NASA), military technology, vaccines against particular diseases, sustainable energy, etc. Public authorities also establish specialised research institutions and funds in order to boost research and development (R&D). In some cases, the aim is to strengthen the general knowledge and know-how of society by stimulating basic research. In other cases, the aim is to steer R&D into applied knowledge creation

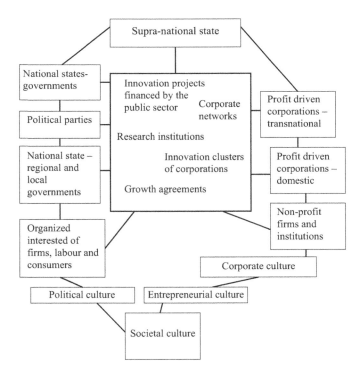

Figure 8.1   Overview of factors of collective entrepreneurship

which supports economic and social objectives. Examples of such measures are universities, national and international research funds and innovation centres.

Regional growth agreements are further examples of collective entrepreneurship that have been implemented in many Western countries. Such agreements are contracts signed by the state, regional authorities, research institutions, development corporations and firms which agree to improve local know-how, education, and R&D in the region in question. In many cases, governmental ministries take part in the agreements and partly finance the activities (A. Östhol and B. Svensson, 2002). The main purpose of growth agreements is to create a permanent partnership of collaboration between regional actors concerning industrial development and innovation. The measures public authorities take in order to develop partnerships are part of the strategy of the new public governance which aims at decentralising the public sector and out-sourcing public services. The emphasis is on 'governance' as opposed to the traditional system of 'public management' characterised by the 'public administration' of a centralised public sector (O.E. Hughes, 2003). Regional 'growth agreements' are examples of decentralised governance. Usually they aim at developing partnerships between firms and supporting public institutions; thus industrial innovation clusters are organised as part of measures aimed at setting up the collaboration of innovation activities.

As we discussed in Chapter 5, regional innovation clusters are an important method of organising collaboration for the purpose of industrial innovation. The same applies to corporate networks, as we highlighted in Chapter 4 when we observed different forms of alliances and collaboration of firms in the field of research and development.

Figure 8.1 draws attention to the main actors that collaborate in the field of industrial innovation. Actors belonging to the political system are shown on the left hand side of the figure. The right side of the figure indicates corporations; that is, both profit driven and non-profit organisations. The left side presents interest groups, political parties, institutions of the national state and supra-national bodies and the right side demonstrates domestic as well as transnational corporations. All these actors attempt, directly and indirectly, to influence the scale and scope of the innovation activity in the society or societies in question.

Political parties also formulate official innovation policies and members of parliament take part in societal decision-making through legislature, and when parties participate in coalition governments, their ministers realise their policies. Political parties and organised interests also influence innovation policy formation at regional and local level. The state finances and executes both basic research and applied R&D, supporting innovation activity through regional innovation centres. Moreover, the state assists innovation projects planned by regional development organisations. In many Western countries, governments stimulate industrial innovation activity with special tax allowances. As an example, costs related to innovation activities are refunded by public funds and costs reduce taxes. These examples indicate that the nation state plays an important role in stimulating innovation activity within its borders.

In recent years, international collaboration in this field has become more important. Nation states are in some cases part of supra-national bodies such as the European Union (EU) and the European Economic Area (EEA). These bodies foster large R&D and innovation programmes. The EEA member countries pay their way into EU research programmes. The total EU expenditure during 2014–20 on its Horizon 2020 research and development programme is expected to be nearly 80 billion euros (European Commission, 2015). The aim of EU research programmes is to enlarge the scale and quality of scientific research in the EU-EEA countries, foster collaboration between European scientists and improve the competitiveness of the industries of member states. A further goal is to tackle societal challenges. All these examples reflect collective entrepreneurship in which the state participates.

Corporations play an important role in collective entrepreneurship. They collaborate with other firms on R&D, as well as working with public institutions. Transnational corporations (TNCs) often cooperate on R&D projects, developing goods with subcontractors and research institutions in the regions where their R&D-departments and production units are located. In some instances, governments require that TNCs buy inputs for their production from local corporations so that local inputs reach a particular minimum percentage level of the total inputs they need for their production. This policy forces the TNCs to collaborate with local firms on developing the inputs and their production technology. As a result, know-how accumulates in the local economy whose competitiveness increases in the long run. Taiwan and South-Korea are the best known examples of an industrial policy of this kind. The concept of 'state entrepreneurship' reflects cases like these in which the state plays an active and strategic role in realising this type of innovation policy (C. Huang, 1989; R.D. Davis and D.W. Ward, 1990; S. Chan and C. Clark, 1992). In many instances, TNCs and domestic corporations seek to cooperate with research institutions and universities on R&D, but this depends on the stage of development of the new technology in question. The main rule is that the corporations collaborate when basic research is needed and the risk of investing in R&D is high (R.R. Nelson, 1988).

Domestic profit driven corporations participate in various kinds of innovation projects. They often participate in regional innovation clusters, play an important role in defining and realising regional growth agreements and collaborate closely with research institutions. This kind of collaboration is often part of an informal knowledge milieu. As an example, we could mention that the innovation activities of the corporation Marel grew out of an informal network of the founders of the company and scientists at the University of Iceland in the 1970s (S. Eliasen, 2001). Marel is a frontier company in the development and production of fish and meat processing technology. In fact, R&D in research institutions and universities often leads to the establishment of high-tech 'start-ups' and in recent years the number of such companies has increased greatly. The bio-technology firm DeCode is an example of a start-up company. It was founded by a Harvard professor and concentrates on DNA-research (P.E. Auerswald and L.M. Branscomb, 2003, p. 81). In addition to firms like these, many corporations are rooted in applied research which is part of an informal milieu of scientists. Marel is an example of this.[1]

The nonprofit sector in Western countries is large, but often goes unnoticed in research into innovation activities. In the EU, 8 per cent of employees who have full-time work are employed in this sector (OECD, 2003, p. 12). The companies, institutions and organisations in the nonprofit sector have various aims, but they share the objective of social improvement for their members, particular social groups or society as a whole. Their collaboration with social groups and public actors is substantial and their innovation activity is extensive. This is particularly true concerning welfare services, as innovation activity in this field is often more advanced compared to public and private institutions in terms of services for particular social groups, patients, etc. Since the 1970s, the number of nonprofit companies has increased faster than that of profit driven companies. In USA, as an example, the number of nonprofit companies grew by 4.7 per cent on average between 1977 and 1992. During the same period, the number of profit driven companies increased by 3.0 per cent. Between 1992 and 1996, the number of nonprofit enterprises increased on average by 5 per cent each year, while that of profit driven companies increased by 1.7 per cent on average 1992–1997 (J.J. Cordes et al., 2004, p. 117).

In Figure 8.1 culture is presumed to be an important factor affecting collective entrepreneurship. The culture of a country influences its corporate culture, willingness to collaborate and entrepreneurial culture. As an example, students of management have claimed that the traditional culture of Japan which, among other things, stems from centuries old collaboration of rice farmers determines the willingness to collaborate both intra-murally and extra-murally (G. Morgan, 1996, pp. 122–6). Traditional culture is, therefore, an explanatory factor as to why collaboration between governmental bodies, public institutions and corporations is much closer in Japan than USA (M.L. Gerlach, 1997). Culture also appears to influence entrepreneurial culture. Research of immigrants in Western countries indicates that there is a difference between groups in terms of willingness to establish businesses and this depends on where they come from. Their cultural background, social characteristics, size of the respective group of immigrants and the level of their language-related exclusion from the rest of society are among the most important explanatory factors (M.D.R. Evans, 1989; J. Rath and R. Kloosterman, 2000).

It appears from our discussion above that collective entrepreneurship takes place both within and between organisations. In Table 8.1 we highlight 'external' forms of collective entrepreneurship; that is, collaboration between independent actors (see I. Jonsson, 1994b and 1995).

---

1   For a detailed discussion of the development in this field in USA, see N. Rosenberg, 2003.

Table 8.1   Various forms of collective entrepreneurship

The state: governments, municipalities and institutes	Organised interests	Firm	Individual
Supporting international R&D projects e.g. EUREKA, ESPRIT, ERASMUS; developmental plans for R&D on regional level; establishing R&D funds and institutions, science parks, etc.; tax reductions for R&D, procurement, etc.	Collaboration between employer's organisations, trade unions and the state in developing R&D and innovative institutes run by organised interests	Procurement, science parks, tax allowances for innovative firms, etc. Technological transfer via foreign MNCs (cf. Taiwan. S-Korea, Singapore, etc.)	Centres and laboratories for inventive individuals
R&D projects in the welfare state, health and work conditions. Collaboration in the field of transformation of skills and flexibility of labour and technology as well as spatial flexibility of labour	R&D funds and institutes stablished and run by employer's organisations and/or trade unions from different branches of industry	R&D funds and institutes established and run in collaboration with employer's organisations and/or trade unions from different branches of industry	R&D contracts with individuals and access arranged to laboratories and other facilities
R&D projects related to the improvement of the environment, consumer information and health standards and gendered technology and discrimination	R&D collaboration by new social movements related to the interests of the new social movements	Collaboration as concerns definition of market niches and access to laboratories and other facilities	R&D contracts with individuals
		R&D and Innovation networks of firms; user-producer relations	firms provide innovative individuals with risk capital, mass produce products and bring them to the market
			Groups of individuals initiate and finance R&D projects

8.3 Theoretical Principles of Collective Entrepreneurship

An entrepreneur is a person who takes financial risks, invests in factors of production and implements organisation and technology that he or she presumes will increase productivity and surplus relative to current practices in particular production or services at a particular time and place. Modern business requires knowledge and technology which most often presumes the participation of more than one actor. Consequently, entrepreneurship is characterised by collaboration of many actors, both within and between organisations. Innovation and entrepreneurship must, therefore, be analysed as a process situated in a societal context such as Figure 8.2 highlights.

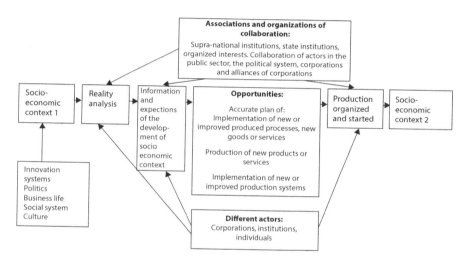

Figure 8.2   The process of entrepreneurship in societal context

The main problem facing entrepreneurs and those who engage in innovation activity is financial risk and imperfect information concerning relevant organisation of production of new goods and services, different assembly of inputs and demand. Collaboration between actors reduces risk and improves quality and accessibility to information. As the diagram above indicates, the actors of innovation and entrepreneurship are many and various. Hence, it is interesting to observe why these actors decide to collaborate and what hinders collaboration.

Let us start with game theory and the concept of 'collective action'. William Baumol (1952) has described how the logic of game theory works in a community setting.

> ... (T)he individual as a citizen, having his share of local pride, may desire
> an improvement in the general future state of welfare in the community. If,
> however, he alone directs his activities in a manner conducive to it, the effects
> of his action may be quite negligible. It is true that in the process he may also be
> improving the value of his own assets, but his private return must be discounted
> by a risk factor which does not apply when calculating expected gain to the
> community. Thus neither private interest nor altruism (except if he has grounds
> for assurance that others, too, will act in a manner designed to promote the future
> welfare of the community) ... can rationally lead him to invest for the future, and
> particularly the far distant future, to an extent appropriate from the point of view
> of the community as a whole. Taken as a commodity, improvement in the future
> state of the community as a whole is one that must serve as a group demand and
> not just the demand of isolated individuals. (W.J. Baumol, 1952, p. 92)

According to Baumol, the individual evaluates his or her willingness to act,
both in terms of utility that he or she will gain as a consequence of the contribution
and in terms of his or her expectations of the participation of others. It is clear
that the individual's utility depends on whether other individuals share his or
her worries for the future welfare of the society (D.J. Connell, 1999). The 'logic
of collective action' calculates the willingness to act. Mancur Olson (1965) has
expressed this phenomenon accordingly: $Ai = Vi - C$. C refers to cost, Vi is the
individual's (i) gross benefit (utility), Ai refers to his or her net utility from the
contribution to a group's collective good. Olson claims that:

If the net benefit for Ai is positive for some i, the group is *privileged* and likely
  to successfully organise;

If the net benefit for Ai is negative for all i, the group is *latent* and likely to fail
  (i.e., not organise).

Moreover, this logic also states that large groups will fail; small groups
may succeed.

Olson gives three arguments to explain why larger groups will fail to further
their own interests:

1. The individual incentive not to contribute increases with group size;
2. Larger groups are less likely to be privileged; and,
3. The larger the number of people who must be coordinated, the higher
    the costs of organising them to an effective level (Hardin, 1982, cited in
    D.J. Connell, 1999, pp. 12–13).

A decision on collective action, or collaboration as Olson describes it, is
essentially a utilitarian decision; that is the actors attempt to maximise their utility
and minimise related costs. A decision of this kind is the more difficult the more

risk it involves and the less perfect information is. Situations like this characterise innovation activity and therefore the explanatory power of game theory is limited concerning innovation and entrepreneurship. In order to explain the reasons collective entrepreneurship is based on when the logic of a utilitarian decision making is inadequate, we need different explanations.

In Figure 8.3, explanatory factors which illustrate collective entrepreneurship are highlighted. Utilitarian decisions are of two kinds. *On the one hand*, they are non-contextual. An example of non-contextual decisions are transactions in simple markets where dealings between actors are random, impersonal and do not imply any relations other than what formal law on transactions prescribes. Decisions of this kind are basic to Adam Smith´s classical economics and orthodox neoclassical economics. The explanatory power of decisions of this kind is very limited with regard to the logic of collective entrepreneurship. *On the other hand*, utilitarian decisions are game theoretical and presume that decisions concerning collaboration and collective action are dependent on time and space; that is, the context in which individuals find themselves at the moment of decision.

We would argue that more factors are needed to explain decisions of collective entrepreneurship than those that determine contextual game theoretical decisions. At hand are factors such as force, Weberian relations of authority and trust. Max Weber explained how people persuade other persons to collaborate. He analysed three kinds of reasons for accepting the authority of others. Firstly, he mentioned 'charismatic domination', that is people obey other persons, or follow their course, because of their personality traits, such as rhetorical skills, manners, looks, etc. Secondly, Weber observed what he called 'traditionalist authority' which hypothesises that people obey other individuals because they have done so for a

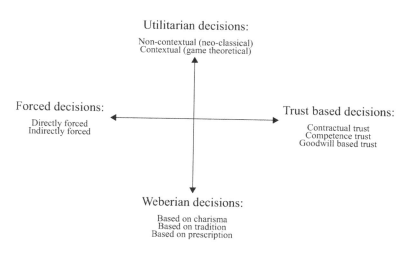

Figure 8.3   Explanatory factors of decisions on collective entrepreneurship

long time or it is traditional to obey persons in those particular positions. Thirdly, he mentions 'legal authority' or what we prefer to call 'prescriptive authority' which refers to a situation when people follow other persons' demands due to law, regulations or formal rules of conduct (M. Weber, 1974, pp. 295–6 and 299).

Innovation activity characterised by 'charismatic domination' is exemplified by cases in which strong personalities and enthusiasts motivate other persons to join a team of innovators organised around the charismatic leader. An example of decisions based on traditionalist authority is the case when firms or governmental bodies organise an R&D project in collaboration with particular research institutes because they have traditionally done so. Finally, there are examples of prescriptive decisions concerning innovation activity such as in corporations that have particular R&D departments and it is clearly defined which members of the staff are responsible for R&D. Furthermore, it is often prescribed by law which actors are authorised to execute R&D in particular fields, such as in the case of medical research and the development of military technology.

Collaboration in R&D is sometimes based on force. Totalitarian societies are instances in point. In the Nazi era, many German corporations were forced to take part in R&D of military technology which strengthened the military production of the Third Reich. Some of the corporations took active part in the rise of Nazism in order to secure their interests (D. Guerin, 1994). The situation was similar in Mussolini's Italy and probably is in China today.

Trust in communication is the opposite of force. As we discussed in Chapter 5, trust appears in three forms: Contractual trust, competence trust and goodwill trust. Contractual trust exists between trading partners and results in the belief that goods will be delivered on time, be of the required specification and agreed quantity and quality. Competence trust refers to the belief that the trading or collaborating partner will fulfil a particular task. Goodwill trust appears in situations where initiatives are undertaken beyond the specific remit of a contract (M. Danson and G. Whittan, 1999). Goodwill trust presumes that participants in an innovation project will not keep ideas or new technology to themselves but share them with other participants in the project.

The three categories of trust are different from Weber's analyses of authority. The concepts of trust-based decisions are founded on the idea that collaboration results from rational and logical evaluation built on clear propositions; that is, information concerning objectives of collaboration and that there is more than one partnership or collaboration available to participate in. However, often these conditions are not at hand, as information on the experience of potential partners is not available. This knowledge is often missing in innovation activity, because of high uncertainty as to what will be the specific characteristics of the goods or services developed and what will be the best organisation of R&D work. Thus it is a matter of considerable uncertainty with whom one should collaborate. The concept of 'cultural capital' (P. Bourdieu) which we discussed in Chapter 5 is useful in explaining reasons for trust among actors and their willingness to collaborate despite uncertainty. Knowledge of participants' social background or 'habitat' is often the critical factor that determines the possibility of collaboration. In particular, if they have the same social background in terms of class, education and social space and share the same cultural and discursive reference world. The right mix of cultural capital makes communication easier and helps generate the informal entrepreneurial milieu which is an important precondition for fast information flow within innovation communities. Figure 8.4 highlights the relationship between cultural capital, trust and Weberian decisions.

New institutionalist economists presume that decisions and actions are determined by convention if they are not utilitarian or 'extrarational' as they call them. This train of thought is based on the game theoretical philosophy of David K. Lewis (1969). It accepts that utilitarian explanations are not sufficient. However, new institutionalist explanations are too abstract to be useful in explaining innovation activity. The above model of decision-making factors is more in tune with everyday reality of people who work on innovations. It also highlights the fact that tradition which generates cooperation grows from concrete experience and is reproduced in the concrete collaboration of innovation actors. Consequently, the precondition for collective entrepreneurship is not simply the belief that the welfare of the community will increase in the future (cf. Hardin, 1982, pp. 160 and 175). Rather, the precondition is experience of collaboration in the past, the image and the reputation the actors have created as well as their reference world.

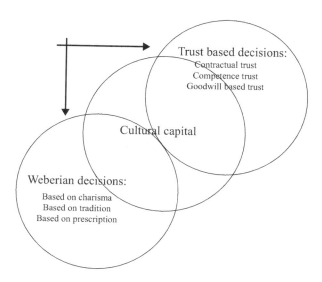

Figure 8.4   Explanatory factors of participation in collective entrepreneurship

8.4 Conclusion

In this book, we have observed various theories and research into innovation and entrepreneurship. A common feature of most of these theories is that they are 'monistic' rather than general. Their point of departure is that one or only a few factors adequately explain the dynamics of innovation and entrepreneurship. They do not emphasise the importance of actors and the interaction of diverse explanatory forces. These theories point at factors such as inventions in science and technology, market demand, egoism, profit maximisation of firms, etc. In this book, we have argued that innovation activity is so complicated that it can neither be reduced to a sole factor nor explained in terms of the narrow theoretical framework of a single discipline. A general theory is needed to explain innovation and entrepreneurship; that is, a theory which can clarify why particular explanatory factors of innovation and entrepreneurship are important in the different fields of innovation and entrepreneurship during specific historical periods or in particular countries. In this concluding chapter, we have sketched a framework which includes the main factors such a general theory should incorporate. The main emphasis is on the societal and collective nature of innovation activity. This view postulates that the main precondition for innovation activity is a culture which breeds the willingness to collaborate, creativity and tolerance concerning new ways of thinking and generating knowledge. Market mechanisms alone do not generate these preconditions and therefore other actors than competing corporations play an important role. The state and the public sector, the nonprofit sector, political actors and organised interests have a significant function in this respect. The increasingly important role of these actors has become ever more apparent as the capitalist system has matured and corporations increasingly need more productive innovation systems.

The paradox of capitalism is that as it matures, it needs ever more intensive socialisation of the process of capital accumulation. This goes both for 'externalities' of production and intra-mural management strategies, as we discussed in the last two chapters of this book. The socialisation of capital accumulation has become ever more focused and better organised in the public sphere (J. Habermas, 1975). Efficient production systems are an increasingly important factor in the competitiveness of nations and innovation systems are an essential aspect of the competitiveness of firms, regions and countries in the context of the new regionalism, especially in Europe (M.M. Keating, 1998). Our general theory of collective entrepreneurship is a contribution to an interdisciplinary, institutional analysis of these general developmental tendencies of the social economies of capitalism.

References

Abelson, D.E. (2009). *Do Think Tanks Matter?: Assessing the Impact of Public Policy Institutes*. Montreal: McGill-Queen's University Press.

Abowd, P. (2015). *Koch Brothers Pour more Cash into Think Tanks*. Center for Public Integrity. Retrieved from publicintegrity.org

Adam Smith Institute (1989). *The First Hundred*. London: The Adam Smith Institute.

Andersen, K.V., Bugge, M.M., Hansen, H.K., Isaksen, A., and Raunio, M. (2010). 'One Size Fits All? Applying the Creative Class Thesis onto a Nordic Context' in *European Planning Studies*, 18(10). London: Routledge.

Archer, M. (1995). *Realist Social Theory: The Morphogenetic Approach*. Cambridge: Cambridge University Press.

Armstrong, P., Glyn, A., and Harrison, J. (1984). *Capitalism since World War II: The Making and Breaking of the Great Boom*. London: Fontana Paperbacks.

Arrow, K.J. (1962). 'The Economic Implications of Learning by Doing' in *Review of Economic Studies*, XXIX.

Atladóttir, Kristín (2007). *Tacit Knowledge as a Driver for Innovation*. MA-Dissertation in Innovation and Entrepreneurship Studies. Bifröst: Bifröst University.

Auerswald, P.E. and Branscomb, L.M. (2003). 'Collective Entrepreneurship between Invention and Innovation' in Hart, D.M. (ed.), *The Emergence of Entrepreneurial Policy; Governance, Start-ups, and Growth in the U.S. Knowledge Economy*. Cambridge: Cambridge University Press.

Baldwin, C. and Hippel, E. von (2009). *Modeling a Paradigm Shift: From Producer Innovation to User and Open Collaborative Innovation*. Boston: MIT Sloan School of Management Working Paper # 4764–09. Retrieved papers.ssrn.com

Baran, P.A. and Sweezy, P.M. (1973). *Monopoly Capital; An Essay on the American Economic and Social Order*. Harmondsworth: Penguin Books.

Barnes, B., Bloor, D. and Henry, J. (1996). *Scientific Knowledge: A Sociological Analysis*. London: Athlone Press.

Baron, S., Field, J. and Schuller, T. (2000). *Social Capital; Critical Perspectives*. Oxford: Oxford University Press.

Baumol, W.J. (1952). *Welfare Economics and the Theory of the State*. Cambridge, MA: Harvard University Press.

Baumol, W.J. (1959). *Business Behavior, Value and Growth*. New York: Macmillan.

BBC (2015). *In Quotes: Margaret Thatcher*. Retrieved from bbc.com.

Bell, D. (1960). *The End of Ideology: On the Exhaustion of Political Ideas in the Fifties*. Glencoe: Free Press of Glencoe.

Berle, A.A. and Means, G.C. (1932). *The Modern Corporation and Private Property*. New York: Macmillan.

Bernhard, V. (1976). 'Cotton Mather and the Doing of Good: A Puritan Gospel of Wealth' in *The New England Quarterly*, 49(2). The New England Quarterly, Inc. Retrieved from jstor.org

Bessant, J. (2005). *High-Involvement Innovation; Building and Sustaining Competitive Advantage through Continuous Change*. Chichester: Wiley.

Bion, W.R. (1959). *Experiences in Groups*. New York: Basic Books.

Blair, T. (2011). *A Journey*. London: Arrow Books.

Bloem, J., van Doorn, M. and van Ommeren, E. (2007). *Open for Business: Open Source Inspired Innovation*. Paris: Research Institute for the Analysis of New Technology.

Blois, K. (1972). 'Vertical Quasi-integration' in *Journal of Industrial Economics*. 20(3).

Bontje, M. and Musterd, S. (2009). 'Creative Industries, Creative Class and Competitiveness: Expert Opinions Critically Appraised' in *Geoforum*, 40(5). New York: Elsevier.

Bornstein, D. (2004). *How to Change the World; Social Entrepreneurs and the Power of New Ideas*. New York: Oxford University Press.

Boulding, K.E. (1981). *Evolutionary Economics*. London: SAGE.

Bourdieu, P. (1993). *Outline of a Theory of Practice*. Cambridge: Cambridge University Press.

Bourdieu, P. (1997) [1983]. 'The Forms of Capital' in Halsey, E.H. (ed.), *Education: Culture, Economy and Society*. Oxford: Oxford University Press.

Buckley, S. (2006*). Prime Minister and Cabinet*. Edinburgh: Edinburgh University Press.

Callinincos, A. (1999). *Social Theory. A Historical Introduction*. Cambridge: Polity Press.

Callo, J.F. (1999). *Legacy of Leadership: Lessons from Admiral Lord Nelson*. Central Point: Hellgate Press.

Cantillon, R. (1755). *Essai Sur la Nature du Commerce en Général* [Essay on the Nature of Trade in General]. Retrieved from archive.org.

Casson, M. (1982). *The Entrepreneur; An Economic Theory*. New Jersey: Barnes & Noble Books.

Castells, M. (2000). *The Rise of the Network Society (The Information Age: Economy, Society and Culture)*. Vol. 1, 2nd edition. London: Wiley-Blackwell.

Chamberlin, E. (1948) [1933]. *The Theory of Monopolistic Competition*. Cambridge, MA: Harvard University Press.

Chan, S. and Clark, C. (1992). *Flexibility, Foresight, and Fortuna in Taiwan's Development: Navigating Between Scylla and Charybdis*. London: Routledge.

Chesbrough, H. (2006). *Open Innovation: Researching a New Paradigm*. Oxford: Oxford University Press.

Clark, J.M. (1940). 'Toward a Concept of Workable Competition' in *American Economic Review*, 30. Pittsburgh: American Economic Association.

Coase, R.H. (1937). 'The Nature of the Firm' in *Economica*, 4. London: Blackwell Publishing.

Cockburn, C. (1981). 'The Material of Male Power' in *Feminist Review*, 9(1). London: Palgrave.

Cohen, D. and Prusak, L. (2001). *In Good Company; How Social Capital Makes Organizations Work.* Harvard: Harvard Business School Press.

Cole, G.D.H. (1917). *Self-Government in Industry*. London: Bell & Sons.

Cole, G.D.H. (1920). *Guild Socialism Re-stated*. London: Leonard Parsons Ltd.

Coleman, J. (1994). *Foundations of Social Theory*. Harvard: Harvard University Press.

Collins, R. and Makowsky, M. (1998). *The Discovery of Society*. Boston: McGraw-Hill International Editions.

Connell, D.J. (1999). *Collective Entrepreneurship: In Search of Meaning*. Retrieved from djconnell.ca

Cordes, J.C., Steuerle, C.E. and Twombly, E. (2004). 'Dimensions of Nonprofit Entrepreneurship: An Exploratory Essay' in Eakin, D.H. and Rosen, H.S. (eds), *Public Policy and the Economics of Entrepreneurship*. Cambridge: MIT Press.

Craib, I. (1976). *Existentialism and Sociology: A Study of Jean-Paul Sartre*. Cambridge: Cambridge University Press.

Crepaldi, C., De Rosa, E. and Pesce, F. (2012). *Literature Review on Innovation in Social Services in Europe: Sectors of Health, Education and Welfare Services*. Milano: IRS – Instituto per la Ricerca Sociale.

Crewe, I. and Searing, D.D. (1988). 'Ideological Change in the British Conservative Party' in *American Political Science Review*, 82(2). Cambridge: Cambridge University Press.

Danson, M. and Whittan, G. (1999). 'Clustering, Innovation and Trust: The Essentials of Clustering Strategy for Scotland' in Fischer, M.M., Suarez-Villa, L. and Steiner, M. (eds), *Innovation, Networks and Localities*. Berlin: Springer-Verlag.

Davis, R.D. and Ward, D.W. (1990). 'The Entrepreneurial State; Evidence from Taiwan' in *Comparative Political Studies*, 23(3). SAGE Publications.

Denham, A. (1997). *British Think Tanks and the Climate of Opinion*. London: Routledge.

Dicken, P. (1992). *Global Shift, Second Edition*. New York: Guilford Press.

Douglas, D. (1989). 'Breakthrough of the Brotherhood' in *Herald Scotland* (1989, 3 October) Retrieved from heraldscotland.com.

Drucker, P.F. (1964). *Managing for Results*. London: Heinemann.

Drucker, P.F. (2004). *Innovation and Entrepreneurship*. Oxford: Butterworth-Heinemann.

Duijn, van J.J. (1985). *The Long Wave in Economic Life*. London: George Allen & Unwin.

Eatwell, J. and Milgate, M. (1983). *Keynes's Economics and the Theory of Value and Distribution*. London: Dockworth.

Edwards, L. (2002). *The Conservative Revolution: The Movement that Remade America*. New York: The Free Press.

Eliasen, S. (2001). *Lokal innovation og produktion af teknologi til fiskeindustri – Betingelser for lokalisering af innovation og produktion af maskiner og udstyr til fiskeindustri i Alaska og Island* [Local innovation and production of technology for the fishing industry – Opportunities for localising innovation and the production of machinery and equipment for the fishing industry in Alaska and Iceland]. Doctoral dissertation, Institut for Geografi og Internationale Udviklingsstudier. Roskilde Universitetscenter.

Elster, J. (1985). *Explaining Technical Change*. Cambridge: Cambridge University Press.

European Commission (1995). *Green paper on Innovation*. Brussels: European Commission. Retrieved from europa.eu.

European Commission (2015). *HORIZON 2020; The EU Framework Programme for Research and Innovation*. Retrieved from ec.europa.eu.

Evans, E.J. (1997). *Thatcher and Thatcherism*. London: Routledge.

Evans, M.D.R. (1989). 'Immigrant Entrepreneurship: Effects of Ethnic Market Size and Isolated Labor Pool' in *American Sociological Review*, 54(6). London: SAGE.

Etzkowitz, H. (2008). *The Triple Helix: University-Industry-Government Innovation in Action*. London: Routledge.

Fagerberg, J. (1988). 'International Competitiveness' in *The Economic Journal; The Quarterly Journal of the Royal Economic Society*, 98(June). The Royal Economic Society, Cambridge: Cambridge University Press.

Fellner, W. (1961). 'Two Propositions in the Theory of Induced Innovations' in *Economic Journal*, 71. London: Blackwell Publishing.

Fine, B. (1999). 'The Development State is Dead – Long Live Social Capital' in *Development and Change*, 30. London: John Wiley and Sons.

Fine, B. (2001). *Social Capital versus Social Theory; Political Economy and the Social Science at the turn of the Millennium*. London: Routledge.

Fisher, S.G. (1903). *The True Benjamin Franklin*. Philadelphia: J. B. Lippincott Company. Kindle: Project Gutenberg.

Fisher III, W.W. and Oberholzer-Gee, F. (2013). 'Strategic Management of Intellectual Property: An Integrated Approach' in *California Management Review*, 55(4). Berkeley: CMR.

Fligstein, N. (2002). *The Architecture of Markets; An Economic Sociology of Twenty-First Century Capitalist Societies*. Princeton: Princeton University Press.

Florida, R. (2002). *The Rise of the Creative Class and How it's Transforming Work, Leisure, Community and Everyday Life*. New York: Basic Books.

Florida, R., Mellander, C.P.A. and Stolarick, K.M. (2010). 'Talent, Technology and Tolerance in Canadian Regional Development' in *The Canadian Geographer / Le Géographe canadien*, 54(3). Canadian Association of Geographers / L'Association canadienne des géographes.

Foster, J. (1991). 'The Institutionalist (Evolutionary) School' in Mair, D. and Miller, A.G. (eds), *A Modern Guide to Economic Thought; An Introduction to Comparative Schools of Thought in Economics*. Aldershot: Edward Elgar.

Franklin, B. (2006). *Autobiography of Benjamin Franklin*. Retrieved from Gutenberg.org.

Freeman, C. (1984). *Long Waves in the World Economy*. London: Pinter Publishers.

Freeman, C. (1987). *Technology Policy and Economic Performance: Lessons from Japan*. London: Pinter.

Freeman, C. (1994) 'The economics of technical change. A critical survey of the literature' in *Cambridge Journal of Economics*, 18(5). London: Academic Press.

Freeman, C., Clark, J. and Soete, L. (1982). *Unemployment and Technical Innovation; A Study of Long Waves and Economic Development*. London: Frances Pinter Publishers.

Freeman, C. and Perez, C. (1988). 'Structural Crises of Adjustment: Business Cycles and Investment Behaviour' in Dosi, G., Freeman, C., Nelson R., Silverberg, G. and Soete, L. (eds), *Technical Change and Economic Theory*. London: Pinter Publishers.

Friedman, M. (1968). 'The Role of Monetary Policy' in *American Economic Review*, 58(1). Pittsburgh: American Economic Association.

Fukuyama, F. (1989). 'The End of History?' in *The National Interest*. Washington: Center for the National Interest.

Fukuyama, F. (1997). *The End of Order*. London: Social Market Foundation.

Gabora, L.M. (2000). 'The Beer can Theory of Creativity' in P. Bentley and D. Corne (eds), *Creative Evolutionary Systems*. San Francisco: Morgan Kauffman.

Gabora, L.M. (2002). 'Cognitive Mechanisms Underlying the Creative Process' in Hewett, T. and Kavanagh, T. (eds). *Proceedings of the Fourth International Conference on Creativity and Cognition*. UK: Loughborough University.

Gadamer, H.-G. (1977). *Philosophical Hermeneutics*. London: University of California Press.

Galbraith, J.K. (1974). *The New Industrial State*. Harmondsworth: Penguin Books.

Gambetta, D. (1988). *Trust: Making and Breaking Cooperative Relations*. Oxford: Blackwell.

Gamble, A. (2001). 'Neoliberalism' in *Capital & Class*, 25(3). London: CSE.

Gamble, A. (2009). *Spectre at the Feast: Capitalist Crisis and the Politics of Recession*. Basingstoke: Palgrave Macmillan.

Garud, R. and Van de Ven, A.H. (1992). 'An Empirical Evaluation of the Internal Corporate Venturing Process' in *Strategic Management Journal*, 13(S1). London: John Wiley and Sons.

Gee, J. M.A. (1991). 'The Neoclassical School' in Mair, D. and Miller, A.G. (eds), *A Modern Guide to Economic Thought: An Introduction to Comparative Schools of Thought in Economics*. Aldershot: Edward Elgar.

Gelderen van J. (J. Fedder) (1913). Springvloed: beschouwingen over industriële ontwikkeling en prijsbeweging'[Observations on industrial development and price fluctuations] in *De Nieuwe Tijd Jaargang*, 18. Amsterdam: Fortuyn.

Gerlach, M. (1992). *Alliance Capitalism: The Social Organization of Japanese Business*. Berkeley: University of California Press.

Glaeser, E. (2005). 'Review of Richard Florida's The Rise of the Creative Class' in *Regional Science and Urban Economics*, 35(5). Elsevier Ltd.

Glyn, A. and Sutcliffe, B. (1972). *British Capitalism, Workers and the Profits Squeeze*. London: Penguin.

Gorz. A. (1978). *Division of Labour*. Brighton: Harvester.

Granovetter, M. (1973). 'The Strength of Weak Ties' in *American Journal of Sociology*, 76(6). Chicago: University of Chicago Press.

Granovetter, M. (1985). 'Economic Action and Social Structure: The Problem of Embeddedness' in *American Journal of Sociology*, 91(3). Chicago: University of Chicago Press.

Gray, J. (1999). *False Dawn: The Delusions of Global Capitalism*. London: Granta Books.

Gregg, P. (2011). 'New Labour and Inequality' in *The Political Quarterly*, 81(S1). Oxford: Blackwell Publishing Ltd.

Grint, K. (1998). *The Sociology of Work: An Introduction; 2nd Edition*. London: Polity Press.

Gruening, G. (2001). 'Origin and Theoretical Basis of New Public Management' in *International Public Management Journal*, 4. Oxford: Taylor & Francis Group Ltd.

Guerin, D. (1994). *Fascism and Big Business*. New York: Anchor Foundation.

Habermas, J. (1971). 'Technology as Ideology' in *Toward a Rational Society: Student Protest, Science and Politics*. London: Heinemann.

Habermas, J. (1975). *Legitimation Crisis*. Boston: Beacon Press.

Habermas, J. (1978). *Knowledge and Human Interests*. London: Heinemann.

Hall, P.A. and Soskice, D.W. (2001). *Varieties of Capitalism: The Institutional Foundations of Comparative Advantage*. Oxford: Oxford University Press.

Hall, P.D. (2003). 'Doing Good in the World: Cotton Mather and the Origins of Modern Philanthropy', in *Documentary History of Philanthropy and Voluntarism in America*. Harvard. Retrieved from hks.harvard.edu

Hall, S. and Jacques, M. (1983). *The Politics of Thatcherism*. London: Lawrence and Wishart.

Halldórsdóttir, Kristín (2005). *Samspil nýsköpunar og hönnunar; Samanburðarrannsókn á stoðkerfum Íslands og Danmerkur* [The Interaction between Innovation and Design: A Comparison of the Support Systems of Denmark and Iceland]. M.A. dissertation, University of Bifrost, Iceland.

Hames, T. and Feasey, R. (1994) 'Anglo-American Think Tanks under Reagan and Thatcher' in Adonis, A. and Hames, T. *A Conservative Revolution? The Thatcher-Reagan Decade in Perspective*. Manchester: Manchester University Press.

Hardin, Russell (1982). *Collective Action*. Baltimore: Johns Hopkins University Press.

Harding, S. (1991). *Whose Science? Whose Knowledge?: Thinking from Women's Lives*. Ithaca: Cornell University Press.

Hayek, F.A. von (1934). 'Capital and Industrial Fluctuations' in *Econometrica*, 2(2). New York: The Econometric Society. Retrieved from jstor.org.

Hayek, F.A. von (1935). *Prices and Production*. London: Routledge and Kegan Paul.

Hayek, F.A. von (1937). 'Economics and Knowledge' in *Economica*, IV. Retrieved from jstor.org.

Hayek, F.A. von (2008). *The Road to Serfdom* (The Collected Works of FA Hayek, Vol. II), B. Caldwell (ed.). London: Routledge.

Hayek, F.A. von (2009). *A Tiger by the Tail: The Keynesian Legacy of Inflation*. S.R. Shenoy (ed.), 3rd edn, Auburn: Institute of Economic Affairs and Ludwig von Mises Institute.

Hills, J., Brewer, M., Jenkins, S., Lister, R. and Lupton, R. (2010). *An Anatomy of Economic Inequality in the UK – Summary Report of the National Equality Panel*. London: Government Equalities Office.

Hippel, E. von (1988). *The Sources of Innovation*. Oxford: Oxford University Press.

Hippel, E. von (2014). *Open User Innovation*. Retrieved from interaction-design. org.

Hirschman, A. (1984). 'Against Parsimony: Three Easy Ways of Complicating Some Categories of Economic Discourse' in *American Economic Review: Papers and Proceedings*, 74(2). Pittsburgh: American Economic Association.

Hodgson, G.M. (1993). *Economics and Evolution: Bringing Life Back into Economics*. London: Polity Press.

Holton, R.J. (1992). *Economy and Society*. London: Routledge.

Holzmann, T., Klaus, S.K. and Katzy, B.R. (2014). 'Matchmaking as Multi-sided Market for Open Innovation' in *Technology Analysis & Strategic Management*, 26(6). London: Routledge/ Taylor & Francis.

Hoplin, N. (2008). *Funding Fathers: The Unsung Heroes of the Conservative Movement*. Washington DC: Regnery Publishing.

Huang, C. (1989). 'The State and Foreign Investment: The Case of Taiwan and Singapore' in *Comparative Political Studies*, 22(1). SAGE Publications.

Hughes, O.E. (2003). *Public Management and Administration: An Introduction*. Houndsmills: Palgrave Macmillan.

Hume, D. (1739). *A Treatise on Human Nature: Being an Attempt to Introduce the Experimental Method of Reasoning into Moral Subjects*. Retrieved from archive.org

ILO (2008). *World of Work Report 2008*. Geneva: International Labour Organization.

Imai, M. (1986). *Kaizen: The Key to Japan's Competitive Success*. McGraw-Hill/ Irwin.

Isaksen, A. and Hauge, E. (2002). *Regional Clusters in Europe*. Observatory of European SMEs 2002, No. 3, Brussels: European Commission.

Jensen, M. (1989). 'Eclipse of the Public Corporation' in *Harvard Business Review*, 67(5).

Johnson, P. (2008). 'The Tax System under Labour' in *The Political Quarterly*, 79(S1). London: The Political Quarterly Publishing Co. Ltd.

Jones, D.S. (2012). *Masters of the Universe – A History of Neoliberalism*. Princeton: Princeton University Press.

Jonsson, F. and Jonsson, I (1992). *Innri hringurinn í íslensku atvinnulífi* [The Inner Circle in Icelandic Business Life]. Reykjavík: National Institute of Social and Economic Research.

Jonsson, I. (1988). *Tækniþróun og samkeppnisstaða; smáríki og nýja tæknin*, Skýrsla unnin fyrir ársfund Iðntæknistofnunar Íslands í apríl 1988 [Technical Change and Competitiveness: Small States and the New Technology], Reykjavík: National Institute of Social and Economic Research.

Jonsson, I. (1989). 'Capitalist restructuring' in Þjóðmál, *1*. Reykjavík: National Institute of Social and Economic Research.

Jonsson, I. (1990, 4 January). 'Háskólinn á Akureyri í ljósi raunsærrar byggðastefnu' [The University of Akureyri and realist regional policy] in *Tíminn*. Reykjavík: Framsóknarflokkurinn.

Jonsson, I. (1991a). 'Keynes's General Theory and Structural Competitiveness' in Þjóðmál, 2. Reykjavík: National Institute of Social and Economic Research.

Jonsson, I. (1991b). 'Velferðarkerfi heimilanna og fyrirtækjanna'.[Welfare state of households and corporations] in Þjóðmál, *2*. Reykjavík: National Institute of Social and Economic Research.

Jonsson, I. (1991c). *Hegemonic Politics and Accumulation Strategies in Iceland 1944–1990: Long Waves in the World Economy, Regimes of Accumulation and Uneven Development. Small States, Microstates and Problems of World Market Adjustment*. D.Phil. dissertation, University of Sussex.

Jonsson, I. (1994, 18 May). 'Nýsköpun, tæknigarðar og erlendar fjárfestingar' (Innovation, science parks and foreign direct investment) in *Viðskiptablaðið*, Reykjavík.

Jonsson, I. (1994b). 'Collective Entrepreneurship and Microeconomies' in Greifenberg, T. (ed.), *Sustainability in the Arctic*. Aalborg: NARF/Aalborg University Press.

Jonsson, I. (1995). *West Nordic Countries in Crisis: Neo-Structuralism, Collective Entrepreneurship and Microsocieties Facing Global Systems of Innovation*. Copenhagen: Copenhagen Business School.

Jonsson, I. (1996). 'Reflexive Modernization, Organizational Dependency and Global Systems of Embedded Development – A Post-Colonial View' in *Cultural and Social Research in Greenland 95/96 – Essays in Honour of Robert Petersen*. Nuuk: Ilisimatusarfik/Atuakkiorfik.

Jonsson, I. (2001). 'Societal Paradigms and Rural Development – the Case of Iceland-' in Granberg, L., Kovách, I. and Tovey, H. (eds), *The Green Ring – De-Peasantisation of Rural Europe*. London: Ashgate.

Jonsson, I. (2012). 'Explaining the Crisis of Iceland – a Realist Approach' in *Journal of Critical Realism*. Sheffield: Equinox Publishing.

Keating, M. (1998). *The New Regionalism in Western Europe: Territorial Restructuring and Political Change*. Cheltenham: Edward Elgar.

Keen, S. (2001). *Debunking Economics: The Naked Emperor of the Social Sciences*. Annandale: Pluto Press Australia.

Kersbergen, K. van (1995). *Social Capitalism: A Study of Christian Democracy and the Welfare State*. London: Routledge.

Keynes, J.M. (1983). *General Theory of Employment, Interest and Money*. London: Macmillan.

Klein, M. (1981). *Love, Guilt and Reparation and Other Works*. London: Hogarth.

Kline, S.J. (1985). 'Research is not a linear process' in *Research Management*, 28(4). New York: Industrial Research Institute.

Kline, S.J. (1989). *Innovation Styles in Japan and the United States: Cultural Bases; Implications for Competitiveness*. Report INN-3B, Thermosciences Division, Mechanical Engineering, Stanford University.

Kline, S.J. and Rosenberg, N. (1986). 'An Overview of Innovation' in Landau, R. and Rosenberg, N. (eds), *The Positive Sum Strategy. Harnessing Technology for Economic Growth*. Washington DC: National Academy Press.

Kolko, G. (1971). *Wealth and Power in America: An Analysis of Social Class and Income Distribution*. Twelfth printing, New York: Praeger Publishers.

Kondratieff, N.D. (1926). 'Die lange Wellen der Konjunktur' in *Archiv für Sozialwissenschaft und Sozialpolitik*, 56(3).

Kropotkin, P. (1904). *Mutual Aid: A Factor of Evolution*. London: William Heinemann.

Kuhn, T. (1970). *The Structure of Scientific Revolutions*. Chicago: University Of Chicago Press.

Kuttner, R. (1999). *Everything for Sale: The Virtues and Limits of Markets*. Chicago: University of Chicago Press.

Kuznets, S. (1940). 'Schumpeter's Business Cycles' in *American Economic Review*, 30(2). Pittsburgh: American Economic Association.

Kuznets, S. (1953). *Economic Change*. New York: W.W. Norton.

Lagendijk, A. (1999). *Innovation, Networks and Localities*. Berlin: Springer.

Levine, S.S. and Prietula, M.J. (2014). *Open Collaboration for Innovation: Principles and Performance*. Retrieved from arxiv.org.

Lewis, D.K. (1969). *Convention: A Philosophical Study*. Cambridge: Cambridge University Press.

Lewis, P. (2000). 'Realism, Causality and the Problem of Social Structure' in *Journal for the Theory of Social Behavior*. 30(3), London: John Wiley and Sons.

Lindegaard, Stefan (2010). *The Open Innovation Revolution: Essentials, Roadblocks, and Leadership Skills*. Hoboken: John Wiley & Sons.

Locke, J. (1690). *Two Treatises of Government*. Retrieved from archive.org

Lowery, D. and Brasker, H. (2004). *Organized Interests and American Government*, New York: McGraw-Hill.

Lundberg, E. (1961). *Produktivitet och räntabilitet. Studier i kapitalets betydelse inom svenskt näringsliv* [Productivity and Profitability. Studies in the Role of Capital in the Swedish Economy]. Stockholm: Studieförbundet näringsliv och samhälle.

Lundvall, B.-Å. (1988). 'Innovation as an Interactive Process' in Dosi, G., Freeman, C., Nelson, R., Silverman, G. and Soete, L. (eds), *Technical Change and Economic Theory*. London: Pinter Publishers.

Lundvall, B.-Å. (1992). *National Systems of Innovation: Towards a Theory of Innovation and Interactive Learning*. London: Pinter Publishers.

Lundvall, B.-Å. Aaen, N. and Olesen, M. (1983). *Det landbrugsindustrielle kompleks: teknologiudvikling, konkurrenceevne og beskæftigelse* [The agricultural industrial complex: technical development, competitiveness and employment.]. Ålborg: Ålborg University Press.

Lundvall, B.-Å. and Foray, D. (1996). *Employment and Growth in the Knowledge-based Economy*. Paris: OECD.

Maddison, A. (2004). *World Economy: Historical Statistics on C-rom*. Paris: OECD.

Mahan, A.T. (1897). *The Life of Nelson*. Vol. 1, London: Sampson Low, Marston, & Company Limited. Kindle Edition.

Malerba, F. (1992). 'Learning by Firms and Incremental Technical Change' in *The Economic Journal*, 102(413). Oxford: Blackwell Publishers.

Mandel, E. (1974) [1962]. *Marxist Economic Theory*. London: Merlin.

Mandel, E. (1976). *Late Capitalism*. London: NLB.

Mandel, E. (1984). 'Explaining Long Waves of Capitalist Development' in Freeman, C. (ed.), *Long Waves in the World Economy*. London: Frances Pinter (Publishers).

March, J. and Simon, H.A. (1958). *Organizations*. New York: Wiley.

Marrocu, E. and Paci, R. (2012). 'Education or Creativity: What Matters Most for Economic Performance?' in *Economic Geography*, 88(4).New York: Wiley.

Marshall, A. (1890/1920). *Principles of Economics*. London: Macmillan and Co., Ltd. Retrieved from econlib.org

Marshall, M. (1987). *Long Waves of Regional Development*. London: Macmillan.

Marx, K. (1976). *Capital*, Vol. 1. Harmondsworth: Penguin Books.

Marx, K. (1981). *Capital*, Vol. 3. Harmondsworth: Penguin Books.

Maslow, A. (1943). 'A Theory of Human Motivation' in *Psychological Review*, 50(4). Retrieved from psychclassics.yorku.ca

Massey, D., Quintas, P. and Wield, D. (1992). *High-Tech Fantasies: Science Parks in Society, Science and Space*. London: Routledge.

McGregor, D. (1960). *The Human Side of Enterprise*. New York: McGraw Hill.

Mendner, J.H. (1975). *Technologische Entwiklung und Arbeitsprozess: zur reellen Subsumtion der Arbeit unter das Kapital* [Technical Development and Work Processes: towards a real subsumption of work under capital]. Frankfurt am Main: Fischer Taschenbuch Verlag.

Mensch, G. (1975). *Das Technologische Patt* [Stalemate in Technology]. Neustadt an der Weinstraße: Umschau Verlag.

Mensch, G. (1979). *Stalemate in Technology*. New York: Ballinger.

Mescon, T.S., Montanari, J.R. and Tinker, T. (1981). 'The Personalities of Independent and Franchise Entrepreneurs: An Empirical Analysis of Concept Counterpoint' in *Journal of Enterprise Management*, 3(2). Pergamon Press: Oxford.

Midgley, D.F., Morrison, P.D. and Roberts, J.H. (1992). 'The Effect of Network Structure in Industrial Diffusion Processes' in *Research Policy*, 21(6). Melbourne: Elsevier.

Mill, J.S. (1843). *A System of Logic*. Retrieved from Gutenberg.org

Mill, J.S. (1845). 'Claims of Labour' in Edinburgh Review, *LXXXI*. Published in Williams, G.L. (1976). *John Stuart Mill on Politics and Society*. Glasgow: Fontana/Collins.

Mill, J.S. (1848). *Principles of Political Economy*. Retrieved from Gutenberg.org

Mills, C.W. (1956). *The Power Elite*. Oxford: Oxford University Press.

Mises, L. von [1949] (1980). *Human Action: A Treatise on Economics*. Auburn: The Ludwig von Mises Institute. Retrieved from mises.org

Montesquieu, C-L. (1748). *The Spirit of Laws*. Retrieved from archive.org

Morgan, G. (1996). *Images of Organization*. London: SAGE Publications.

Mort, G.S., Weerawardena, J. and Carnegie, K. (2003). 'Social Entrepreneurship: Towards Conceptualisation' in *International Journal of Nonprofit and Voluntary Sector Marketing*, 8(1), London: Henry Stewart Publications,

Mourdoukoutas, P. (1999). *Collective Entrepreneurship in a Globalizing Economy*. London: Quorum Books.

Mowery, D.C. and Rosenberg, N. (1979). 'The Influence of Market Demand upon Innovation: A Critical Review of some Recent Empirical Studies' in *Research Policy*, 8.

Mulé, R. (2001). *Political Parties, Games and Redistribution*. Cambridge: Cambridge University Press.

Mumford, M.D. (2002). 'Social Innovation: Ten Cases from Benjamin Franklin' in *Creativity Research Journal*, 14(2). Mahwah: Lawrence Erlbaum Associates.

Mumford, M.D. and Gustafson, S.B. (1988). 'Creativity Syndrome: Integration, Application, and Innovation' in *Psychological Bulletin*, 103(1), Washington: American Psychological Association.

Murlis, M.A. and Murlis, H. (2004). *Reward Management: A Handbook of Remuneration Strategy and Practice*. London: Kogan Page.

Myrdal, G. (1957). *Economic Theory and the Underdeveloped Regions*. London: Duckworth.

Nelson, R.R. (1959). 'The Simple Economics of Basic Scientific Research' in *Journal of Political Economy*, 67(3). Chicago: The University of Chicago Press.

Nelson, R.R. (1988). 'Institutions Supporting Technical Change in the United States' in Dosi, G., Freeman, C., Nelson R., Silverberg, G. and Soete L. (eds). *Technical Change and Economic Theory*. London: Pinter Publishers.

Nelson, R.R. and Winter, S.G. (1982). *An Evolutionary Theory of Economic Change*. Cambridge, Massachusetts: The Belknap Press of Harvard University Press.

Nicolas, H.N. (1846). *The Dispatches and Letters of Vice Admiral Lord Viscount Nelson: With Notes by Sir Nicholas Harris Nicolas, G.C.M.G, The Seventh Volume. August to October 1805*. London: Henry Colburn, Publisher. Retrieved from archive.org.

Nicholson, L. (ed.) (1989). *Feminism/Postmodernism*. London: Routledge.

Norton, R.D. (1999). 'Where are the World's Top 100 I.T. Firms and Why?' in Fischer, M.M. and Suarez-Villa, L. *Innovation, Networks and Localities*. Berlin: Springer.

Oakley, A. (2011). 'New Labour and the Continuation of Thatcherite Policy' in *POLIS Journal*, 6, (winter 2011/2012). Leeds: University of Leeds.

OECD (2001). *New Patterns of Industrial Globalisation: Cross-border Mergers and Acquisitions and Strategic Alliances*. Paris: OECD.

OECD (2003). *The Non-Profit Sector in a Changing Economy*. Paris: OECD.

OECD and Eurostat. 3rd ed. (2005). *Oslo Manual – Guidelines for Collecting and Interpreting Innovation Data*. Paris/Brussels: OECD/European Commission. Retrieved from oecd.org.

Olson, M. (1965). *The Logic of Collective Action*. Cambridge, MA: Harvard University Press.

Ouchi, W. (1980). 'Markets, Bureaucracies and Clans' in *Administrative Science Quarterly*, 25(1).

Owen, S. and Yawson, A. (2013). 'Information Asymmetry and International Strategic Alliances' in *Journal of Banking & Finance* 37/2013. Melbourne: Elsevier.

Padfield, P. (2000). *Nelson's War*. Ware: Wordsworth Military Library.

Palmer, M.A. (1988). 'Lord Nelson: Master of Command' in *Naval College of War Review*. Winter, Philadelphia: Naval Publications and Forms Center.

ParenteBeard (2013). *Subsidiary Consolidated Financial Statements, June 30, 2012 and 2013*: ParenteBeard.

Parvus (1901). *Die handelskrisis und die gewerkschaften, nebst anhang: Gesetzentwurf über den achtstündigen normalarbeitstag*. München: Verlag M. Ernst.

Peck, J. (2005). 'Struggling with the Creative Class' in *International Journal of Urban and Regional Research*, 29(4).Oxford: John Wiley & Sons, Inc.

Perrow, C. (1986). 'Economic Theories of Organisation' in *Theory and Society*, 15. New York: Springer.

Petersen, R. (1992). *Den Grønlandske organisation i det traditionelle samfund. Samt eksempler fra Canada og Alaska* [The Greenland organisation of a traditional society. With examples from Canada and Alaska]. Nuuk: University of Greenland.

Pettigrew, T.J. (1849). *Memoirs of the Life of Vice-Admiral Lord Viscount Nelson, K. B. Duke of Bronté.* Vol. 2, London: T. and W. Boone.

Piore, M. and Sabel, C. (1984). *The Second Industrial Divide.* New York: Basic Books.

Polanyi, M. (1967). *The Tacit Dimension.* Garden City, N.Y.: Doubleday Anchor.

Porter, M. (1980). *Competitive Advantage.* New York: Free Press.

Porter, M. (1985). *Competitive Strategy.* New York: Free Press.

Porter, M. (1990). *The Competitive Advantage of Nations.* New York: Free Press.

Porter, M. (1998). 'Clusters and the New Economics of Competition' in *Harvard Business Review.* November-December.

Powerbase (2014). *Peter Jay.* Retrieved from powerbase.info

Pratt, A.C. and Hutton, T.A. (2013). 'Reconceptualising the Relationship between the Creative Economy and the City: Learning from the Financial Crisis' in *Cities,* 33. New York: Elsevier Ltd.

Putnam, R.D. (1993). *Making Democracy Work: Civic Traditions in Modern Italy.* Princeton: Princeton University Press.

Putnam, R.D. (1995). 'Bowling Alone: America's Declining Social Capital' in *Journal of Democracy,* 6(1). Washington: The Johns Hopkins University Press.

Putnam, R.D. (1996). 'Who Killed Civic America?' in *Prospect,* March 1996.

Putnam, R.D. (2000). *Bowling Alone: The Collapse and Revival of American Community.* New York: Touchstone.

Ranelagh, J. (1991). *Thatcher's People: An Insider's Account of the Politics, the Power, and the Personalities.* London: HarperCollins.

Rath, J. and Kloosterman, R. (2000). 'Outsiders' Business: A Critical Review of Research on Immigrant Entrepreneurship' in *The International Migration Review,* 34(3). New York.

Ray, G. (1980) 'Innovation in the long wave' in *Loyds Bank Review,* 135.

Reich, R.B. (1992). *The Work of Nations: Preparing for the 21st Century.* New York: Vintage Books.

Reinert, E.S. (2002). 'Schumpeter in the Context of Two Canons of Economic Thought' in *Industry and Innovation,* 9(1/2). Oxford: Taylor & Francis Group Ltd.

Richardson, G.B. (1972). 'The organisation of industry' in *The Economic Journal,* (82). St. Andrews: The Royal Economic Society.

Robinson, J. [1933] (1954). *The Economics of Imperfect Competition.* London: Macmillan.

Root-Bernstein, R. et al. (2013). 'Arts, Crafts, and STEM Innovation: A Network Approach to Understanding the Creative Knowledge Economy' in Rushton, M. (ed.), *Creative Communities: Art Works in Economic Development.* Washington: Brookings Institution Press.

Rosenberg, N. (1982). *Inside the Black Box: Technology and Economics*. Cambridge: Cambridge University Press.

Rosenberg, N. (2003). 'America's Entrepreneurial Universities' in Hart, D.M. (ed.), *The Emergence of Entrepreneurial Policy: Governance, Start-ups, and Growth in the U.S. Knowledge Economy*. Cambridge: Cambridge University Press.

Rosenfeld, S.A. (1997). 'Bringing Clusters into the Mainstream of Economic Development' in *European Planning Studies*, 5. Oxford: Taylor & Francis Group Ltd.

Rostow, W.W. (1960). *The Stages of Economic Growth: A Non-Communist Manifesto*. London: Cambridge University Press.

Rostow, W.W. (1978). *The World Economy: History & Prospect*. Austin: University of Texas Press.

SA Navy (2006). *SANGP 100: MARITIME DOCTRINE FOR THE SA NAVY*. South-Africa Navy.

Salamon, L.M. et al. (1999). *Global Civil Society: Dimensions of the Nonprofit Sector*. Baltimore: Johns Hopkins Center for Civil Society Studies.

Salamon, L.M., Wojciech Sokolowski, S. and List, R. (2003). *Global Civil Society: An Overview*. Baltimore: The Johns Hopkins Comparative Nonprofit Sector Project, Center for Civil Society Studies, Institute for Policy Studies, The Johns Hopkins University

Salamon, L.M. et al. (2012). *The State of Global Civil Society and Volunteering: Latest findings from the implementation of the UN Nonprofit Handbook. Working Paper No. 49*. Baltimore: Johns Hopkins Center for Civil Society Studies.

Sartre J.P. (1972). *Being and Nothingness*. London: Methuen & Co, Ltd.

Saul, R. (2005). *The Collapse of Globalism and the Reinvention of the World*. New York: The Overlook Press.

Say, Jean-Baptiste (1803). *A Treatise on Political Economy or the Production, Distribution, and Consumption*. Philadelphia: Claxton, Remsen & Haffelfinger. Retrieved from socserv.mcmaster.ca

Sayer, A. (2000). *Realism and Social Science*. London: SAGE.

Schmookler, J. (1966). *Inventions and Economic Growth*. Cambridge, Massachusetts: Harvard University Press.

Schumpeter, J.A. [1911] (1934). *The Theory of Economic Development*. London: Transaction Publishers. This book was first published in German in 1911.

Schumpeter, J.A. (1936). 'Review of the General Theory of Employment, Interest and Money', by John Maynard Keynes' in *Journal of the American Statistical Association*, 51(4). New York: Academy of Political Science.

Schumpeter, J.A. (1939). *Business Cycles: A Theoretical, Historical and Statistical Analysis of the Capitalist Process*. New York: McGraw-Hill. Retrieved from archive.org

Schumpeter, J.A. (1942). *Capitalism, Socialism and Democracy*. New York: Harper.

Schumpeter, J.A. (1954). *History of Economic Analysis*. London: George Allen & Unwin.

Scott, J. (1986). *Capitalist Property and Financial Power*. Brighton: Wheatsheaf Books.

Scott, J. (1991). *Social Network Analysis: A Handbook*. Thousand Oaks: SAGE.

Scott, J. and Griff, C. (1984). *Directors of Industry: The British Corporate Network 1904–76*. Cambridge: Polity Press.

Sen, A. (1977). 'Rational Fools: A Critique of the Behavioural Foundations of Economic Theory' in *Philosophy and Public Affairs, 6*. Also published in A. Sen (1982). *Choice, Welfare, and Measurement*. Oxford: Blackwell. Retrieved from jstor.org

Senge, P. (1990). *The Fifth Discipline: The Art and Practice of the Learning Organization*. New York: Doubleday.

Simon, H.A. (1959). 'Theories of decision-making in economics and behavioral science' in *American Economic Review*, 49(3). Pittsburgh: American Economic Association.

Simon, H.A. (1982). *Modes of Bounded Rationality*. Cambridge, MA: MIT Press.

Sklair, L. (2003). *The Transnational Capitalist Class*. Oxford: Blackwell Publishing.

Smith, A. [1776] (1904). *An Inquiry into the Nature and Causes of the Wealth of Nations*. London: Methuen & Co., Ltd. Retrieved from archive.org

Smith, M.J. (1998). *Social Science in Question*. London: SAGE Publications Ltd.

SourceWatch (2015). Information on think tanks on the link. Retrieved from sourcewatch.org

Steedman, I. and Sweezy, P. (1981). *The Value Controversy*. London: Verso.

Storper, M. (1997). *The Regional World, Territorial Development in a Global Economy*. London: The Guilford Press.

Storper, M. and Walker. R. (1989). *The Capitalist Imperative: Territory, Technology, and Industrial Growth*. London: Basil Blackwell.

Stuart, R.W. and Abetti, P.A. (1990). 'Impact of Entrepreneurial and Management Experience on Early Performance' in *Journal of Business Venturing*, 5(3). New York: Elsevier Ltd.

Sundbo, J. (1998). *The Theory of Innovation: Entrepreneurs, Technology and Strategy*. Cheltenham: Edward Elgar.

Swedberg, R. (2000). *Max Weber and the Idea of Economic Sociology*. Princeton: Princeton University Press.

Tarde, G. (1890). *Les lois de l'imitation* [The Laws of Imitation]. Paris: Félix Alcan.

Tarde, G. (1890). *L'opposition universelle* [The Universal Opposition]. Paris: Félix Alcan.

Tarde, G. (1894). *La logique sociale* [The Social Logic]. Paris: Félix Alcan.

Teasdale, S. and Buckingham, H. (2013). *Job Creation through the Social Economy and Social Entrepreneurship*. Paris: OECD Publishing.

Thatcher, M. (2013). *Margaret Thatcher: The Autobiography*. HarperCollins Publishers. Kindle Edition.

Tidd, J., Bessant, J. and Pavitt, K. (2000). *Managing Innovation: Integrating Technological, Market and Organizational Change*. Chichester: John Wiley & Sons.

Tieben, B. and Keizer, W. (1997). 'Introduction: Austrian Economics in Debate' in Keizer, W., Tieben, B. and van Zijp, R. (eds), *Austrian Economics in Debate*. London: Routledge.

Timmons, J.A. (2000). *New Venture Creation: Entrepreneurship for the 21ˢᵗ Century*. Boston: McGraw-Hill International Editions.

Torsvik, G. (2000). 'Social Capital and Economic Development: A Plea for the Mechanisms' in *Rationality and Society*. London: SAGE.

Tyler, B.B. and Steensma, H.K. (1995). 'Evaluating Technological Collaborative Opportunities: A Cognitive Modeling Perspective', *Strategic Management Journal*, 16(S1). London: John Wiley and Sons.

UNCTAD (2014). *World Investment Report 2014*. United Nations.

Van de Ven, A.H. and Garud, R. (1989). 'A Framework for Understanding the Emergence of New Industries' in *Research on Technological Innovation, Management and Policy, 4*. Bingley: Emerald Group Publishing Ltd.

Wallerstein, I. (1997). 'Long Waves of Capitalist Development: A Marxist Interpretation by Ernest Mandel' in *Science & Society*, 61(2). New York: Guilford Publications.

Weber, M. (1958). *The Protestant Ethic and the Spirit of Capitalism*. New York: Scribner's.

Weber, M. (1974). *From Max Weber*. Gerth, H.H. and Mills, C.W. (eds). London: Routledge and Kegan Paul Ltd.

Weber, M. (1978). *Economy and Society: An Outline of Interpretive Sociology*. Berkeley: University of California Press.

Weiss, L. (1998). *The Myth of the Powerless State*. Ithaca: Cornell University Press.

Westney, D.E. (1987). *Imitation and Innovation: The Transfer of Western Organizational Patterns to Meiji Japan*. Cambridge, Mass.: Harvard University Press.

WhoFundsYou (2014). Information on think tanks on the link. Retrieved from whofundsyou.org.

Wickham, P.A. (2006). *Strategic Entrepreneurship*. Harlow: Prentice Hall.

Williamson, O.E. (1964). *The Economics of Discretionary Behavior: Managerial Objectives in a Theory of the Firm*. Englewood Cliffs: Prentice-Hall.

Williamson, O.E. (1975). *Markets and Hierarchies: Analysis and Anti-Trust Implications: A Study in the Economics of Internal Organisation*. New York: Free Press.

Wilson, J. (2001). *John Franklin: Traveller on Undiscovered Seas*. XYZ Publishing: Montreal.

Winnicott, D.W. (1959). 'Transitional Objects and Transitional Phenomena' in *Collected Papers*. London: Tavistock.

Winter, S.G. (1982). 'An Essay on the Theory of Production' in Hymans, S.H. (ed.), *Economics and the World Around It*. Ann Arbor: University of Michigan Press.

Wolff, de, S. (1924). 'Prosperitäts- und Depressionsperioden' [Periods of Prosperity and Depression] in Otto Jensen (ed.), *Der lebendige Marxismus, Festgave zum 70. Geburtstage von Karl Kautsky* [The living Marxism, a celebratory publication in honour of Karl Kautsky's 70th birthday]. Jena: Thüringer Verlagsanstalt.

Wolff, de, S. [1913] (1929). *Het economische getij* [The Economic Tide]. Amsterdam: J. Emmering.

World Trade Organisation (2003). *World Trade Statistics 2003*. WTO

Yáñez, C.J.N. (2013). 'Do 'Creative Cities' Have a Dark Side? Cultural Scenes and Socioeconomic Status in Barcelona and Madrid (1991–2001)'. in *Cities*, 35. New York: Elsevier Ltd.

Zeitlin, M. (1974). 'Corporate Ownership and Control: The Large Corporation and the Capitalist Class' in *American Journal of Sociology*, 75. Chicago: University of Chicago Press.

Östhol, A. and Svensson, B. (2002). *Partnership Responses – Regional Governance in the Nordic States. Future Challenges and Institutional Preconditions for Regional Development Policy*, 4. Nordregio Report 2002:6. Stockholm: Nordregio.

Index

For Product Safety Concerns and Information please contact our EU
representative GPSR@taylorandfrancis.com Taylor & Francis Verlag GmbH,
Kaufingerstraße 24, 80331 München, Germany

Printed and bound by CPI Group (UK) Ltd, Croydon, CR0 4YY
01/05/2025
01858432-0003